Where Did I Go Wrong? How Did I Miss The Signs?

Dealing with Hostile Parenting and Parental Alienation

WHERE DID I GO WRONG? HOW DID I MISS THE SIGNS?

Dealing with Hostile Parenting & Parental Alienation

A Prevention and Intervention Book
To Guide and Teach Tools to Families of High
Conflict Relationships and Divorce

JOAN KLOTH-ZANARD
Sponsored by
PAS Intervention
Is a Tax-Exempt charitable organization approved
for tax deductible contributions under Sec. 501(c)(3)
of the IRS.

LULU.com
Online Self-Publishing

LuLu.com
Online at www.LuLu.com

This book is a work of non-fiction based on research, studies and work with victims of Parental Alienation Syndrome and Hostile Parenting since 1997. Some of the names and information have been altered to protect the innocent and identities. Other than those who have agreed to have their comments and information included in this book, any resemblance to the comments made by anonymous participants is coincidental, as all of their factual details have been altered completely to protect them.

Copyright © 2009 by Kloth Consulting
Copyright © 2012 by PAS Intervention

All rights reserved, including the right to reproduce this book or portions thereof in any form whatsoever, without express permission of the author.

For further information on Kloth Consulting, please go to www.KlothConsulting.com or email at KlothConsulting@aol.com

Design by Joan T. Kloth-Zanard

Manufactured in the United States of America
10 9 8 7 6 5 4 3 2 1

Library of Congress Cataloging-in-Publication Data

ISBN: 978-0-557-44779-4

DEDICTION
For all of my family and friends who suffer daily to fight for their rights to be a parent to their children.

And a special thanks to Annette, Al, Karen, Greg, Fran, Amy and everyone else who helped or tried to help edit and proofread this book for me.

Legal Disclaimer:
I am NOT an attorney, therefore all legal ideas and information is just that, information that I and others have amassed through years of research using places open to the public such as on the internet, in law libraries and from our personal experiences. It is always best to consult with an attorney about the many ideas presented to you by anyone, whether in this book or by others.

PAS INTERVENTION
Is a Tax-Exempt charitable organization approved for tax deductible contributions under Sec. 501(c)(3) of the IRS.

TABLE OF CONTENTS

INTRODUCTION	i
CHAPTER 1 - Divorce A Negative Dirty Word	1
CHAPTER 2 – Where Did I Go Wrong? How Did I Miss The Signs?	4
CHAPTER 3 – Parental Alienation is Domestic Violence	11
CHAPTER 4 – All About The Alienator	20
CHAPTER 5 – Types of Abusers	30
CHAPTER 6 – Why do Alienators Alienate	35
CHAPTER 7 – Nature Via Nurture	42
CHAPTER 8 – The Pendulum Effect	52
CHAPTER 9 – The Amusement Park Ride	55
CHAPTER 10 – Dysfunctional Child Development	66
CHAPTER 11 – Parental Alienation is Ageless	94
CHAPTER 12 – Statistical Information	104
CHAPTER 13 – Blasting Through the Mountain	109
CHAPTER 14 – Combating the Negative Responses – Putting Your Foot Down	140
CHAPTER 15 – Helping Children to Understand & Learn Compassion	148
CHAPTER 16 – Borderless Boundaries & Alternative Terms for Court	153
CHAPTER 17 – Ethical & Legal Challenges	159
CHAPTER 18 – Proactive Approach To Divorce Court	162

CHAPTER 19 – Choosing Which Battles to Fight	184
CHAPTER 20 – Dealing With Educational Institutions & Parental Rights	190
CHAPTER 21 – Documenting Evidence & Tape Recording Properly	193
CHAPTER 22 – 167 Red Flags & Child Behavior Indicators	201
CHAPTER 23 – Deprogramming Centers	227
CHAPTER 24 – Divorce Rules	245
CHAPTER 25 – The Healing Power of Laughter	250
CHAPTER 26 – Moving Forward & Letting Go: Healing the Festering Wounds	252
CHAPTER 27 – Stress Management	259
CHAPTER 28 – Parental Character Analysis & Indicator Scaling Test	262
CHAPTER 29 – Solving for PAS & HAP	276
CHAPTER 30 – Article, Book & Movie Recommendations	310
CHAPTER 31 – Parentectomy Redefined and New Insights to Family Dynamics Newsletter	314
Abbreviations	333
References	334

HHSS

Happiness comes from inside of all of us. Thus the greatest control you can have over this form of abuse is to stand up for your self while being Happy, Healthy, Successful and Spiritually Positive.

INTRODUCTION

Someday PAS will need no introduction. It will be well established as a form of abuse in the Diagnostic and Statistical Manual of Mental Diagnosis's. Until then...PAS begins as Hostile Aggressive Parenting (HAP), which leads to Parental Alienation (PA) or the estrangement of the children from one parent and the effects on the children are called Parental Alienation Syndrome (PAS).

If you are reading this book, you are either getting divorced or are in the middle of a nasty High Conflict Divorce (HCD). You are doing something good right now, by trying to prepare yourself or at least learn how to deal with the aftermath that has hit your children and you. Early intervention is the best prevention for this debilitating form of psychological abuse called PAS.

My involvement with PAS began in 1996, when it affected my family. I began studying it and researching it and by 1999, I was heavily involved in numerous online support groups trying to figure out how to stop it from happening. Today, I voluntarily run 3 International non-profit support groups for Parental Alienation Syndrome (PAS). The groups are completely run voluntarily with at least 2 moderators/owners per group. These yahoo groups known as PAS-Guardian Angels, PAS 2nd Wives Club and stopPAS, provide an invaluable resource for parents, grandparents, wives of fathers who are being alienated, husband's of wives that are alienate and so on. The groups are international with members all over the United States, Australia, New Zealand, Canada, Spain, England, Port Rico and so on. The type of support provided ranges from giving the members a place to cry, scream, yell, vent, ask questions and give advice to providing research work, studies and other information to help them navigate the family court system and the abuse they are dealing with on a daily basis. The groups also provide resources to articles, study's and professionals such as counselors, doctors, lawyers and advocates.

From my work with these groups and the research work I have done, I began to construct this book. The information contained herein comes from years of work with victims of this horrific abuse. My only hope is that this book can be an asset and tool used to prevent and intervene in stopping the psychological abuse of HAP and PAS.

As you read through this book, some chapters are really short and some are very long. But each chapter will be like a growing living organism. Because this is a growing, new field of work, I will try to keep things updated on my website, http://www.KlothConsulting.com.

While reading things, certain concepts or ideas are sometimes repeated. This is in part because of their importance or how they were originally written in the article I included in the book. Just take it all in, mark up the book, do what you need to do to keep the key points that interest or concern you available at your figure tips. Just remember this book is a tool to help intervene and hopefully prevent HAP and PAS from snowballing out of control.

Speaking of this book, coming up with a title was challenging, as there was so much I wanted it to say. So I gave it as a question to my support group members and clients. The suggestions were amazing because they said it all in just one line. So I am including them here in the Preface because these lines give definition and meaning to the feelings, emotions and pain from PAS. I want to give a huge thanks to all those members and clients for their help and input.

- *From HAP to PAS and Back Again: Dealing with Parental Alienation and the Psychological Abuse from High Conflict Divorce*
- *Breaking through the Mountain While Riding a Roller Coaster: Dealing with Parental Alienation and the Psychological Abuse from High Conflict Divorce*
- *Divorce, the Dirtiest Word in Any Language: Dealing with Parental Alienation and the Psychological Abuse from High Conflict Divorce*
- *What Happened? From HAP to PAS and Back Again: Dealing with Parental Alienation and the Psychological Abuse from High Conflict Divorce*
- *Beyond Normal Parenting Relationship: When you child does not want to have anything to do with you after the Divorce.*
- *Abnormal Child Parent Relationship Before, During or After Divorce: When your Spouse impedes your relationship with your children*
- *Where Did I Go Wrong? How Did I Miss The Signs? Am I Still A Good Parent? Dealing with Hostile Aggressive Parenting and Parental Alienation.*
- *"Spread the hatred. My Ex tried to kill me through the kids."*
- *"My Ex turned the kids into scud missiles."*
- *Are you a Target Parent?*
- *Toxic Spouses/Toxic Kids: Dealing with Parental Alienation and the Psychological Abuse from High Conflict Divorce*
- *"When your ex tries to ruin your life through the kids: Dealing*

- *with Parental Alienation and the Psychological Abuse from High Conflict Divorce*
- *"What happened?: Dealing with Parental Alienation and the Psychological Abuse from High Conflict Divorce*
- *Toxic Spouses: Dealing with Parental Alienation and the Psychological Abuse from High Conflict Divorce*
- *Support Group Suggestions:*
- *In One Fell Swoop: The destruction of a parent child relationship*
- *Normal to Hatred in 60 days*
- *The Nightmare of PAS*
- *Parental Alienation Syndrome; Dodging the Slings and Arrows*
- *Parental Alienation Syndrome after Divorce; Tempest after the Storm*
- *Parental Alienation Syndrome; American Gulag*
- *Breaking through the Mountain on a Roller Coaster: Dealing with Parental Alienation and the Psychological Abuse from High Conflict Divorce*
- *I Divorced My Spouse - Not My Kids! How Parental Alienation Syndrome Ruined Our Parent/Child Bond*
- *I Split from My Ex - But Not From My Kids! How Parental Alienation Syndrome Ruined Our Parent/Child Bond*

PLEASE NOTE: I am not a lawyer. I relate all my statements to my personal experience and research.

CHAPTER 1

DIVORCE IS THE MOST NEGATIVE, DIRTY WORD IN ANY LANGUAGE AND IT DOES NOT HAVE TO BE!

Divorce, UGH, is one of the ugliest, most negative words; no matter what language you speak. It immediately conjures up negative thoughts, ideas, tears, broken hearts, broken homes and a landslide of financial troubles. But it really does not have to be this way. If people looked at divorce in a positive framework, we would see much less damage, heartache and emotional turmoil. If the courts, families, counselors and agencies took on a more positive attitude toward divorce, it would filter its way throughout the family system.

When the institution of marriage was created, people only lived to be at most 35. They were married for not more than 20 years. Today, people live into their 70's, 80's and 90's. This is three times as long and marriages must endure for three times that length as well. And that means marriages must last for nearly 50 years or more, not 15 years. This is a lot to ask of human beings who go through major personal changes every 7 years or so. And it puts a lot of pressure on the two adults to continue to love, honor, cherish and continue to grow together. If we do not grow and learn together in the marriage, then we grow apart.

To look at divorce positively, one must first understand that a failed marriage is not about failing in life but about life changes and growing apart. It is about a new stage in their life, much like going from being an infant to a toddler, from a toddler to a pre-juvenile, from a pre-juvenile to juvenile, from juvenile to adolescent, from adolescent to young adult, from young adult to adult and adult to elder. Throughout this entire process we are growing, learning and going through emotional, physical and personal changes.

With this theory in mind, unless the couple is growing in the same perspective and direction, it is no wonder that so many marriages end in divorce. But this does not have to be viewed as a negative concept. Like when an infant becomes a toddler and is just learning to walk, or when an adolescent is finally becoming a young adult with new aspirations and responsibilities, people grow through life cycles changes and sometimes grow apart. When this happens this should not be a time of revenge, hatred and anger. Instead, we should be seeing this as a new stage or cycle in our lives. It should be viewed as a new opportunity to do the things we might not have done or thought about when we were married. It is a chance to explore a new self.

If we look at divorce as just being another step or stage in our life cycle, then we can view it as just another process in our aging. It should be a time for growth, letting go and going on. It can be a time for us to explore things we dared not do while married. It can be a time to find new partnerships and relationships, which are more compatible with whom we have matured into. And for our children it is a chance to gain new relatives and extended family members. It is a chance to increase our networking potential and have more family and friends to communicate with and count on and even get the other necessary ingredients that make up their hierarchy of needs.

With divorce being so prevalent and the ravages so detrimental, it just stands to reason that we need to find another way of understanding and accepting this new change in our lives, without making it into a horrific event. If we can change our attitude to see divorce as a stepping-stone to the next level or stage in our life, it will open up endless doors of opportunity for all involved.

But what about the children? Isn't this teaching them to give up too easily on their marriages? Well, this is a fair question. But instead, maybe we should look at this as having more tolerance and understanding. We could teach them to not be so afraid and freaked out about change. Instead, they can view this as a time to get some space from each other and see if they grow back together or further apart. It is a chance to work on our own personal selves, which quite often is very difficult to do in a marriage.

So how do the couples do it that stick it out and stay together all those years? Maybe they still have a special connection to each other. Maybe they have allowed each other to grow and continue to become a better person? Maybe their life stages and cycles coincided together in such a way that they could work through things together instead of alone? This would be a great area of research to help couples find a way to work through their marriages and life stage changes, rather than part.

In the meantime, it would seem to make much more sense to not think of divorce or separation, for that matter, as the end of life, but instead as a new beginning. If we could find a more positive approach to dealing with divorce, we might just find fewer high conflict divorces, fewer troubled and angry children and fewer incidents of hostile aggressive parenting, which ultimately rip the children and parents apart. There would be much less disruption in our children's lives and they could maintain a healthy relationship with both parents. Then, just maybe, we could break the cycle of psychological abuse that accompanies so many divorces these days. Maybe we can make a difference in divorce.

Until the time that divorce and separation can be seen with a more positive approach, it is important to learn all we can about protecting ourselves, our extended families and the children we love from the psychological abuse of Parental Alienation and Hostile Aggressive Parenting.

CHAPTER 2

WHERE DID I GO WRONG?
HOW DID I MISS THE SIGNS?
AM I STILL A GOOD PARENT?

So many targeted parents ask," How could I not see this coming? How could I have not known this was what was going to happen? How could I have been so blind?"

Don't blame yourself. You just were not raised this way. You do not think this way. So why would you have thought otherwise? Unfortunately, the signs were probably there all the time but we just did not know to look for them, or we were struggling so hard to survive that we just did not want to see it or hear it or maybe it was something we thought was normal because that is the way we were raised. Either way, in most of the cases I have dealt with, the signs and symptoms of Hostile Aggressive Parenting (HAP) and Parental Alienation Syndrome (PAS) were always there but we just did not recognize them. Denigrating our families, refusing to allow the kids to keep gifts from the other side of the family, berating the targeted parent (TP) with the kids there, and bad-mouthing the TP in front of friends and family, are strong indicators of HAP AND PAS. But sometimes the signs are even subtler, like ignoring the other parent when they talk, or throwing out their personal stuff "accidentally", or not including them in decisions or making snide comments that indirectly put the TP down. These are all signs, but when we are in the thick of it, we just cannot see through the muck. In reality, the TP is just as much of a victim of the AP's bullying as the children are.

AN writes:
I don't think the behavior comes up all of a sudden. I think there are hints and under currents. There were in my case. And, I think our culture convinces us that everything will be ok, to turn the other cheek, that "God only gives us whatever to make us stronger, etc."

RH writes:
It's been over 5 years. Oh I know now that ex was committing HAP for a very long time. I wasn't aware of it when it was happening. That's how sneaky they (AP) are. Everything is done behind your back. My older one assisted him in the alienation too. And I know she has been paid off. I have proof from an old online diary she had been keeping for several years, which I found last year. Unfortunately, none of this could be brought out into the open, such as showing it to the judge. My older one was always treated like a princess and the younger one like a 2nd class citizen (same as me). In fact, the younger one has had a student loan in her name for a community college and I know that my ex could very well afford a few thousand dollars a year for a community college. Also, I know that he goes around telling people that I'm not allowed to have contact (and everyone believes him.... including my daughters) and that I'm violating court orders (which are non-existent) and that I'm not paying child support (untrue). This is a sick parent who goes around telling people lies and of course the kids don't even question him.

Anonymous writes:
Yes, my family member's ex was committing HAP all along too. She started it while they were married, putting the husband down in front of the kids, his friends and anyone else that would listen, right in front of him.

And she denied the children a relationship with anyone on their father's side of the family; even making the kids return Christmas gifts when they were 4 and 6 years old. In this case, she actually made enemies out of all the other people, because they knew what a nasty narcissistic woman she was. But this did not stop the kids from believing her because she kept them away from anyone who would have set the kids straight.

In another of my family members cases, the ex was also doing it all through the marriage. At first she only directed it at her husband's side of the family. She even tried to convince her then husband, how horrible his side of the family was, including claiming that my daughter was a bad influence. Yes, a child, who was a competitive figure skater, competitive dancer, advanced art and honor roll student, who was always so busy and involved after school, that she was a troublemaker. Yes, my daughter, who was nice to every one; was extremely focused, disciplined; hates drugs and alcohol, was not safe to be around. Yes, my daughter was such a horrible influence that she was constantly asked to assistant teach ice skating and dance and work with other kids in school who were struggling to learn things. Yes, my daughter who would not hurt anyone because she thinks it is mean. Yet, her own daughter is down right rude, nasty, arrogant and could careless whose feelings she hurts. Oh, and my whole side of the family is crazy.

But of course this ex's own mother is the perfect mom, a chronic gambler, whom the Targeted Parent had to bail out constantly. Oh, and the ex's father is no better, having cheated on the ex's mother all through their marriage with his secretary whom he had two kids out of wedlock with. Yes, her family is so much better than everyone else's. But you get the point; they were setting these spouses and their kids up from the start because of their own insecurities.

AP's are very insecure and just like the bully at school; they need to make sure that they are revered. They pick fights,

Where Did I Go Wrong? How Did I Miss The Signs?

start rumors and lie just to boost their own image. They pick on anyone they think they can over- power and control. It is the definition of a bully. I think these Dictionary definitions of bullies describe the AP perfectly. If this is illegal for children to do to another child, then why is it allowed by an adult to do to another adult or child?

bul·ly [1] (bl)
n. pl. bul·lies
1. A person who is habitually cruel or overbearing, especially to smaller or weaker people.
2. A hired ruffian; a thug.
3. A pimp.

v. bul·lied, bul·ly·ing, bul·lies
v.tr.
1. To treat in an overbearing or intimidating manner. See Synonyms at intimidate.
2. To make (one's way) aggressively.
v.intr.
1. To behave like a bully.
2. To force one's way aggressively or by intimidation.

Free Dictionary 2009 on line at
http://www.thefreedictionary.com/bully

bully[1]
n pl -lies
1. a person who hurts, persecutes, or intimidates weaker people
2. *Archaic* a hired ruffian
3. *Obsolete* a procurer; pimp
vb -lies, -lying, -lied
(when tr, often foll by into) to hurt, intimidate, or persecute (a weaker or smaller person), esp. to make him do something

Collins English Dictionary – *Complete and Unabridged 6th Edition 2003.* © *William Collins Sons & Co. Ltd 1979, 1986* © *HarperCollins Publishers 1991, 1994, 1998, 2000, 2003*

In hindsight, the APs were probably hostile aggressive people all along, while the TP started out as the passive one who would do anything to keep the peace. When the balance of control is shifted, the relationship begins to fall part. If these tendencies are picked up on early on during either the marriage or the divorce process that maybe effective therapy can result in a healthier relationship and the prevention of PAS should the couples' relationship ultimately break up. Below is an excerpt from a letter by a client who did just this and got therapy for both her and her spouse.

PC writes:

My husband and I have been in counseling with several local services for over a year. The counseling I feel made a HUGE impact, and I honestly think that if that had not happened, we might still be in an extremely tense and stressful situation, for all of us, including the kids. Though we continue to live separately with separate households, we have been able to work through this and are working on saving our marriage as we both do still love each other very much. Currently, we share custody of all 3 children, and are able to cooperate very well and be flexible with that.

The other day, my husband told me our kids would not be better off without me, and that I am a good mother. That is the point both parents must be at, knowing that for their kids sake, their kids need both parents, not just the one parent. Both parents have to keep trying, and sometimes the alienated parent must try even harder, to make the other parent open up and talk about why things have gotten so difficult, how they both can make things better, and how they can both be a part of their kids' life.

There are no easy or quick answers. Both parents must cooperate together, and maybe even work on themselves, in order to make the situation better, especially for the kids. We continue to make sure our kids know they are important and we love them, and that it is ok for them to love us:)

I think one of the many huge reasons the

counseling helped, is it made it possible for us to realize why this happened (a combination of midlife crisis brought on by our 3rd planned pregnancy; my husband's parents both dying; and him suddenly thinking I would kidnap our kids back to the US when he demanded a divorce). Counseling also helped us understand that in spite of everything, we still deeply love and like each other, still share a deep friendship, humor, numerous common interests, etc. and that we both wanted to have a better relationship again, share custody, and work on our marriage. I think that as much as I want our marriage and love to keep us together, and to be a family together with our kids in our house...at this point, I feel the counseling has made it possible to also, in the worst scenario to be divorced amicably and sharing custody, amicably.

* So, maybe it helps to know WHY the alienating parent feels so strongly they must alienate the other parent, and counseling helps by helping that alienating parent realize they don't have a reason to be so scared/angry to keep the other parent from their own children.* Counseling also helps the alienated parent deal with all their emotions, pain, anger, hurt, frustration...and forgive, so they can move on and continue to be a good parent.

SO ARE YOU A GOOD PARENT, PARENTING TEST: ARE YOU PRACTICING GOOD PARENTING TECHNIQUES?
Created by Alison Benitz

Take the following test to find out how good you are at parenting after a separation or divorce.

1) When talking to your child do you ever refer to their other parent by their first name?
2) If your child refers to their other parent by their first name, do you allow it?

3) Do you allow your child to decide whether or not they want to spend time with the other parent?
4) Do you have fights with the other parent in front of your children?
5) Are you so honest with your children that you tell them everything including about divorce court and child support?
6) Do you ever tell your child they are just like the other parent?
7) If your child has done something wrong, do you tell the other parent the child is just like they are?
8) Do you ever tell the child to ask the other parent for something you know they cannot deliver?
9) Do you tell the other parent about school functions, doctor visits, and the children's accomplishments/disappointments?
10) Do you ask your child to sit with you to write encouraging/positive letters and send good happy pictures to their other parent?
11) Do you call the other parent just so your child can talk to them?
12) Do you help your child remember the other parent's birthday, Mother's or Father's day, Christmas or other special holidays?

If you answered "yes" to any of the question from 1-8 or "no" to any of the question from 9-12, you may be practicing a form of abuse known as parent alienation. For the sake of your child, please seek help. It's your child who will be hurt far more than your ex.

If your responses indicated that you are a good parent, DO NOT STOP HERE. This book is not about being just a good parent. It is about being a better parent and preventing the other parent from stopping you from being the best parent you can be to your children.

CHAPTER 3

PARENTAL ALIENATION IS DOMESTIC VIOLENCE

Abuse is one of the most gut wrenching issues in our times. Whether it is the abuse of a child, a women, an elder or a man, it is heinous. Abuse comes in three main forms: physical, sexual and psychological (also known as emotional abuse.). It is the mental and emotional abuse caused by a spouse's deliberate attempt to destroy the Targeted Parent in the eyes of the children that will be the focus of this chapter. Parental Alienation, also classified as Hostile Aggressive Parenting, Enmeshed Relationships, Cross-Generational Coalitions, Relationship Triangles and Alienation, is a growing epidemic in divorce proceedings. It is time to change this and make a difference for the children and Targeted Parent of these psychological abuses.

During a high conflict divorce involving visitation or custody, there are more false cases of domestic violence and abuse filed according to the various departments of protection and the courts. (DHHS, 2001 Statistics) This issue is one of international alarm because false reporting takes massive amounts of resources away from true victims. In addition, the psychological ramifications and loss of reputation for the accused can ruin their lives forever, which is usually the intention with the false allegations. Unfortunately, these types of abusers drag their innocent children into their bogus stories, which force the children to lie and go through horrendous tests and interviews, which emotionally scar them for life. Even if the accused parent has not committed the crime, the accusations cost the accused thousands of dollars and years to prove their innocence, while the abuser commits defamation and slander. By all documented accounts, (see Fiebert's Reference) it is apparent that the gender of the abuser does not matter. Both genders are equally aggressive using both physical and psychological abuse.

It is the mental end of this abuse that Bill Kuhl speaks about in his article "Violence Knows No Gender". Abusers are devious and use covert physical attacks to catch their prey off guard. Kuhl refers to this as the "element of surprise". (Kuhl, Violence Knows No Gender) This is not only devious but also psychologically stressful. The targeted parent never knows if and when it is coming or how; much like a soldier during a sniper attack. They must live their lives as if they are constantly at war, on edge and in fear. Psychologically they become worn out with nowhere to turn to for help.

This psychological abuse and the toll that these victims pay come at a great price. If they stay, they chance being seriously injured if not killed. If they leave, they are faced with the humiliation of 'allowing' someone to abuse them. In the course of this, they will lose everything, including their children. Most victims stay in their abusive marriages for the same reason; that is they have nowhere to go, are being threatened with losing everything, scared for their children and have been beaten down emotionally and they can no longer stand on their own anymore. For men this is a double indemnity, because it is the humiliation and ridicule that a woman has abused them, which prevents most men from reporting the abuse they encounter and prohibits them from leaving home. For women, it is not so much the humiliation as the fear of further attacks as well as fear of not being able to make it on their own. The one fear that stigmatizes both genders is the loss of their children and that relationship.

When a parent is denied a relationship, it is the same as isolating the children from the parent. It can be legally termed as an alienation of affection, criminally referred to as domestic violence and psychologically referred to as Parental Alienation, Parental Alienation Syndrome (soon to be in the DSM V), Hostile Aggressive Parenting, an Enmeshed Relationship, Triangles in Relationships, Cross-Generational Coalitions or Alienation and Denigration. No matter what it is named, it is not

Where Did I Go Wrong? How Did I Miss The Signs?

only abusive to the Targeted Parent (TP), but also abusive to the children. The Alienating Parent (AP) sees the children and/or their relationship with the other parent as a possession that they have power over, which in turn controls the TP. By refusing to allow a healthy relationship to exist between the children and the TP, the AP maintains a sense of control and what they feel is a bargaining chip to possess the other parent. Whether it is returning the TP to the AP's life or revenge 'for not loving them anymore', the AP has absolutely no regard for any of the other victims. Their only goal is to destroy the TP anyway they can.

This abuse is so subtle and slow, that when the parent realizes what is occurring, it is often too late and the children are refusing to have a relationship with the TP, especially in the case of high conflict divorce with custody/visitation issues. The once naturally healthy relationship and bonds of a parent with their offspring have been destroyed; their children's lives are filled with treachery and uncharted waters. The psychological community is just now beginning to understand the ramifications of this type of abuse, while examining a definition to be included in the DSM. Alienation is an insidious type of abuse because proving its existence is a nightmare that is still on going. The psychological community is baffled as to how to stop it and correct the damages to the children.

PAS OR PARENTAL ALIENATION SYNDROME DEFINED

Dr. Richard Gardner, of Cresskill, NJ, a child psychologist, was one of the leading authorities on children of dysfunctional families. What he found in his research is that no matter the financial or cultural background, alienation of one parent from the other could occur. (www.rgardner.com)

According to Dr. Richard Gardner, PAS is described as "a disturbance in which children are obsessively preoccupied with depreciation and/or criticism of a parent. In other words, denigration that is unjustified and or exaggerated." (www.familycourts.com/pas.htm) In effect, these children are taught to hate the other parent to the point of wanting to eliminate them from their lives. Dr. Gardner considers this psychological abuse and it is the only form of psychological abuse that has clear-cut unmistakable signs and symptoms and therefore the only psychological abuse that can be easily diagnosed.

PAS can be further described as a form of psychological kidnapping (www.familycourts.com/pas.htm) where the child's mind has been forced to prejudicially believe and discriminate against the other parent. This is perpetrated by creating fear, not of the only of the TP/outsider parent, but of the parent whom the child must reside with, or as Gardner calls it, the "hostage taker" parent. (www.familycourts.com/pas.htm) It is also called the Stockholm Syndrome and best compared to the Patti Hearst kidnapping.

In these cases, the hostages are so isolated from the outside world that they begin to associate with their hostage takers. Actually refusing to accept any overt actions from the outside that contradict their captor's motives. This has been documented in cult situations where the followers are literally brainwashed to believe that the cults objectives are the only way to think, act or believe.

This also applies in PAS where the children learn to side with the aggressor and avoid being victims of the same abuse. As Roland Summit (Kemp, P. 16) and John Briere (Kemp, P. 239-240) call it, *Abuse-Related Accommodation.* Abuse-related accommodation occurs when a person's natural survival instincts have enabled them to "adapt" to the abuse. This adaptation includes distortions of thought, altered emotions (such as depression and anxiety), and dissociation by disconnecting from the trauma. It is these adaptive techniques that will determine whether a child will develop personality disorders such as multiple personalities, anti-social behaviors or psychotic tendencies. (Kemp P. 239). Briere further breaks it down into 3 stages of adaptation. First is the initial reaction stage of fear, anxiety, hurt, betrayal or abandonment, because they are so isolated they have nowhere to turn. In the second stage, accommodation to on-going abuse, they try to pacify and soothe the abuser. With children of PAS this might be avoiding issues that trigger anger, such as positive comments about the other parent. Finally in the 3rd stage called Long-Term Elaboration and Secondary accommodation, the victims life centers around avoiding and living with the abuse, which now affects every

Where Did I Go Wrong? How Did I Miss The Signs?

mechanism for coping and behavior. The abuse actually becomes so internalized that their entire world changes to accommodate it. A PAS victimized child might denigrate and spew hatred about the targeted parent with no valid and justifiable reasons.

No matter how we describe it or compare it, the ultimate truth is that PAS destroys the children and the parents it is directed at. Despite our courts supposed protection of children from this kind of abuse, it is happening even more. This type of abuse is directly correlated with marital issues involving parental separation, divorce, custody and visitation. It became even more prevalent in the 60's with the introduction of No-Fault Divorce. Despite the high incidence of this type of abuse, it is barely recognized in the courts until recently when it passed the Frye Test, to determine admissibility of scientific evidence, validating its existence (wwwr.gardner.com/ref/pas), which now permits it's open testimony and use in court. With the passage of the Frye test, the State of Connecticut mandated Court Support Family Services to get training in Parental Alienation Syndrome. Unfortunately, at present this training is very inadequate and riddled with missing data. If only we can finally get the courts to put aside their prejudices against men and non-custodial parents.

HOW DO WE RECOGNIZE AND DIAGNOSE PAS?

The following is a list of behaviors exhibited by children of PAS according to Richard Gardner. See link below. www.rgardner.com/ref/pas_intro.html)

1) A campaign of denigration
2) Weak, absurd, or frivolous rationalizations for the deprecation.
3) Lack of Ambivalence
4) The "independent thinker" phenomenon
5) Reflexive support of the AP in the parental conflict
6) Absence of guilt over cruelty to and/or exploitation of the Alienated Parent
7) The presence of borrowed scenarios
8) Spread of the animosity to the friends and/or extended family of the Alienated Parent.

In effect, PAS is a form of prejudice and discrimination that isolates the children from the TP, and extended family and friends. Through a series of actions, the alienating parent is able to influence the children to hate the targeted parent and extended family. In particular, the AP instills such loathing and anger toward the TP that it could easily be classified as a hate crime.

CLASSIFYING PAS AS DOMESTIC VIOLENCE

According to Kemp in his book <u>Abuse in the Family</u>, domestic violence is defined as "A form of Maltreatment perpetrated by a person with whom the victim has or had a close personal relationship." (Kemp, P.36) Furthermore, the clinical and textbook definitions and categories of Child Psychological Maltreatment found in Table 3-1 of Alan Kemp's book, <u>Abuse in the Family</u>, on pages 72-77, can easily be applied to PAS showing it as a form of Domestic Violence via Psychological Maltreatment. This book is a technical training book for Students studying for their Masters in Counseling and Social Work. It is just one of many textbooks used to teach the students and professionals about Psychological Maltreatment and the categories that make it up. Those categories are:

- Rejecting (spurning)
- Terrorizing
- Corrupting
- Denying essential stimulation, emotional responsiveness, or availability
- Unreliable and inconsistent parenting
- Mental health, medical, or educational neglect
- Degrading/devaluing (spurning)
- Isolating
- Exploiting

As we correlate the above definition, we will see how it fits in classifying PAS as Psychological Maltreatment and thus Domestic Violence. For example, by deliberately alienating the victims from other family members and social supports, isolation is occurring. The whole premise of PAS is to isolate and alienate the children from the Targeted Parent or any other individual who supports the Targeted Parent. If the alienator uses threats or

Where Did I Go Wrong? How Did I Miss The Signs?

denigrating tactics, to force the victims to comply, this can be seen as terrorizing. (Kemp, P. 225-228) As well, verbal denigration, harassment and exploitation of the Targeted Parent is very prominent and a key indicator of PAS. In addition, DV includes the exploitation and use of the children for personal gain. Thus in PAS when the children are used to destroy the Targeted Parent by denying visitation or a relationship between TP and the children or is used for monetary gains such as excessive expenses beyond child support, they are in affect committing Domestic Violence. It is for these reasons that PAS or alienating the children from the Targeted Parent can be considered as a form of domestic violence.

Let's take this a bit further in it's application. When a parent REJECTS a child because the children show any love or affection for the Targeted Parent that is a form of abuse. This is not only a form of rejection, but TERRORIZATION. In fact, a child's refusal to come to the Targeted Parents home for fear of losing the Alienating Parent's conditional love is fear and fear is terror.

Next, there is CORRUPTING. When an Alienating parent refuses to comply with court orders and tells the children they do not have to either, this is corrupting. It is teaching the children that they are above the law and therefore immune to the courts authority. When a parent files false allegations of abuse and convinces the children to do the same, this is corruption. When an Alienating parent tells the children lies about the Targeted Parent, and that anything having to do with the Targeted Parent is illegal, immoral and disgusting, this is corrupting. In fact, this is a form of discrimination and prejudice, which corrupts the children's minds.

Next, let's look at DENYING ESSENTIAL STIMULATION, EMOTIONAL RESPONSIVENESS, OR AVAILABILITY. By refusing to allow the children to have a relationship with the Targeted Parent, for no reason other than their own need to control the ex-spouse, the Alienating Parents are denying them the basic elements of stimulation, emotions and availability with the Targeted Parent. In fact, the Targeted Parent has little to no opportunity to defend themselves against the false allegations. Though they will have you believe that they or the children feared for their lives and that the Targeted Parent was abusive, this is usually unsubstantiated or proven by the courts to be a fabrication. With no basis for this denial, the Alienator refuses their children a warm and loving relationship with the Targeted Parents. Thus it causes UNRELIABLE AND INCONSISTENT PARENTING. Since the children have been denied a relationship with the Targeted Parent, they have also been denied a reliable and consistent parenting situation and the Alienating Parent has proven that they cannot parent consistently and reliably in the supporting of a two-parent relationship with the children.

This brings us to the MENTAL, MEDICAL AND EDUCATION NEGLECT. When an Alienating Parent refuses to comply with numerous separate court orders for counseling, they are denying their children's mental health. Thus mental neglect has occurred as defined in the DSM IV as Malingering. (V65.2) and by Neglect of Child (V61.21).

If despite numerous court orders or request and recommendations, the alienator continues to insult, verbally abuse and denigrate the child's Targeted Parent in front of them, this behavior DEGRADES AND DEVALUES someone the children once respected and loved and in most cases, secretly want a relationship with. This disdain and disrespect for the Targeted Parent in front of the child(ren) is another form of Psychological Maltreatment as it permanently affects their view of that Targeted Parent, which transfers to their view of themselves. This creates a distorted sense of reality, of themselves and their ability to trust and accurately judge others.

When a parent deliberately sabotages a relationship with the Targeted Parent by refusing to allow visits, calls, or any form of healthy communication, with no evidence of abuse, this is called ISOLATION. Furthermore, when a parent has initially allowed continuous contact with the children during the separation and divorce period, but reneges on this refusing them visitation, especially when they find out their ex-spouse has a new partner, this is isolation and abuse. This is also called Remarriage as a Trigger for Parental Alienation Syndrome and can be further reviewed in an article by Dr. Richard Warshak,

Where Did I Go Wrong? How Did I Miss The Signs?

There is no doubt this is isolation and thus psychological abuse. (http://www.fact.on.ca/Info/pas/warsha00.htm)

And finally, EXPLOITATION. When a parent uses the children as pawns to get back at their ex spouse for not loving them anymore or to control them further, this is exploitation. When an Alienating Parent uses the children and makes false allegations of abuse, terrorizing the children to state they hate the Targeted Parent, this is EXPLOITATION. When a parent uses the children for monetary gains, but yet does not allow the children a relationship with the targeted parent, this is EXPLOITATION.

When you add all these factors up, it is easy to see how Cross-Generational Coalitions, Parental Alienation, Parental Alienation Syndrome, Enmeshed Relationships, Triangles and Borderless Boundaries can be classified as Child Psychological Maltreatment in a divorce situation. When you put it all together, the DSM sums up the Alienator quite nicely under Cluster B Personality Disorder, Antisocial Personality Disorder, (301.7). The Alienating Parent willfully and without regard to the child(ren) or the targeted parent's welfare, or the innocent extended families welfare, continually violated their rights and disregarded their needs for a relationship. The Alienating Parent uses and exploits the children. The Alienating Parent isolates the children from a nurturing parent and family. The Alienating Parent denies the children their basic needs of love and belonging from the Targeted Parent. The Alienating Parent thus neglects the children's mental welfare. They rejected the children's and Targeted Parent's testimony of love and need for each other. The Alienating Parent terrorizes and corrupts the children. The Alienating Parent callously puts their own desires, wants and needs above those of everyone else including their own children. This all adds up to one thing, PAS is Domestic Violence in the form of Psychological Maltreatment.

CHAPTER 4

ALL ABOUT THE ALIENATOR
THE ALIENATING PARENT'S PSYCHOLOGICAL MAKE-UP

NOTE: In the 1980's it was believed that women only committed PAS. Over the years this belief has changed to a non-gender specific issue. For that reason, I have chosen to use gender neutral terms such as AP (Alienating Parent) for any person who refuses or destroys the relationship between the children and the other parent; and TP (Target Parent) to represent the targeted parent.

Why does the AP do what they do? To begin with, it may come from unfounded feelings of entitlement. When a person feels slighted by another, even if only in their imagination, they experience intense emotions of anger and use every tactic they can conceive of to harm the target and fill the void in their heart. They have no impulse control over this anger and rage that triggers a need for revenge.

They actually believe that filling this hole in their heart using revenge and anything that will hurt the other person will actually make them feel better. It is as if they were never taught how to self soothe or feel better using positive actions. This is especially true in high conflict divorces where the AP will use contrived scenarios of domestic violence or rape to manipulate the children, courts, attorneys and counselors. They must convince them that they are the better parent and that the other parent is a horrible, terrible person. They will denigrate the TP, alter information and do anything to maintain control over the ex because they want to continually inflict pain, suffering and they fear abandonment.

Where Did I Go Wrong? How Did I Miss The Signs?

Further research reveals that that they are probably narcissistic or megalomaniac, believing that the world evolves around them and only them. (Baron and Byrne, P. 456). In other words, rules are made for everyone but them. For example, the AP may refuse to abide by court orders regarding visitation, counseling and denigration of the other parent. The rules do not apply to them. Then, hypocritically, they will immediately file contempt charges if child support is one day late.

Furthermore, narcissistic individuals are especially affected by negative interpersonal experiences, which explain why the AP might deliberately destroy the TP's relationship with the kids. If the AP cannot have the TP, then no one, not even the children, should be allowed to have anything that resembles a relationship with the other parent. The TP is not permitted any happiness.

Their egotism causes them even more frustration by not being able to manipulate everything they want. They have lost control and their "holier than thou" image appears tarnished. In fact, re-marriage by the TP can trigger even more abuse when they realize that the ex-spouse is no longer available. (Warshak, http://www.fact.on.ca/Info/pas/warsha00.htm) Their pronounced anger and loss of control is evidenced by their methods of retaliation, which include denied visitations, and further denigration of the TP.

Also known as Frustration-Aggression, they became exceedingly more dangerous in their disregard for the children and ex-spouse's safety, security and emotional states. (Baron and Byrne, P. 443) In their mind, they depersonalize the TP and all associated with them. In fact, the covert aggression gets so out of control that they will deliberately lie about such things as telephone contact and mail contact from the other parent. Another example of Frustration-Aggression might be repeatedly telling the other parent the children are not around and then telling the children that the other parent never tries to contact them.

AP's belligerently try to control the formation of any relationship between the children and the other parent. Their anger is so consuming that it extends to any family member who sides against them. Repeatedly, they will even try to destroy the new marriage by using continual court harassment, which may include the serving of a subpoena in the middle of the night. They will also try to destroy the new marriage by backstabbing the TP and his family, which further alienates the children.

The above examples of outrageous responses are forms of Obstructionism. (Baron p. 466) Although this term usually applies to business situations, Obstructionism is classified as behaviors designed to impede the TP's relationship and performance. (Baron & Byrne, P. 466) In some cases, their refusal to let the children receive telephone calls, have visitation and see their mail, are clearly obstructive and classifiable as isolation and thus a form of domestic violence. Returning mail and failing to give sport schedules to the TP are also obstructive. Sometimes, they attempt to control contact times and allow visitation only when the other parent is supposed to be working. They know this interferes with the TP's ability to pay child support and could force the TP to postpone his visitation. Their attempts to get revenge are similar to crimes of passion. (Baron & Byrne, P. 453)

Though most do not use physical force, they use indirect aggression techniques intended to destroy any close relationships for the TP or their family. In fact, their hostile personality and intentions are indicative of a very stressful Type A personality. (Baron & Byrne, P. 455) They aggress with the prime objective of committing intentional harm upon innocent people. And though, according to Kemp (*Abuse In the Family*), females are thought to be less physically aggressive, this fact has been clearly refuted by the numerous reports and research by Mark Fiebert (Feibert, M. S. *References Examining Assaults By Women on Their Spouses or Male Partners: An Annotated Bibliography.* http://www.csulb.edu/~mfiebert/assault.htm). In addition, if a woman attacks, they often sustain injuries from the man who is trying to defend or protect himself. When this happens, the women are quick to file false accusations of domestic violence in order to frame the men.

These false accusations, in fact, are one of the prime indicator issues that Dr. Richard Gardner speaks about repeatedly (http://www.rgardner.com). According to Dr. Gardner, false allegations of abuse associated with PAS can surface in two

Where Did I Go Wrong? How Did I Miss The Signs?

ways. First they may be the result of thwarted efforts to be rid of the TP or they may be related to an underlying psychiatric disorder of the AP and surface prior to the separation or immediately after the separation. (Rand, Deirdre, http://www.robin.no/-dadwatch/pasdir/rand)1.html). In fact, these behaviors are quite typical of Narcissistic APs and can be more detrimental to the children than if the actual abuse had occurred because the children are not emotionally able to handle the discrepancies between illusory truth and lies. (Rand, Deirdre, http://www.robin.no/-dadwatch/pasdir/rand1.html)

The AP's personality can further be described as Manipulated Affiliation behavior. When an AP does not have people who are thinking and behaving their way, they deliberately do everything in their power to make sure that at least the children are on their side. This reaction comes out of fear that they will be abandoned and alone in their own thoughts and anger toward the other parent and that eventually the children might turn against them. AP's biggest fear is that of abandonment. To boost their own self-esteem and to perpetuate their "demented" perceptions of the ex-spouse, they psychologically abuse the children with fear or terror to enlist the children in the denigration and hatred of the other parent. With the children on their side, they preserve their self-esteem, self-concept and other personal images. Without the children's support, they are alone and vulnerable to the truth about their own anger, fear and irrational behavior. Without the children, their biggest fear, (a fear of abandonment), becomes a reality to them. All of this anger and hatred has traumatic life-long effects upon the children. If nobody intervenes and immediately corrects the maltreatment it will persist into the children's own adulthood and affect their own relationships and families, and become a multigenerational process.

When anger becomes this evolved it is abuse. Abuse of any kind is about control, not gender. When a person feels that they have lost the power to control their ex-spouse, they resort to various methods of abuse from physical to mental to gain back that control. For example, in a relationship situation where one partner refuses to do as the other partner demands, the aggressor or abuser will attempt to force the person to listen and do, as the abuser wants. Furthermore, if the relationship is failing but one spouse does not want it to end, they might use the children as pawns to keep the spouse. This is the same idea as a female who deliberately gets pregnant with the hopes that the man will love them more and that it will fix the marriage or relationship. In a situation where the children are already in existence, the spouse might feel that denying a relationship between the other spouse and the TP's children will put the control in their hands because they believe they can make them return. If the first denial of visitation does not work, then they begin to manipulate the children to change how the children feel about the other parent. The ultimate motive is to gain and keep control.

With their inability to act and think rationally or with appropriate emotions and feelings, they become a megalomaniac and damage all around them, particularly their children. In fact, these people are stagnant in this stage of understanding of how their actions affect others. Their emotional development becomes stunted and they continue on this downward spiral, unable to function in their own lives. It is a selfish stage and one where they are afraid of being abandoned. Taking this idea one step further, we can look at their emotional development as being immature or underdeveloped. They are usually narcissistic, a personality trait that stems from low self-esteem and low self-worth. Because they truly do not think they have what they need to be loved and wanted, they resort to all sorts of horrible tactics to get that love and devotion. One way to guarantee this love and devotion is to make sure the children hate the other parent and refuse to have anything to do with them. The children become solely dependent upon the AP for all their human needs, especially love. The TP is pushed out of the picture and the AP is guaranteed lasting love and devotion from the children.

Experts are uncertain whether the cause of the AP's disorder is organic. That is, there has been some speculation that the Alienating Parent (AP) may have a physical or mental dysfunction in the Amygdala of the brain. The Amygdala is located at the base of the brain and is responsible for understanding and sensing emotions and the feelings of others. (http://www.sci.uidaho.edu/med532/amygdala.htm) Some scientists feel that if the Amygdala shrinks, atrophies or is damaged in some way, it prevents the person from appropriately responding to emotions or causes the person to respond inappropriately to emotions. Optimistically, if this dysfunction is not caused by physical damage, it can be corrected, but only if the person is willing to go to counseling and therapy. This is the crux of the problem for an AP. They refuse to believe they have a problem. AP's are so narcisstic and self-centered, that they refuse to admit they may have a physical problem, mental problem or an uncontrollable rage problem. They vehemently refuse to attend counseling or if they do go, they cause such havoc that no progress can be attained. In addition, they interfere with their children's counseling even when it is court ordered. Unfortunately, the courts refuse to sanction the offending parent for fear of monetarily hurting or otherwise jeopardizing the children, and thus the AP continues to get rewarded for their poor behavior, dysfunction and manipulation.

In the next section, I will go into more detail about various aspects of the Alienator's personality and in particular, their fear of abandonment.

ABANDONMENT ISSUES IN RELATION TO PARENTAL ALIENATION SYNDROME

What causes abandonment issues? How do they develop? How does this fear affect people? And how do you handle it when it arises during a divorce and/or Parental Alienation.

Abandonment issues involve the fear that you will be left alone with no one there for you, to hear you, to be friends with you, to even care about you. This is a learned behavior from past experiences such as having someone leave and never return, having someone lie to the person and now they trust no one. Abandonment issues reach to the depth and core of the person's heart and soul and could be part of a grieving process. It triggers every imaginable emotion they have and creates a devastating fear that causes the person to do just about anything to prevent that abandonment from happening. In addition, any action deemed as abandonment such as a separation or divorce or even a simple disagreement, will send this person into hyper vigilance mode to protect himself or herself from any further abandonment by anyone else. This person's self-esteem is based entirely on being loved, wanted, needed and cared about. Any thing that contradicts this is considered a black mark on them personally and a preliminary to abandonment by anyone connected to the person or event that is causing them to believe they are being abandoned. This is a large part of what we see in Parental Alienation and Hostile Aggressive Parenting.

In fact, their own biological reactions to this fear become heightened including increases in hormone levels, pulse, heart and more. At the website, www.abandonment.net, they state the following, there is an "acute neuro-biological crisis…a rush of stress hormones…such as adrenaline and norepinephrine….glucocorticoids. Their brain chemistry shifts in response to imminent danger…. causing hyper-vigilant, obsessively focused, and on edge, as if prepared to sustain a life and death battle." (www.abandonment.net) This is similar to the flight or fright response where they are in an emergency situation. In this heightened state of awareness and fear of being left behind, these people fight back to prevent any further losses and disappointments. In a sense, their natural instincts to protect at any cost are misdirected by the fear of being abandoned. They are afraid that this loss will be like the black plague and everyone else will follow because if the one person they loved and counted on has left them, then they themselves must not be any good and so therefore everyone else is going to leave them unless they can prove that it was not them but the other persons fault. They work tirelessly to prove that they are the perfect ones and that the other person is the weak and terrible one. They work endlessly to maintain the control they feel they have lost. In reality, they are grieving a loss of a relationship and cannot process it completely and appropriately, leaving them in angry denial.

They are not able to truly grieve this loss because they are too afraid that it is contagious or an indication of them not being perfect. If instead, these people could properly grieve this loss of the relationship and understand that it does not mean that life cannot move forward and continue in a positive way, we might be able to help them to get past this fear of abandonment. As part of a grieving process, one needs to go through several stages, i.e. denial, anger, bargaining, depression and acceptance. What seems to happen with alienators and people with abandonment fears is they get stuck in the denial and anger stage, making it impossible to move forward. They refuse to bargain or work things out with the other person. Consequently, they never get to the depression step and then acceptance. If proper grief counseling were initiated at the start of a separation or divorce, it is quite possible that this type of person could move forward from the loss and not hang onto the anger. If the anger could dissipate, they would not use it against the other parent and chances are they would not destroy the relationship between the other parent and the children.

Interestingly, the psychological trauma they perpetuate between the children and the other parent causes a grief related to loss. The children are stuck grieving for a parent they cannot have a relationship with because it goes against the Alienating Parent (AP). For the Targeted Parent (TP), they are stuck grieving the loss of their relationship with their children. However, the TP cannot completely grieve because the children are still alive but physically dead to them. It is like a living death for both the children and the Targeted Parent.

As mentioned previously, for the person with abandonment issues, it feels like they are losing control and that is something they cannot have happen. If they lose control, how are they going to keep from losing the people they love? How are they going to maintain the status quo? How are they going to continue on in life, if they have no control over the lives around them? They believe that in order to be a whole person, they have to have control of all the parts of their lives including others and how they feel or think about them. They are so self-absorbed and afraid of being exposed as imperfect, that they must protect their self-image at all costs. Hence, there is the heightened biological stress related changes of the fright or flight response.

Part of this above scenario, also includes the fact that these people are terrified that if they are not perfect, they will be abandoned. Somewhere in their pasts, they experienced a loss and equated it to their own inadequacies. They mistakenly believed that it was their own imperfections that caused the loss. They have no faith in who they are. They do not understand that it is the imperfections in each of us that make each of us who we are and why we are all so different. These imperfections are what make life worth living because we grow and learn from them and that's what life is about. It's about growing and learning from the world and our experiences. If we can help them to understand that "being perfect" is not what life is about and isn't the norm, then maybe we can help them to accept the beautiful person they can be. They can be someone who gets to move forward in their life and someone who has lots of new experiences that will help them grow.

This fear of being left behind is traumatizing for these people. Can it be resolved? Well, that depends on the situation. In a intact family, it can be resolved with loving and caring relationships if the person with the abandonment issue is willing to work on accepting that this is their personal fear and does not mean that the whole rest of their world is untrustworthy. But if there is an impending divorce, the person is already feeling on the outside. This person needs to learn how to trust and understand that a relationship that falls apart does not mean the end of the world and that everyone else will abandon them too. By teaching them unconditional love and trust in themselves and their own abilities to move forward with their lives and gain more friends and wonderful life experiences, these individuals can get past this issue of abandonment related to divorce and separation. It can take years, but with proper counseling and support, it can be accomplished.

Part of the treatment for this person would need to include helping them with their insecurities and inability to trust others. In his or her mind, no one can be trusted. They are living with past experiences that they are still angry about and never properly grieved about. Helping them to come to terms with trust issues (who to trust and who not to trust) will give them the confidence to properly read people and situations. With this confidence, they will be able to bolster their self-esteem and discover their own personal abilities. They will learn how to protect themselves and finally have a chance to grieve about their past losses.

The big question here is how do we get these people to even go to counseling to help them work through this, when they believe that counseling means they are no good and not loveable. First, we can teach them that no one is perfect and everyone

Where Did I Go Wrong? How Did I Miss The Signs?

needs someone on the outside to talk to. Next, we can teach them how to be aware of the biological changes that occur when they are overreacting. We can show them when to step back and take a breath. We can also teach them when it's necessary to call someone and talk about their feelings before they overstep their boundaries.

From here we can help them to see that though a relationship has ended, it does not mean that the memories and experiences from that relationship are gone and forgotten. In fact, maybe being able to recall those memories with the person from the failed relationship can help them to see the wonderful things that are worth remembering. And maybe it will help them to understand that they are not being left behind because all of those wonderful memories will always be with both partners.

From there, various conversations can be had about how scared each of them is by this relationship falling apart and that it feels like their life is falling apart and that moving forward seems out of reach. This is where talks about their future visions and dreams could be useful. Helping them to state what their original dreams had been and where they can move forward to from here might help give perspective. Helping each other to see the positive adventures and experiences that could be in their future if they have this chance to separate and move forward separately may also be rewarding in this type situation. If one partner cannot think of their future without this person, then maybe it would help to ask them about things they have always wanted to do but never thought they could do because of the marriage. Try to help them explore their own personal attributes and skills that they have never fostered. With just these exercises alone, we are building confidence and positive thinking into the future and about who they are or could be.

CHAPTER 5

TYPES OF ABUSERS

PIT BULL VS. COBRA
TWO TYPES OF DOMESTIC VIOLENCE ABUSERS
IS THERE HOPE FOR THEM TO REGAIN CONTROL OF THEIR AGGRESSIVE BEHAVIOR?

There are two main types of abusers, the Pit Bull and the Cobra that were discovered by researchers, J. Gottman and N. Jacobson. They discovered that both abusers are aggressive physically and psychologically. Both abusers will stop at nothing to keep their victim under their control. Both abusers can, and may feel remorse. But there are differences.

The Pit Bull is like a magnet. They cement themselves to you out of fear of abandonment and loss of control. They are the stalker. They typically will only aggress toward family members and usually have no criminal record. But they are harder to get rid of because they are desperate to keep the victim in their lives. They never accept that the relationship is over. They keep going and going. If they cannot have the victim, then no one can and they are the most likely to commit suicide/murder. As Gottman and Jacobson say, "they cannot and won't let go."

The Cobra, by contrast, is anti-social in their behavior, usually having a criminal record and they do not care. The world revolves around them. As Jacobson and Gottman say, "they strike without warning". But, if they cannot control their victim, they will move on to their next prey. If a victim can get away from a cobra abuser, there is a good chance, they will survive and the cobra will just go away.

Where Did I Go Wrong? How Did I Miss The Signs?

There are more differences. Pit Bulls have actual physical changes to their bodily functions when they are about to get aggressive. These changes include and are not limited to, increased heart rate, increased blood pressure, sweating, increased breathing, and so on. Their attack is not without forewarning. They have signs and symptoms when they are about to lose control. And it is these signs and symptoms that could help reform a Pit bull.

This is in stark contrast to the Cobra, who has no physical bodily changes. They literally stay calm, cool and collected before they aggressively attack their victims and even during it. Prior and even during the attack, they never miss a heartbeat. Their pulse never races. Their breathing never increases. They do not even sweat. They just attack, like a cobra, striking without warning. They have no conscience. They have an agenda. And that is Control.

So what does this mean? It means that the Cobra, though more deadly at first, is easier to get rid of once the victim leaves them. The problem is "the leaving". The Cobra is so controlling, that it is "the leaving" that is hard to do. The Pit Bull is easier to leave because they feel more remorse but they never truly let go and continue to be fixated on the victim and their family. They fasten themselves to the victim and will not release their grip even after the victim has physically left them. They are more dangerous after the fact.

On the brighter side, since the Pit Bull has physical indicators that they are about to lose control i.e. increased heart rate, breathing and pulse, they can be taught to step back and walk away. With proper counseling, using behavior modification and other techniques, a Pit Bull can be taught to recognize these warning signs. Since the Pit Bull's aggressive behavior is related to their fear of abandonment, a counselor can work through this with them and delve deeply into their past to understand why they feel this way. Then, they can move forward and away from the fear of abandonment. In other words, Pit Bulls can be reprogrammed.

Cobra's, on the other hand, are socio-paths, with no conscience, no understanding and no care for others. They are narcissistic in their attitude. And since they don't feel any physical changes (increased heart rate, etc.) there is no way to help them see or feel the warning signs that they are about to lose control. Cobras don't care about being out of control. They only want to control everyone and everything. They cannot be rehabilitated in the normal traditional setting of a counselor's office.

So which is better? This will depend on the situation the victim is in. If the Pit Bull is willing to work things through and go to counseling, then there is a chance for them and the victim to make things work in their lives, whether together or separately. But if they are not willing, then this is a deadly combination. If it is the Cobra, and the victim can wrestle free from their hold and control, they have a better chance of survival. But if they cannot get free of the Cobra, they are destined to a life of torture, pain and suffering at the hands of a sociopath.

For more information and to figure out which you are the victim of, please check the following resources.

Gottman, J. & Jacobson, N. 1998. When Men Batter Women: New Insights into Ending Abusive Relationships. Simon and Schuster. P. 28-33.
Kemp, A. (1998) Abuse in the Family. An Introduction. NY: Brooks/Cole Publishing Company, Albany.

THE ALIENATOR AS TERRORIST
IS THERE A TERRORIST IN THE HOME WHO IS ESTABLISHING FEAR, ANGUISH, AND APPREHENSION IN THE CHILDREN?

What do you call it when a parent or person instills such fear and hatred in a child that he/she is afraid to love their other parent? What do you call it when a parent uses condescending words and actions to describe the other parent to the point of creating fear of that Targeted Parent? What do you call it when a parent threatens to not love a child if the child shows any love, compassion or feelings for the other parent? I call it Parental Alienation or Hostile Aggressive Parenting, but someone else might call this Terrorism.

Where Did I Go Wrong? How Did I Miss The Signs?

Terrorism: the word strikes fear in most people's hearts. But what is the actual definition of Terrorism? According to Encarta World English Dictionary, it is:

>ter·ror·ism n
>violence or the threat of violence, especially bombing, kidnapping, and assassination, carried out for political purposes.

The synonyms for Terrorism are not better: Violence, intimidation, terror campaign and bombing. Wow, some pretty strong words. And what about the word Terrorist? What does it mean?

>ter·ror·ist n
>somebody who uses violence or the threat of violence, especially bombing, kidnapping, and assassination, to intimidate, often for political purposes.

And what about the word Terror? This is a strong one, too.

>ter·ror n
>1. intense or overwhelming fear
>2. violence or the threat of violence carried out for political purposes
>3. something such as an event or situation that causes intense fear
>4. an annoying, difficult, or unpleasant person, particularly a naughty child (informal)

Encarta® World English Dictionary © 1999 Microsoft Corporation. All rights reserved. Developed for Microsoft by Bloomsbury Publishing Plc.

Parental Alienation utilizes all of these tactics and more. There are threats of violence if a child does not follow the parent's orders. There is fear that the Alienating Parent will no longer love them if he/she does not follow the parent's orders and there is fear of being treated just like the Targeted Parent by the alienator. A child's mind is kidnapped and held hostage under the guise of love, honor and just reward. Parental Alienation is the assassination of one parent's good name and character for the sole, selfish purposes of depriving a child of a relationship with the other parent. It's "the bombing" of all the child's positive feelings and memories of their other parent.

Parental Alienation has been compared to cults while the actions of Cult Leaders are compared to the Alienator. Just like a Cult Leader, a Parental Alienator indoctrinates their followers to believe in only them and that no one else matters or is safe. But isn't that what a Terrorist leader is? A Cult Leader for a fanatical group believes their way is the only way. In some cases, this narcissism is so extreme that the alienator/terrorist will kill to get what they want.

A Parent who alienates their children from the other loving parent, barring no true and proven abuse has occurred, is doing the same thing. The alienator is bribing and brainwashing their children and even brainwashing friends and family, to believe that the other parent is a worthless, terrible person who could never be trusted. The alienator sets up extreme scenarios to push their campaign to destroy the other person, in much the way a terrorist incites their disciples to become suicide bombers and blow up others who do not believe their way. The alienator kills their child's soul and heart, making sure that any feelings between the children and their other parent are destroyed. Cult Leaders and Terrorists are really no different in their actions and thoughts. It is all for them.

We need to stop these family terrorists from destroying any more children and their relationships with the other parent. Terrorism, whether it is an assault on a nation or on a family, is a crime and should be penalized appropriately. Until the courts and therapists appreciate the gravity of the Parental Alienator's terrorist tactics, children and their Targeted Parents will continue to be decimated by narcissistic control freaks, i.e., the alienating abusive parents.

CHAPTER 6

WHY DO ALIENATORS ALIENATE? AND WHEN WILL IT STOP?

Why is this happening?
Why do they want to hurt us so badly?
Why do they want to hurt innocent children?
Why can't they see what they are doing is wrong?

I've heard the same questions asked over and over again. How can a parent do this to a child? Why do they do this? How can they be so mean and evil? I wish there were simple answers. Instead, I am going to give some plausible explanations. These are not going to make the Alienator stop, but they might put some perspective on the situation and help to direct you in a better way to deal with the Alienator. The scenarios I list below are not necessarily all the possibilities. They can be the main issue or could be combined together to make these Alienators who they are and why they do what they do.

1. The Alienator is so filled with anger, rage and hatred that they cannot see any further past that and their whole entire world is wrapped around making sure the other person hurts as much as they do. It is like they are blinded by their anger and hatred.

2. It is a warped sense of pleasure. They are narcissistic and probably several other things. So

for them, they cannot derive pleasure from truly happy and meaningful things, as they do not know how. They are so mentally warped that the only pleasure they derive is from hurting others around them to boost their own self-esteem and ratings.

3. They were raised in a home where one of their parents was an Alienator and the only thing they know about relationships, is that one person controls everyone. If you do not have control, then you are nothing. Consequently, they do not know how to have any other kind of relationship nor would they know how to handle it. They fear losing control over everyone, because not to be in total control means you are a loser.

4. The Alienator could have such low self-esteem that anyone putting them down or any inference with anything they were involved in, such as their failed marriage, would set them off. They will fight to defend their honor and reputation. They are so protective of their image that they will do anything to make sure that they stay looking like the perfect person and will destroy everyone else around them to maintain that image.

5. The Alienator's own parents put them down constantly and told them they would never amount to much. When their own marriage fails, they are desperate to prove their parents were wrong and will do anything to make it appear that it was not their fault.

6. Alienators have warped views of themselves from low self- esteem issues. It puts them in such a fragile state of fear that they are no good unless they are seen as all good.

Where Did I Go Wrong? How Did I Miss The Signs?

7. Alienators cannot accept responsibility for their actions and blame their faults on everyone else. How could they possibly be wrong? Everyone else is wrong. Alienators are so narcissistic in their belief that they are never wrong, that they will do anything to protect their image. They must make sure they are always on top and that it is everyone else who is at fault.

8. Alienators were never taught to take responsibility for their own actions and to be humble when they have made a mistake. They were raised believing they could do no wrong, just like their own parents could do no wrong. Thus, it is everyone else who is wrong. So instead, they were raised to blame everyone but themselves for their own mistakes.

9. The Alienator is so terrified of losing their children and being abandoned that they need to paint this perfect picture of themselves. At the same time, they make the other person look extremely bad or guilty in order to ensure they do not lose their children or control.

10. The Alienator is so terrified that they are not lovable that they try to force others to love them.

11. The Alienator is not a real good sharer. In other words, they do not know how to share love and happiness. Maybe because they had to share their parents and never understood that sharing is not only a nice thing, but it also feels really good.

12. Insane, Unrealistic, Irrational Jealousy of the other parent's relationship with the children. In other words, the targeted parents close and attentive relationship with the children causes extreme jealousy in the alienating parent, who wishes the same attention was being paid to them by the

targeted parent. In turn, this spurs on the alienating parents fear of abandonment by the children for the other parent. In the case of grandparents who alienate children, it is a jealousy of the relationship that their child has with their grandchildren but that they, the grandparent, never had with the alienated parent. This jealousy could clearly explains the alienator's actions and absolute fear of abandonment.

What this boils down to is possible DSM (Diagnostic and Statistical Manual) Diagnoses such as functional Borderline Personality (BPD), Bi-Polar Personality (BPP), Post Traumatic Stress Syndrome (PTSS), Narcissistic Personality Disorder and other mental conditions. But, the more I hear, the more I see, and the more I read, the more the Alienators behavior fits a co-morbid diagnosis of BPD in combination with at least one other DSM diagnosis. In particular, I see BPD and being stuck in the grieving process as the main diagnosis because of their extreme fears.

1. They are afraid of being abandoned.
2. They fear people finding out they are not perfect and become desperate to point the finger at anyone but themselves. They must deflect their imperfections. (In other words, they project their imperfections on you and everyone else.)
3. They fear that if everyone who is important in their life does not love them, they are worthless.
4. They are ashamed of how they act, but do not understand why.
5. Their world is either black or white. There is no gray area in between and therefore no compromise.
6. They must deny that anything is wrong with them, because otherwise they are admitting they are NOT perfect and thus worthless.
7. To avoid the pain and suffering inside their heads, they project all of their insecurities and pains onto

the other people in their lives, hoping it will stop their own pain.

When is this going to stop? When will you feel normal? When will the Alienator figure out how wrong all of this is? This is a good question but there's no simple, single answer. In the meantime, you can make a difference for yourself and those around you by knowing:

1. You have the power to make it stop by not engaging or allowing the Alienator to cross over your boundaries. You need to protect your personal boundaries and determine what is acceptable and not acceptable behavior. Only you have this control. When you put your foot down, the Alienator/BPD is being taught where you draw the line and what you will or will not tolerate. You are helping them to actually understand and create their own boundaries so they do not cross them with others. They can only learn by watching, seeing, hearing and getting stopped in their tracks. And this includes the children's behavior. You have the control to not allow their projection to get to you and you can say to the Alienator, "This is your problem and I will not accept you pushing your problems and issues on me. I am sorry if you feel abandoned, but just because our relationship is over, it does not mean that I will not be there to help raise the children. No one is perfect and parents are no exception. It is okay to make a mistake so long as you own it and learn how to correct it. I will not be held accountable for your imperfections, only mine"

2. It will feel normal when you finally take back control of your life and when you stop letting others cross over your personal boundaries. This is your space and you decide what you will and will not tolerate. If you continue to allow them to beat

you up emotionally and mentally, you are allowing them into your space. When you tell them NO, I am not going to be your whipping post. NO, I am not going to tolerate your fears and problems being projected onto me, and then you will start to feel normal, because you will be back in control of your own life and destiny. If you have to tell them to "Piss-Off" then do it. But get the point across loud and clear. If it means hanging up on them when they are abusive, then do it. If it means closing the door in their face, then just do it.

3. The Alienator cannot get it, if they are not learning the right lessons. If we continue to allow them to control us and continue to cross our boundaries and borders, they will not get it. When we act by example, the Alienator will have to start learning to work with us, not against us, or they will never get their pain resolved. They will always feel abandoned, imperfect and out of control.

4. You cannot change them, but you can change how you react to them and block the hurt. And the best way to do that is to become more successful in your life with each passing day. I would suspect that the more you succeed or make any headway with your children, the more it upsets their warped and wobbling apple cart. And the more you upset this apple cart, the more they try to straighten it up. But because it is warped and wobbling, it will never sit straight and so eventually, one day, it will come crumbling down and when it does, you need to be there for your children.

5. What this means is that you need to stop worrying about why they do it, because in reality, they can't help it. They know no other way but to take from others and make them hurt. This makes them feel

Where Did I Go Wrong? How Did I Miss The Signs?

better inside. Instead you need to concentrate on your success and remain healthy and happy so that you can be there for your kids. HHS or Happy, Healthy and Successful in life.

We could go on and on and come up with excuses for the Alienator's behavior. But what it boils down to is the very first one on this list. They are so filled with hatred, rage and anger that they just cannot move on with their lives. It consumes them to the point that they will do anything to win or get revenge. Added together, or even in small combinations, this amounts to DSM diagnoses that explain so much of what goes on in an Alienators mind. But is this natural? Is this learned or is it a combination of both?

CHAPTER 7

NATURE VIA NURTURE: WHAT'S NATURE GOT TO DO WITH NURTURE?

AN AGE OLD QUESTION: WHICH IS MORE IMPORTANT HEREDITY OR ENVIRONMENT?

Nature occurs naturally or by innate processes versus Nurture, which is learned and becomes habitual. But not all is, as it seems. Which came first, the chicken or the egg, Nature or Nurture? At first, when you start to read this chapter, you will think, "What does this have to do with Parental Alienation?" But as you read on, it will all begin to make sense, so be patient.

Which is stronger nature or nurture? This is a loaded question that has plagued scientists, psychologists, psychiatrists, physicians and philosophers for centuries. Do our genes control who and what we become or do our life experiences control who and what we are? Causality or Teleology? According to Matt Ridley's interview with Craig Venter for the research of his article and book, Mr. Venter states that there is no way that genes and biology alone dictate who we are and what makes us special. It is, which is the title of Ridley's latest book and the premise for his article in Time Magazine called *What Makes You Who You Are*. (June 2, 2003, P.54-63).

Nature describes all those things that we come by through genetics or heredity. This includes our traits of skin, hair, eyes and physical structure as well as our abilities and disabilities or

Where Did I Go Wrong? How Did I Miss The Signs?

"limitations and capacities." (Berger, P.52-53) To some extent, even our personality and intellectual ability are inheritable according to Murray Bowen.

Nurture, by contrast, is related to what we learn, and is influenced by our environment. All of which, can affect our personality, intelligence and physical traits. If just one of these is not properly nurtured, even naturally, their development can be dysfunctional. Thus, ultimately, there is a case to be made for equal contribution from nature and nurture as they intersect or "interact", helping to form and develop who we are. (Berger, P. 52)

According to Ridley, Venter states it is simply impossible for the limited amount of genes that we posses, to be the total sum of who we are and will be. Our personal experiences are what make us different and special as our biological make-up responds to those experiences. That is, the more genes are exposed to experiences, or as Ridley says, "lifting the lid on the genome", the more variables in genetic make-up occur.

Furthermore, genes are more than just handed down by our parents. Genes are affected by everything that they come in contact with. Whether it is a strong influence or weak one, our genes draw upon these experiences. And it is these experiences, which are the tools for learning, directing us in our pursuit of who we are and what we will or want to be. Without experiences our genes would be lost in a sea of unknown direction, excelling and propelling to nowhere.

Ridley explains the premise of genetic experiences as genes being the "puppets", which are controlled by our behaviors, which in turn are affected by the environment. He states that our instincts, which are those things we innately know, are more than just inborn, they can be learned. Furthermore, he believes the environment is less adjustable and thus less adaptable to change. And he believes nature was meant to back up nurturing. That is to say, what occurs by itself unimpeded is meant to be cultivated to be distinct and different. Hence, if we nurture the innate abilities of a child, then we promote the growth of a child's strengths naturally.

He explains this further by saying that human's natural fear of snakes comes from learned experiences of our ancestors as innate as well as learned from watching others fear snakes. His premise is that it is not the fear of the snake, but that we are programmed to learn to fear snakes and that this involves a genetic tendency for a protective form of nurturing.

Ridley goes on to make some profound statements about our genetic makeup and hox genes or the nature of organism development. Apparently, our genes are not much different from earthworms, according to another scientist that Ridley interviewed. It is all about which genes are turned on or off. It seems that everything has the same genes, it just depends on how they are turned on and off by a promoter. Going on this biological premise, promoters might be affected to turn on or off according to hormones in the mother's blood stream. For example, these chemicals could then account for homosexual and heterosexual tendencies. Thus, as Ridley says, "Bodies are not made, they grow." (Ridley, P. 60). They are part of a mixture of ingredients that is varied in amounts to create not only differences from human beings and other species but from one human being to another.

This difference can even include such things as antisocial behavior. We know for a fact that hatred is learned and not innate. In other words, hatred is bred into the psych and behavior patterns of an individual either by experience or by significant others. And for years it has been assumed that deviant behavior was only the result of mistreatment in childhood. Under new research it seems that this is only true for small genetic groups. It seems there is a genetic correlation to the amount of the monoamine oxidase gene found in a person. Apparently, if one has a high amount of monoamine oxidase, they are more likely to be immune to mistreatment and thus less likely to become antisocial. If one has low levels of this genetic trait, they are more likely to have socialization problems if they were mistreated. In light of this information, it is apparent that genetics and environment are more involved in our personality makeup than we ever thought.

In fact, it seems that even homosexuality is related to the amount of chemicals left or produced by an older male sibling in the mother. A recent study concluded that gay men were more likely to have an older brother as a sibling than lesbians or

Where Did I Go Wrong? How Did I Miss The Signs?

heterosexual men. But this brings up a big dilemma. If a woman knows that her chances of having a homosexual son are greater because she has already had a son, how should she handle it? Someone who is homophobic might say, "lets have an ultrasound immediately" upon hearing that they are pregnant again. Their response might be to decide to terminate the pregnancy for fear of having a homosexual child. But should these assumptions be used to determine the future of families?

From empiricists to naturists to mathematicians to scientists, the development of nature and nurture even in relation to personality has been debated, researched and studied. People like Immanuel Kant, Francis Galton, Konrad Lorenz and Noam Chomsky believed that nature was our destiny and the deciding factor in our human development. On the other side of the coin are John Locke, Ivan Pavlov, Sigmund Freud and Franz Boas who believed that nurture, in the form of learning, designed our futures.

I think one of the best examples of natures influence on human development is that of the acquisition of language. Man did not just learn this out of the blue. There had to be an inborn skill to help acquire the ability to formulate words and thoughts. This is innate and without this ability our experiences in life would be totally different.

According to Noam Chomsky, all humans have an innate ability to learn language. He calls it LAD or Language Acquisition Device. (Berger, P. 199-200) Theoretically, it is the human brains ability, using structures and organization, to understand and utilize the rules associated with grammar that they hear. In other words, they innately know how to place a noun before a verb. But this also seems to miss the mark as to how much of this is also dependent on Social contact. Without the experience of hearing grammatically correct statements, a child would not be influenced. But, in the same token, being able to recognize these grammatical patterns requires an inborn human ability.

And in the same sense, nurturing creates and sustains naturally occurring issues such as maturity. According to Ridley's article, girls raised in fatherless homes were more likely to begin puberty at an earlier age than girls raised in a two-parent home. This issue seems to tie genes to the environment. Though scientists are not quite sure how this works, it seems that emotional changes and maturity involved with responsibility allow the genes for female hormones to advance in their stages of development. This is quite interesting concept when one sees the statistical reports which state that more and more girls are menstruating at earlier ages, such as 9 and 10 years of age. Can we correlate this to the increased divorce rate in our country? Or the fact that more and more parents are being alienated from their children? Or to hormones being pumped into our foods? Right now, no one knows for sure, but it is a statistical fact that girls from fatherless homes are more likely to have teenage pregnancies and this has everything to do with environment and their biological time clocks ticking out of sync with normal growth patterns.

To further this theory of survival, recently, in one of my on line support groups, one of the moderators spoke about a study that was done in Africa in relation to children's innate mechanisms for survival in psychologically abusive situations. The premise of the study was to show how temperament played a part in children's survival. The study began during prosperous times when crops were good and lots of babies were born. These children's were studied and broken down into 4 temperament groups.

Group 1: Easy Temperament
Group 2: Slow to Warm Up
Group 3: Hard Work
Group 4: Bloody Difficult all the time.

Soon the country endured several years of famine. The researchers went back and found some very interesting correlations. Most of the babies had died. All of the children in groups 1 and 2 died and most of group 3 had died. But in group 4, the toughest of all to handle, none of them had died. The fact that they were demanding, difficult and independent ensured their survival. Which leads one to believe that being selfish is natural to a point for survival, but maybe only up to a certain age. (Threlfalll, Penny) After that age and life stage of development, selfishness and controlling behavior, if not appropriately directed,

Where Did I Go Wrong? How Did I Miss The Signs?

leads to detriment in establishing warm and loving relationships, especially if the children are not able to get past these traumas and learn to love.

So from this study we can gleam a very real reason why some children are more easily alienated and programmed to hate the other parent, than others. To further understand what I am talking about, one of the main things we have noticed about the targeted parent, is they are 99% of the time the more calm, nicer, easy going, will do anything for you parent. In fact, they were probably deliberately picked as a mate by the Aggressive parent because they knew they would be easy to control. Many if not all of these target parents had a very strong relationship with their kids prior to the turmoil, and thus their children probably took on much of this persona from the targeted parent of being giving to a fault. Because of this, these children would be more easily molded to fit the needs of the aggressive parent. If the child did not bend to the aggressive parents ways, just like the targeted parent, they would be sent away or treated with distain and wrath. This child would have no choice but to either leave, or endure the wrath or change to suit the aggressor to survive.

I think if you take this theory and the evidence I have amassed from my support group members, you will see that a child can easily be molded to suit an aggressors needs and though I agree that working on the child's issues is paramount, unless the aggressor is taken out of the picture, quite often, the situation only gets worse, especially if the child is not strong enough to stand up to the alienating parent. And thus, alienation of the children from the other parent can easily be accomplished as these children are too easily molded out of fear and guilt.

This study came up in context to an issue on my Parental Alienation Syndrome (PAS) Web support groups concerning survival techniques used by children of PAS. Parental Alienation Syndrome or PAS is preceded by something called Hostile Aggressive Parenting. Hostile Aggressive Parenting (HAP) is a form of psychological abuse, which is perpetrated by parents who mentally destroy their children's psych by belligerently denigrating the other parent. The process destroys a child's love and respect for the other parent and in turn the children fear losing the love of the perpetrating parent, resulting in Parental

Alienation of the Targeted Parent. In effect, Parental Alienation is the breakdown of a relationship between the children and the other parent, which ultimately leads to specific signs and symptoms that can be classified collectively as Parental Alienation Syndrome.

The children become brainwashed and are programmed to believe that the other parent is no good and should be feared or hated. Ultimately, the children come to believe that their thoughts about the Targeted Parent are solely their own and have nothing to do with the programming process by the perpetrating parent. The children will claim to hate the Targeted Parent for no constructive reason, or for false reasons with no proof, and actually join in the denigration of the Targeted Parent. The children show no remorse or empathy for this Targeted Parent. It is at this point that the syndrome of Parental Alienation has become full blown. This type of abuse can lead to psychological problems for the children, as their basic human needs of belonging and being loved are not being met with the Targeted Parent. In addition, the Alienating Parent will only love them under the condition that they hate the Targeted Parent. The stress of this enmeshment and fusion with the Alienating Parent causes psychological social and self-esteem issues in the children.

From this scenario, one can see how the nurturing of hatred in the children leads to natural reactions to avoid the Targeted Parent. In order to survive the torment and wrath of the aggressive parent, these children learn to block out all their natural emotions and feelings for the Targeted Parent and substitute them with placated reactions and emotions learned from the aggressive parent. Eventually, these new emotions and feelings become natural for them to the point that they believe they are true and their own. In other words, they believe that their hatred and anger toward the Targeted Parent is something they developed naturally all by themselves. It is easy to see how nature versus nurture can get muddled here and how easily a parent's hostile nurturing can destroy the natural love and affection a child has for the other parent.

This destruction of the children's love for the other parent disrupts their natural developmental stages of growth and hierarchy of needs according to Abraham Maslow. For the child

Where Did I Go Wrong? How Did I Miss The Signs?

who is controlled and manipulated, especially in the last scenario, their ability to actually become an independent and self-actualized individual is impossible.

Self-actualizing is a concept equated with Abraham Maslow. (Maslow, A. H. *Toward a Psychology of Being. New York, Norstand, 1962)* He speaks about a hierarchy of needs to keep us alive. He depicts these needs as a triangle starting with our most basic "deficiency needs". (See Figure 1) The first of which are the physiological needs of food and water, thus making up the base of the triangle. Without food and water, we will surely die. Once these needs are met, the next most important need for our survival is safety and security. Without a safe and secure environment, our chances of survival go down, such as in countries were war is constant.

As we progress in our endurance to live on, our need for love and devotion to and by someone else becomes important to our happiness. With love, the child learns and develops self-esteem, which helps them to be proud of who they are and where they come from. If a child does not feel loved or wanted by his parents or guardians, then their belief in themselves as a good person are shattered and so goes their self-esteem. Without feeling good about themselves, a child will see no reason to live life as society expects and so their survival rate drops.

At the top two levels of the triangle are the needs for Self-Actualization and Spirituality that are not necessary to our physical survival as much as our emotional growth and psychological survival. Self-actualization is our ability to see ourselves honestly and openly, while continuing to grow and develop to the best of our ability. Self-Actualization enables sacrifice without guilt or worry, unconditionally. At the spiritual level, there is transcendence to being an individual who is part of the whole of this universe. There is no better or worse, there just is.

As we acquire all of these needs in a progression upward in the triangle, we develop into a stronger and stronger individual "able to leap tall building in a single bound" and thus our chances for survival increase at each level. But in all seriousness, our human needs are striving for us to be as superhuman as we can be which is only natural.

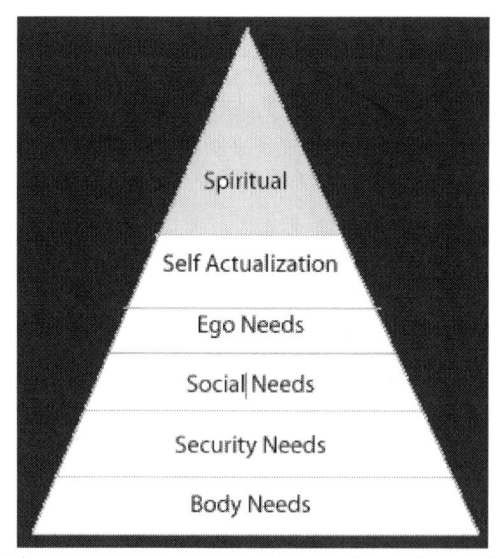

Figure 1. Maslow's Hierarchy of Needs

When this hierarchy of needs is interrupted or not allowed to progress completely in each stage, especially in the four earlier stages, physical and psychological dysfunction occurs. No food and water, we die. No safety and security, we could die or grow up very afraid and weary of everything and everyone around us. No love and belonging and we miss the nurturing of our souls to be good, kind and considerate. No self- esteem and we never believe we can succeed and amount to anything, so we never strive to be our best and instead just settle for anything, especially in relationships.

In PAS children, who are denied these needs, it is apparent that if they make it to the love and belonging stage, but do not get the appropriate response and reaction, they never learn how to give and receive love either. They are left wondering if they are truly loveable, which in turn, lowers their self-esteem. Children caught at this level can never truly understand their true potential or capabilities as a human being. They are left stunted in their emotional growth to develop fully functioning and stable relationships with others. And if they do not have these skills, how can they possibly pass it on to their children. Thus, the vicious circle of multigenerational maladjusted relationships continue to spiral through these families, sending them down a

Where Did I Go Wrong? How Did I Miss The Signs?

road of self-destruction. At this point, do we call this multigenerational behavior pattern natural or nurtured? Since it is now passed on from generation to generation, does this not make it heredity from our families of origin?

The author of the article, *"What Makes You Who You Are"*, Matt Riley, states that Freud "believed in parental influence and early experiences on young minds". (Ridley. P. 58-59). In light of PAS, I would say this is very true. But according to Dr. Bryan Miller, my professor in Graduate School, the core of Freud's personality development was based on Heredity and not Parental Societal experiences and influences. He feels that Freud did not believe so much in environmental problems, but more in a non-completion of the stages of development. But I guess if one were to take these theories just a little deeper, they could be viewed, as Ridley suggests, as parental influences and experiences in the stages of development. In other words, if one of the stages of development is interrupted by divorce or death, then our parent's emotional reactions will affect our maturity and emotional development. In the case of PAS, a child's stage of development related to love and belonging by both parents is interrupted when one parent denigrates and alienates the children from the other parent. This, in turn, sets up a learned lesson that is carried on through the generations by environmental influences in the home. Thus parents, heredity and environment seem to have an equal influence on how we grow up. And one can easily see how PAS is affected by all three elements.

The implications of nature versus nurture and genetics versus environment can bring up some pretty hefty moral values. In addition, genetics, which is something that we really cannot alter accurately, as of yet, has just as big a responsibility in our development as does environment. And environmentally, parents could drive themselves nuts trying to be the perfect parents who provide the perfect atmosphere. I think Ridley may have had it right when he said Nature via Nurture. We are who we are because of our natural tendencies, which can be further enhanced by our environment and the nurturing by our parents. It is all a part of the developing process of human beings, like a pendulum swinging between nature and nurture.

CHAPTER 8

THE PENDULUM EFFECT

Pendulum – Various Definitions
pen·du·lum (pnj-lm, pndy-, pnd-)
n.
1. A body suspended from a fixed support so that it swings freely back and forth under the influence of gravity, commonly used to regulate various devices, especially clocks. Also called simple pendulum.
2. Something that swings back and forth from one course, opinion, or condition to another: the pendulum of public opinion.
[New Latin, probably from Italian pendolo, pendulous, pendulum, from Latin pendulus, hanging; see pendulous.]
The American Heritage® Dictionary of the English Language, Fourth Edition copyright ©2000 by Houghton Mifflin Company. Updated in 2009. Published by Houghton Mifflin Company. *All rights reserved.*

pendulum
Noun
1. a weight suspended so it swings freely under the influence of gravity
2. such a device used to regulate a clock mechanism
3. a movement from one attitude or belief towards its opposite: the pendulum has swung back to more punitive measures
Collins Essential English Dictionary *2nd Edition 2006* © *HarperCollins Publishers 2004, 2006*

Where Did I Go Wrong? How Did I Miss The Signs?

pendulum (pnj-lm)
A mass hung from a fixed support so that it is able to swing freely under the influence of gravity. Since the motion of pendulums is regular and periodic, they are often used to regulate the action of various devices, especially clocks.
The American Heritage® Science Dictionary Copyright © 2005 by Houghton Mifflin Company. Published by Houghton Mifflin Company. *All rights reserved.*

Years ago, in the early 1800's to 1920's, fathers were always allowed first rights to the custody of the children. Once the women's movement and their rights became established, the pendulum began to swing completely to the other side. Today, the pendulum is lowly starting to equalize as it swings out between the two parents, with more fathers getting custody and more mother's losing custody. Is this okay? No, it's not. This should not be about a pendulum swinging from left to right. It should be about a pendulum that swings equally back and forth in the middle of the road.

Now, if you think this pendulum is difficult for the parents to negotiate in the courts, imagine how this pendulum affects the children? They swing between both of the parents they love and then are forced to love only one of them. It is nearly impossible for them to navigate this emotional swing from a stable, middle of the road, normal loving relationship with both parents, to one that is obsessed with despising the other parent. Their emotional highs and lows are so exaggerated that the children cannot properly gauge right from wrong, good from bad, healthy from unhealthy and so on. They are caught in this suspended position, hanging on for dear life, because if they dare to swing to the other side, and show any love and respect for the other parent, they will be thrown off balance and rejected, like garbage. They are literally suspended in time on one side of the pendulum.

So, how do we get this pendulum to swing back and forth evenly for them again? That is the basis for much of what will be said in the next few chapters. It will not be an easy adjustment, nor will it come about without tears and fears. But, in order to break these old patterns of thoughts and behaviors, all of the participants will be forced to give up something that they struggle to hold on to, as well as to "let go" and trust the "universe" to do the right thing. I know this sounds hokey, but in a way, all of us are hanging onto fears and tears that do not allow us to literally "let go". We hold tight, fearing that if we say or do the wrong thing, our children or parent will be lost forever, especially when it comes to PAS. But, if we are able to move forward, then we have to let go of those weights that are holding us. We are stuck on one side of the pendulum and we can't swing freely to the other side. This topic will come up again in the context of putting our foot down as parents and not allowing us to be abused and used as doormats. But for the children, who do not have the emotional maturity to understand all of these concepts, we must teach them critical thinking so that they can "let go" and move forward with their lives. As parents, this will be the toughest job we will ever have.

Where Did I Go Wrong? How Did I Miss The Signs?

CHAPTER 9

THE AMUSEMENT PARK RIDE
THE EMOTIONS AND ACTIONS CAUSED BY PAS.

During a conversation in one of my support groups, mention was made of amusement park rides in relation to the emotions and actions that are occurring when it comes to PAS. I mentioned the pendulum-swinging ride that goes from one side to the other as it gets higher and higher with the child stuck in the middle and a parent on either side of the pendulum. Eventually, the ride comes to rest smack in the middle so all can get off. But the children often get stuck all the way up on one side, (i.e. one parent's side), and they are just suspended there, unable to move, for fear of falling out of their seat with that parent. But there is also another ride that hits home. This is the roller coaster ride, with the ups and downs and hills and valleys; peaks and dives. It's a metaphor for the emotions each and every person feels when they are living through this drama.

So, what is it about amusement parks that attract so many customers? Is it the rush and high that people get from going to these extreme limits to feel something? I wonder if, for the Alienator, the exhilaration of pushing the control buttons and pushing the envelope gives them a "rush" of exhilaration and thrills. That is why they throw us on these emotional amusement park rides.

Below is an excerpt from this discussion from one of my websites:
RE: The Amusement Park Ride
LU writes:
The THRILL of being in control!

The Author writes:
Not just the thrill of the control, but the ability to actually feel something. Most Alienators are BPD and cannot feel anything. Amusement parks provide not only the thrill, but also the ability to feel something that they actually know what it is, control.

LP writes:
That was good and I agree, my sister and everyone else would also. My sister said she has come to the conclusion that A likes the drama, being the center of attention and having complete control over EVERYONE in the family. I will try my hardest not to give my daughter the satisfaction of drawing negative attention to herself. I can only imagine the woe is me stories she has told to gain false sympathy. That's really weird.

Anonymous writes:
I think it is. In our case the AP has to have complete control of everything & I think sitting back & looking at all she has done and created is how she gets her jollies. The drama created from all this is what creates her excitement & then she gets attention. That is her roller coaster.

LU writes:
I've often wondered about this also. I think/believe the only thing they "feel" is better by seeing us hurt. It's all about, them isn't it? From what I've gathered on them, is they do whatever it takes to feel better... to get the narcissist supply, or needed drama and chaos. Hence I hurt you/messed up your day/week/year/life. So therefore, I feel better!

Where Did I Go Wrong? How Did I Miss The Signs?

CC writes:
I agree with this. I will say, however, that my ex has pretty much left me alone since getting the boys full custody (I'm knocking on wood). Well, except for the child support hearings and the whole school thing. Now that he has the boys, whether it's because he knows it hurt me taking them or if it's because having them fulfills his need to control, I'm not sure. Maybe a combination of both. But, in a sense, by controlling them, he's still controlling me, which I'm sure is the ultimate high for him.

The Author writes:
Interesting again here is my interpretation. He is still controlling the boys, which in turn controls you. So the roller coaster is still going on in all of your lives. Just think about how their emotions are from day to day. One day nice to you, the next not talking to you. The next day asking to come early. The next day, not even responding. Still a roller coaster ride emotionally for all.

From this excerpt, we get a pretty good visual of what the emotional stress of PAS feels like for everyone involved. But how much of this roller coaster ride can one family take? How much of this spinning upside down can one person take? All of which brings us to the most basic thought by almost every Targeted Parent at some point in this process. Is it okay if I stop this merry-go-round and get off? I just want to get off the ride. Is that okay?

WHAT HAPPENS WHEN YOU JUST CANNOT TAKE IT ANYMORE?

Sometimes, the pain and heartache that these Alienators foist upon our children and us is just unbearable. Finding a proper support group, such as PAS-GuardianAngels or PAS2ndWivesClub is paramount. All three of these groups can be found on Yahoo. Below is an excerpt from one mother who was ready to throw in the towel and how supportive a group can be.

> *AK writes:*
>
> *I just can't go on...it's been SO long...5&1/2 years. I've fought SO hard. I've spent all my money on lawyers. I'm broke...in every way. No matter what I've done, it's never enough and he's always a step ahead. Nobody understands...how can they all be so immune??? How can they not at least imagine the pain of losing two children??? How does he make them believe he's such a wonderful person??? I'm crazy now. He did it. He drove me there by taking my babies away from me. I can't leave the house. I can't see anyone. I just can't. There's nothing out there but false hope and pain. I can't take it anymore...the pain is finally unbearable. I have to quit. I can't do this anymore...fighting for my children's lives, and having them spit in my face...they hate me and they always will. He's won...he's poisoned their minds and they will NEVER feel anything but hate and disgust for me......the courts won't help me while he's hiding behind his voluntary Army duty in Africa....he says he'll be unable to be in court until my youngest is 18...it's over...it's all over...I just can't go on.*

> *The Author writes:*
>
> *I know you are hurting and feel like all is lost. But this is exactly where he wants you. If you end it all now, he wins because he has driven you mad and that means he has total control of you. You CANNOT let him win. I have gone over your application and introduction. G still lives with you or, at the least, your eldest son and you have a great relationship. You need to be there for him.*
>
> *You also stated that the ex has three counts of neglect or other charges against him from Child Protective Services. You need to go back to Child Protective Services and tell them what has happened, that he kidnapped your kids to another state, if that is what happened.*

Where Did I Go Wrong? How Did I Miss The Signs?

Also, you should be filing a motion for permanent custody of your minor children based on the child protective cases as well as the taking of the boys out of state and leaving them with someone who is not a legal guardian. And at this same time make a motion for the courts to appoint you a pro-Bono attorney as you are indigent and need help presenting a case on your own.

Also, you need to start asking questions of attorney's about how to deal with taking someone to court who hides behind the US Military. Or go to the law library and find case law, that is, cases that set precedence's, involving military personnel and forcing them back to the US to stand trial etc.

If this is all to overwhelming to do right this minute, then go for a walk, clear your head. And come back to this and figure out what your next step is going to be.

Sitting around the house, moping and drowning in self-pity is not going to help here. One of the reasons you are so distraught is because you have allowed yourself to become a caged animal in your own home and life. Get out, talk to your state representatives, your congressman, child protective services. Start telling your story to anyone that can help you. But do not continue to stay in that house one more minute. Staying there and fearing the outside, is exactly what your ex wants. He wants to make you crawl and beg and cry, so that he can say, he is the master and controller of you. You cannot let him win. You need to move forward and out that door right now. Go down the street to a neighbor. Go to a relative. But get out of there and start thinking about what is best for G and you.

RG writes:

I feel for you. I really do. And yes, THEY don't understand, but every one of us in this forum does understand. Please try to take a breather and get your mind off of this. Go to a movie, a walk, an exercise class or something. I know how easy it is to sit and feel badly about your situation. You can overcome your anguish--if not today, but one day. Please, please do not give up on yourself--you are special and important. And no, you are not the one who is crazy. I too found myself thinking I was the one who was crazy, but I have since broken free of it, and learned to lead a normal, happy, and safe life. Please don't give up! We are all here to lend a shoulder even if it is via cyberspace.

Katrina Daniels Lee writes :
You're not alone in the feelings you have right now. Joani (the Author) is right about him wanting to win by running you down, keeping you weak, and having control of you even if he is not married to you.

Alienation is such a horrible and deep psychological, abusive thing for our children and we, as parents have to live through. For the parents and children alike "it is a mourning process that never ends". For the children, they are in survival mode. Trust me when I say, it goes from a survival mode to a brainwashing very quickly especially when they are young and impressionable. You, like myself, have Alienators that are not just a regular working dad but fathers of Brass. Yours in the military and mine a police Lieutenant.. That status helps them fool the court system easier than the average lying Alienator. Both are taught not to allow emotion rule them or cloud them until the mission is complete.

The mission of all alienators is to destroy the loving relationship that you had with your children and make sure that it never revives.

Your mission, is to make sure that all your children know at all times you are there, you are not passing judgment upon them and you will always have open arms for them when they are ready.

It could be days, months, or years, but the children even if they are grown adults, do seek and have the need to know the other parent. Milestones happen. Maturity happens. Some factors that help the process are

Where Did I Go Wrong? How Did I Miss The Signs?

graduations, going to college, getting married, having children of their own, or just being out of the grasp of the emotional tug of the alienator.

I have been quiet as of late in posting here for a while, but with good reasons. There are many changes that have happened in the dynamics of the alienation of my children. I can honestly say, if they see you and hear you leaving voicemails it does pay off. Also, if you have that open MySpace or Facebook blog saying you love them and wonder how their day was, mail them loving cards, and show up to school events....it pays off even more. You are not forgotten, nor are the feelings they have always had for you. They just have been forced to put those feelings away causing them to say and do such horrible things to you.

Its when the children have the parent who does give up, they feel abandoned. They feel everything they have been told about you is validated and they have no need to seek a person who abandoned them like they were told.

This is a very long emotional struggle and fight. You need to take time out for yourself and I mean a real timeout. Step away and take care of YOU! If you're run down and have no energy left, that is no good for you and your children. You have a long road ahead. You're a good mom! I know just by the way you write that you could not live with yourself if you give up. AND you don't really want to either, you're just so tired.....

Please, take time and rest or this will take its toll on you and your children as well.

If you need an ear, I'm here for you. I'm available to chat anytime. You're strong, not weak! You have made it 5 yrs.....if you rest.......you will feel confident, strong, and your thoughts will come together, and you wont feel hopeless. Try to rest more, and see the sunshine of the day. Meditate, walk, go to the spa, go camping, or take a weekend with relatives or friends and just relax. Or just draw a nice warm bath with some candles and real soothing bath beads.......nice hot cup of tea.....its great for the soul!

I'm here for you and everyone, just as Joani is....you're not alone.
Katrina The Lee P.A.S. Foundation
www.theleepasfoundation.org
Katrina C. Daniels Lee Founder/ Exec. Director
908-303-4817

PG writes:

Yep, no doubt about it, you are in a bastard of a position and it looks like there is no way out of it.

But you have no idea the positives that are at the moment smacking you in the face, because you are too overwhelmed by the gravity and the depth of the despair you currently face.

Mate, I just have one small thing to say to you - SNAP OUT OF IT!!!!!!!!!! I (and many others) understand where you are coming from and I am here to tell you that you have an open door in front of you that you are not seeing and I want you to take time out to actually start counting the trees in the forest instead of being blown away by the size of the bloody forest.

Let me point out a few things for you.
1. *You are strong and healthy, are you not, and you're not about to die!*
2. *Do you have an income and, if so, are you able to save any of it?*
3. *Do you have a car and, if so, you need to start using it?*
4. *Are you able to join some new organization/clubs/sports etc, so you can meet new people and start a new life?*
5. *Is there something that you have always wanted to do or somewhere you have always wanted to go for a holiday, if so, why the hell aren't you trying?*
6. *Believe me when I say that even if it is expensive, if you are able to save a little, you*

Where Did I Go Wrong? How Did I Miss The Signs?

can focus on a set date in the short to long-term future and work toward it. This will give you purpose and strength to continue.
7. *Do you enjoy being a victim?*
8. *If not, then believe me when I say that life is so damn nice when you see yourself as THE most wonderful person in your life and that all the bullets these losers fire at you, simply bounce off your chest. And it is very easy to get to this belief. All it takes is a change of mindset and attitude that can all occur in a matter of minutes. That is if you truly wish to help yourself.*
9. *And lastly - how much longer do you think you will last by wallowing like this? Do you think you may pull the plug, toss the towel in, check out, or what ever way you wish to say it?*

Why would you want to let this jerk win? Why would you want to sentence your children, the ones you love, to a lifetime of only having a criminal parent and not a loving parent? If you are not around, then they can never come to you on the day they finally wake up to themselves and, believe me, they will one day. You need to take a holiday from your life. Doesn't matter whether you go anywhere or not, the act of changing everything about you is what you need to do. Go cut your hair short and change your clothing style, or do the opposite. Go and do something really radical and turn your back on your life and your kids for a short time so you can have some respite to rebuild your strength.

At the moment in the lives of your children, you are the only decent parent they have (and yes they don't know it) and you have an obligation to remain healthy, strong and HERE!!!!

Whenever they speak to you on the phone or in person and it is abusive, hang up or shut the door. As I said to someone else recently, you need to tell anyone

> *who abuses you to Piss Off and don't come back until they are prepared to respect you.*
>
> *You're not a mat, so don't lay down like one and let them walk all over you.*
>
> *I hope I haven't offended you, but I have been in your position on a number of occasions and if people around me didn't care enough to give me a kick up the bum when I needed it, I wouldn't be here today.*
>
> *Let your kids go for the short term and fix your life up. Once you are happy, you will beam with health and love, and when they finally come looking for you again, then they will be shocked at the change and will definitely want some of what you got. They cannot get this from an abuser, it is simply not possible.*

None of this is easy, but if we give up on life, then we give up on our children and ourselves. And if we give up, we cannot be there for our children when they finally "get it" and come around. When these kids finally realize that we were not the bad parent they were brainwashed to believe, they will feel guilty about all the things they said and did to us. And if we are not here for them to apologize and make amen's, they will carry this unnecessary guilty with them to their own graves. And this is not fair to them or to us. And it allows the ex to win their game to destroy us at all costs.

There is no right or wrong answer to these questions. It is about how much we can personally tolerate. Do we give up entirely and hope that some day our kids get it? Or do we just take a break for a bit to get a new perspective on how to handle things? Or do we take a break and just move forward with our lives? All of these answers are the right answer for the person who chooses that option. No one should ever tell us whether we did the right thing or the wrong thing, because this is one of the most difficult choices to make in our lives. It's about what is best for the children as well as ourselves so that we can still be around for them when they do "get it". But one thing for sure, taking our own life is not going to fix the problem.

So my suggestion when these questions come around is to pretend that this is not happening to you but to a best friend or

Where Did I Go Wrong? How Did I Miss The Signs?

another family member. What would your perspective of the situation be and what would your advice to them be? Then you will have a better idea of what to do for yourself.

CHAPTER 10

THE SET-UP FOR DYSFUNCTIONAL CHILD DEVELOPMENT

Taken from my previous work in 2003, you may see some repetition of information below but I felt that repeating it again, in the paper's original format could not hurt and instead, would reinforce the information.

DYSFUNCTIONAL DEVELOPMENT IS NURTURED AT HOME

From early childhood, we learn our attitudes and behaviors from our environment. (That is to say our family of origin or other important relationships.) If the person or environment through which we are being taught is unstable, then inappropriate feelings and thoughts about our family, lives and other relationships develop. In fact, the significant relationships, which exist within a marriage and family of origin, contribute extensively to our emotional development. They are important to our identity and the meaning we give to life. If these inappropriate lessons are not corrected early on in life, or relearned later in life, they can have life-long detrimental effects. (Stinnett, p.2)

Such is the case with Parental Alienation Syndrome (PAS). According to the late Dr. Richard Gardner,

> *The Parental Alienation Syndrome (PAS) is a disorder that arises in children in the context of child-custody disputes. It is the result of the combination of the programming (brainwashing) of children by the Alienating Parent and the children's own contributions to*

Where Did I Go Wrong? How Did I Miss The Signs?

> *a campaign of denigration against the Alienated Parent. A central factor operative in the children's contributions is their empowerment, most often by the indoctrinators, but occasionally by the passivity of the Targeted Parent. In addition to these intrafamilial factors, extrafamilial factors are also operative, especially the legal system and mental health professionals. (Gardner)*

In other words, it is a campaign by a parent to discredit and remove the other parent from the children's lives. An anti-social and irrational reaction to the loss of a relationship, the offending, alienating parent then projects their issues upon the children. The children are used as pawns to elicit the Alienating Parent's irrational anger and emotions for the ex-spouse. These types of Alienating Parents are more reactive to their emotions and are not mature enough to think first, and then consider the consequences of their actions. Their only thought is to exact as much revenge, pain and hurt on the other parent as is possible and through any means that are possible.

In essence, the Alienating Parent wants all the control but none of the responsibility for their own behavior. Instead they blame others for the problems in their lives. They never mature or get past this very important growth lesson in life and thus develop very unstable relationships in the future, passing these instabilities onto their children. This is where the multigenerational process comes into play that is insecurities; fears, differentiation and triangulating behavior patterns are passed from one generation to the next.

In this vein of thought, the structural and functionalism theorists would say that families are supposed to raise, produce and socialize their children as new members of society. (Stinnett, P. 5) If via PAS, the children are taught to hate and disregard the feelings of significant others in their lives, such as a parent, grandparent or other extended family member, then the child does not learn appropriate socialization skills. They think that it is okay to hate, vilify and speak horribly about others and toward others. In addition, they have no feeling of guilt, nor do they take responsibility for these actions. In real life situations, these children will have no remorse or understanding of how this attitude and behavior hurts others and is thus inappropriate; yet, their Alienating Parent has condoned it. Ultimately, it will affect any and all relationships these children attempt to establish both in their home and outside of their home in the real world.

Following this theory through, one comes to the reality that the children cannot understand or accept true honest unconditional love. All these years, they lived their lives pleasing the Alienating Parent by hating the Targeted Parent. So instead of learning unconditional love, they learn that love comes as a condition of being only acceptable under the strict and warped delusion they have learned as a child, to hate and disrespect another human being. Thus, when they attempt to establish an intimate relationship with a significant other, the control and overpowering affect their Alienating Parent has had on them all their lives will continually interfere with their ability to show love and thus have a stable, normal relationship with a significant other. In addition, even if they distance themselves from the family of origin, the behavior patterns they have learned about love and life are still enmeshed into their personality and soul, and reek havoc the minute any anxiety or stressful situation arises. In this state of mind, they will never be prepared to handle the ups and downs of life efficiently without destroying their intimate relationship.

This way of thinking makes me wonder why the high schools are not teaching our children about mate and date selection? It would seem to me that by teaching children appropriate responses, behavior patterns and how to know when a mate is right for them, that we would be helping them to develop longer lasting marriages and less unhappy divorces. It would also seem that we might be able to help prevent the multigenerational trend of divorce.

But more important here, is that these actions or behaviors by the Alienator are just games played to discredit the Targeted Parent in the children's eyes. And it teaches them inappropriate coping skills for life lessons.

Where Did I Go Wrong? How Did I Miss The Signs?

PSYCHOLOGICAL GAMES LEADS TO DYSFUNCTIONAL CHILD DEVELOPMENT

According to Stinnett, Walters and Stinnett, psychological games are "a pattern of interaction between two or more persons that superficially appears legitimate or honest but actually has an ulterior motive." (Stinnett, P. 158-159) In other words, it is a set of irrational reactions with the intent to control and direct behaviors and situations using the most unethical and untrustworthy practices. In the case of PAS, it is filled with revenge, deceit and hatred, which are masks for their own frustration and anger about that their own failed lives, failed relationships and being abandoned. If looked at more deeply, one could say it was almost diabolical. But the reality is that it is a sign of some form of mental instability stemming from unresolved issues in the Alienators family of origin.

There are 13 types of games that can be played. They are:
1. Corner
2. Tell me your problem
3. We should do this for you
4. Sweetheart
5. It's your decision
6. Courtroom
7. Camouflage
8. Martyr
9. Why don't you..
10. Wooden leg
11. We never fight
12. Look how hard I've tried
13. "Crazy making"
(Stinnette, P. 159-164)

I list them here but am more concerned with those more closely associated with PAS, though it is feasible that any of the games could be useful to a PAS Alienator.

The "Corner" game involves the emotional game of never being able to do anything right. No matter what they do, it is always berated and wrong. Whether as a child or an adult, the emotional abuse from this game causes the person to have low self-esteem. They are in a no win situation and seem to never be able to get out. They are literally cornered. (Stinnett, P. 159-160) For example, in PAS, the Targeted Parent may send the kids a letter telling them how much they miss and love them. The Alienator will claim that the other parent is harassing the children or that the other parent is just saying this so they do not have to pay child support. Either way, the targeted other parent is made to look like the bad guy because now, they do not really mean what they say, and besides, the Alienating parent says the Targeted Parent is harassing them. Now, the children have an excuse to use to stay on the good side of the Alienator and not have to fight about going to see their other parent.

In the "Tell Me Your Problem" game, the victim is made to believe that the other parent is really sincere in their interests about them. But instead, the Alienator uses the victim's words against them, twisting them to mean whatever the Alienator wants, while making themselves look good. As they boost their own ego, they send the victimized parent or child running for cover from the demonization of their own words and actions. (Stinnett, P. 160)

In the "Courtroom" scenario we see a defendant and a plaintiff who enlist the outside assistance of a third party. Triangulating their relationship problems puts the defendant and plaintiff in a "He said She said" antagonistic position with each one trying to prove themselves to be the better person. The problem with this game is that with PAS, the accuser is usually making claims of false abuse and so the victim or Targeted Parent gets side tracked defending themselves. The Targeted Parent is constantly being bashed verbally in front of their children and significant others, thus destroying any possibility of being considered a good, honest person. They have to constantly fight back and deny all claims. Ultimately, so much time is wasted defending oneself, that all intertwined relationships become destroyed. If the Target Parent tries to disclaim the accusations, expensive court costs can financially devastate them. And worse, any time spent with the children is tarnished with the TP's fear that the Alienator will manufacture more lies and charges after the visitation. The good times spent with their

Where Did I Go Wrong? How Did I Miss The Signs?

children are blackened by the need to constantly defend themselves. (Stinnett, P.162)

"Martyr" games are used by PAS Alienators to say, "I Suffer So Much Because of You", despite the fact that these supposed sacrifices were designed to put themselves in the position of the Martyr. PAS Martyrs might continually claim that they suffered terribly because the ex-spouse left them to raise the children alone. In reality, they refused to allow the ex-spouse to be part of the children's life and help raise them. (Stinnett, P.162-163)

In the "Why Don't You ... Yes But" game, one spouse tries to out do the other spouse by always positioning themselves in the lead. For example, in PAS, you might see the following scenario between the divorced spouses. (AP = Alienating Parent, TP = Targeted Parent)

AP: Why don't you give me some money to pay for the children's dental care?

TP: I have paid my portion that I can afford.

AP: You see (turning to the kids) he/she doesn't care about you. He/She won't even give me money to take you to the dentist."

TP: But I have taken care of the children's teeth. I have even purchased extra dental insurance for the children.

AP: What insurance? This is the first I have ever heard of this.

TP: The extra dental insurance that I told you about and gave you the cards for.

AP: Oh, that cheap no good insurance. That is just cheap junk insurance you purchased through Sears.

TP: No, it isn't. And it reduces the cost by 33%?

AP: I still won't use it, because I doubt my dentist would accept it. And why don't you just talk to your son about brushing his teeth in the first place? It is your fault his teeth are so rotten anyway because you are not here and don't care. It is you who refused to pay for their dental care.

Here we see a no win situation for the TP. The TP is berated for everything they say and attempt to do to improve the children's dental health. Even if the TP had paid for the children's dental care up front, the AP would have found an excuse to turn the scenario around and blame the TP.

The "Look How Hard I've Tried" game gets to the heart of the matter. This is a refusal to accept responsibility for one's part in the failure of the relationship because I have tried, you just don't care. In a divorce scenario, the parents are usually ordered into Divorce Parenting classes and mediations. In the classes, they are taught not to use the children as pawns to exact revenge or hurt the other parent. During mediation, the parents then discuss their options and how to deal with the children in the divorce with a third party as witness and orders that are ultimately created. When PAS is involved, one parent will "yes everyone to death", but as soon as they walk out the door, all bets are off. They immediately start using the children and bad mouthing the other parent. They interfere with visitation and communication with the children and the other parent. When they are caught doing this, they claim that it is not true and that the other parent is refusing to come to pick the kids up for visits or never shows up. They claim that they have done everything to get the kids to cooperate but children's hatred of the other parent has nothing to do with them. In fact, they claim they have worked very hard to raise their children properly with love and respect and it is all the other parent's fault.

If a parent wants to gain sympathy or avoid the consequences of neglect, they might use the "Wooden Leg" game. It is intended as a way to enlist anyone who will listen to their side of the story because of the "Oh, Poor Me" attitude. In a high conflict divorce with PAS, one might see the Alienating Parent crying uncontrollably in court claiming that they are poverty stricken and could not even afford to take the family dog to the vet to save its life. Meanwhile, this same crying AP has just picked up a new dog for the children, despite being too poor to take care of the old dog. Another example would be the AP

Where Did I Go Wrong? How Did I Miss The Signs?

who claims the children's teeth are in horrible shape because other parent is not paying child support. In actuality, not only is the child support paid, but also extra dental insurance is available and the children were eligible for state medical insurance, which included dental care. However, the AP refused to use the purchased insurance because they wanted the ex to look like the bad parent.

But the best and most illusive is the "Crazy Making" game, which Alienators live for. The point of the game is to make the targeted ex-spouse so angry and upset that they break down. This is done using a variety of methods, but the most commonly used in PAS are the refusal of visitation with their children, false allegations of abuse or constantly dragging the ex into court for child support even when the ex is up to date on child support payments and the custodial parent is receiving the maximum amount. Probably the highlight of their abusive pattern is to make the targeted ex-spouse suffer the most unscrupulous of emotional pain by destroying any possible relationship they could have with their children. This is the crux of PAS. It is to aggravate, antagonize and torture the ex-spouse even after the Alienator has received everything they wanted and more.

Furthermore, in Stinnett's book, Relationships in Marriage and the Family, (P.163-164) the authors mention 6 possible crazy making schemes. They are as follows:

1) Pretending there is no problem as they stomp around the house, 2) Denying any agreements or statements have previously occurred or wanting strict compliance to agreements and issues, 3) Creating false hopes and then crushing them, 4) Blaming others while verbally assaulting them with unprecedented guilt, 5) consciously disregarding the wishes of others, and 6) making up mental instability issues out of every action and reaction that someone else has or doesn't have. Any and all of these tricks can be used to destroy the ex-spouse especially in the eyes of the children. For example, telling the ex-spouse that they will have their children for some special event they have purchased tickets for, but when they call to make arrangements to pick the children up, they are told that the children have gone away for the week to another state entirely.

This is done to exasperate, control and cause the ex-spouse financial harm as well as emotional upset. It is one of the most prevalent 'red flags' of Hostile Aggressive Parenting (HAP), which leads to Parental Alienation (PA).

When one starts to analyze why psychological games like these might be played, there are several reasons. There could be a "lack of trust" which impedes the ability to communicate honestly. There could also be a strong need to avoid or distance oneself from the truth by denying the major issues that broke up the relationship and thus running away from them. Even fear of intimate relationships because of past bad experiences could lead to games to avoid close contact. Sometimes just not knowing there are other alternatives to reacting to situations has stilted their emotional reactivity growth. It could be as simple as a lack of appropriate nurturing because, either they never learned it or they were never exposed to other options while growing up. But the worst reason of all is when the games are viewed as ways to control, use and abuse another person. This is often due to a mental disease process such as Borderline Personality Disorder or Narcissistic Personality Disorder. Especially in PAS, this exacting of revenge for a poor relationship and not being willing to accept one's own part in the relationship problems is extremely dangerous. The PAS game initiator has only one motive. The motive is to destroy the other side at all costs. They will lie, steal, cheat and do just about anything to achieve their intended goal of annihilation of the ex-spouse. (Stinnett, P. 164 –168)

Unfortunately, many of these games are learned from the environment we are raised in. (That is from our parents or caretakers.) So unless, the offending parents are willing to step back and see where their anger and hostility actually come from, they will continue to destroy their children by passing along the emotional response patterns. The multigenerational ramifications, which are astronomical, never stop until one person takes the initiative to differentiate themselves from the rest of their family. Murray Bowen wrote and spoke extensively on differentiation as the primary way to rectify the multigenerational snowballing effect of passing on poor emotional reactions from generation to generation.

Where Did I Go Wrong? How Did I Miss The Signs?

But on the positive side, if one does differentiate themselves, others in their lives will follow them and eventually the pattern begins to break down. And this is when more of our children can be taught and molded more appropriately. A big part of this requires understanding and listening to our children's feelings and emotions, while keeping the door open for them to speak up without severe consequences and retribution.

Unfortunately, the need for retribution is probably one of the biggest problems in PAS. As a child, watching and observing, they know what they feel and want. Those that are allowed to express their love and devotion for both parents are able to develop normal attachments. Those who are berated, denigrated or told they must choose between one parent or the other are forced to deny their feelings. Their feelings are never taken into consideration and their emotional reactions are misconstrued. They never truly know what it is like to love both parents. They never truly know how to separate their feelings from their emotions and then from their thoughts. They are only allowed to feel the anger and hatred that the one parent projects. Growing up like this does not give them much of a fighting chance in interpersonal relationships because they have no true experience with the reality of relationships and dealing rationally and thoughtfully in stressful or anxious situations. Thus, they are destined to live a very dysfunctional adult life unless they finally take the initiative to correct their misconceptions and differentiate themselves from the fused mess they have lived all their lives.

It is probably fairly safe to say that the Alienating Parent is a manipulator. They exploit, control and use anyone and everything around them for their own personal gains. Usually, they cannot be trusted, as their lies are more numerous than their truths. Worst of all, they don't see their children as living and breathing organisms, but rather as pawns on a chessboard to be sacrificed when needed for the king or the queen. One father I interviewed said his ex-wife hated him more than she loved her children, because of the extent to which she would go to destroy him. This always included severe emotional pain for his children, as they were not allowed to express their feelings and have a relationship with him.

There are actually several types of manipulators. In a PAS scenario the least harmful is the "Nice Guy" image that just keeps trying to project this perfect image and is always trying to please others, thus always trying to avoid stigmas and control their image. Probably one of the most obvious in PAS is the "Dictator" or the "Ruler" who has to control everyone and everything. The less control they have of their ex-spouse, the more control they feel they need and the more abuse they inflict upon everyone around them.

But there is also the "Poor Me" or "Weakling Type" which is similar to the "Cling On", where they manipulate the events to look like it was not their fault but the ex's or that they are so weak that they need to be taken care of. Their story makes them look like they are the innocent victims, when all along they plotted and planned the steps to make the ex-spouse look bad and out of control. But this is much like the "Calculating" personality that sets things up with lies, deceit and maneuvers, designed to undermine the ex-spouse.

This behavior leads us to the "Bully Manipulator" who is the meanest of the mean with probably the least amount of conscience of all. They use hostile and aggressive behavior patterns intended to destroy any sense of self-worth or happiness, let alone image of the Targeted Parent. They will go to great lengths to harm their intended victim without any regard for whom else may get hurt in the process.

The last remaining two, the "Judge" and the "Protector" are quite interesting in themselves. The "Judge" manipulator always criticizes and puts down the targets. Shame and guilt is the objective in their game of control.

Ultimately, the most emotionally relationship bound of the manipulators is the PASing parent who is overzealous in their support and protection of the children. They are called the "Protector Type". They control the children's every move and thus are so enmeshed and fused with them, that the children can never grow up and learn to think for themselves. They are never able to truly see how much the other parent, who has been pushed out of their lives, loves and misses them unconditionally. The other parent is not allowed to be felt, heard, seen or otherwise influence the children's lives. (Stinnett, P. 169-172)

Where Did I Go Wrong? How Did I Miss The Signs?

To follow on the next few pages is something that was written from the perspective of a child and what they might see or hear or feel as they are being forced to choose between their two parents.

A CHILD'S VIEW
What Would I Think, How Would I Act?
By Cindy Smith

This is a true depiction about a stepmother, father and their family members' success at pressuring/manipulating a child to sever the bond between the child and her mom. In today's society, both fathers and mothers can be the alienating parent motivated by breaking the bond between their child and the other parent. Step parents can play a huge part in this type of abuse.

Authentically, children are programmed to love both parents, but when children are subjected to the type of emotional abuse mentioned below; they lose their childhood and begin acquiring emotional scars.

The rejected parent is at a loss and often feels helpless. Watching their child being brainwashed, manipulated, used like a weapon of revenge, is like watching their child die a slow death, and there is nothing they can do. The rejected parent cannot prevent their child from the brainwashing effects of parental alienation. The sad part is that the alienators believe they are doing the right thing and succeed at convincing the child that they are "protecting" the child from their other parent.

Could you handle this pressure? We highly doubt it!

- o If I was a small child and saw my stepmother cross off my mom's name from my kindergarten folder what would I think...

- o If I was a small child at the age of three and my father was walking me up my driveway to mommy's house saying "Just two more days here then you are back with us," what would I think?

- If I was four years old and heard my father blame my mommy because I caught a cold at preschool, what would I think?
- If I were this child who was put in the bathtub right after I was picked up from my mommy's house, what would I think?
- If I were this child that was told I could not bring my belongings to my mommy's house because they would get dirty or ruined, what would I think?
- If I were this child and was told that child support money should be spent on whatever I wanted, what would I think, how would I act?
- If I were told to call my father and step mom while at my mommy's house in the wintertime to ask them how I should dress to go outside and play, what would I think?
- If I was in first grade and my daddy, step mom, and extended family told me at the age of 13 I could choose to live with my father, what would I think? How would I act?
- If I was this child and my father told me that if my mommy did not have me at the meeting place on time she would get arrested by the police, right in front of her 7th grade students, what would I think, how would I act?
- If I was this child being mouthy to my mom and she squeezed me behind my neck, then I told my father, who then threatened my mom that if she touched me

Where Did I Go Wrong? How Did I Miss The Signs?

again he would take her to court, what would I think, how would I act?

- o If I was this small child and my mommy asked a neighborhood mom to watch me for a couple hours while taking a class but my step mom told me she did not trust my mommy because she got a babysitter "all of the time," what would I think, how would I act?

- o If I was this child and my father and stepmother told me my mom wanted to abort me, what would I think, How would I act?

- o If I went to the dentist with my mommy and was the best little patient, getting my first tooth pulled but then my father and step mom took me to another dentist and told me that the dentist mom took me to did not know what he was doing, what would I think, how would I act?

- o If I was this child and my daddy told me that my mom did not attend my school play, did not care about me, even though when I asked my mom about the play she said she was there and even knew what I was wearing that night, what would I think, how would I act?

- o If I was this child who learned that complaining about my mom pleased my father, stepmom and their family, what would I think, how would I act?

- o If my mom and I had a special beauty day in the form of haircuts, then my father and step mom told me my bangs were crooked, what would I think, how would I act?

- o If I was this child, excited to show my father a Halloween costume my mommy made and he commented, "There is glue on the wing," then bought me a different costume to wear, what would I think?

- If I was a child and my father told me to call my mommy after a school function and lie to her about something my grade school principal never even said, what would I think, how would I act?

- If I was this child and went to the store to pick out a new book bag with my mom, then went to my dad's and they took me to buy another one, what would I think; how would I act?

- If I was this child and my father and family bought me a new bedroom set, a TV, a phone, game boy, clothes, a mini bike and more for Christmas, what would I think, how would I act?

- If I was a child and told my father that I went to a different church and had fun, and despite my father never attending church he then told my mommy's church was not a church, what would I think, how would I act?

- If I was this child and my mom called my dad's house to see how I was feeling and my step mom answered the phone and in a very angry voice said, "Your mother's on the phone," what would I think, how would I act?

- If I was a teen and my mom was going to teach me how to mow the grass with her supervision but as I was getting my shoes on my father called and said my foot was going to get cut off, what would I think, how would I act?

Where Did I Go Wrong? How Did I Miss The Signs?

- If I was a teen asked to find out my mom's income tax information right before a support hearing, and I did, what would I think, how would I act?

- If I was this young teen and my dad took me to the courthouse for a child support meeting, what would I think, how would I act?

- If I was this teen and told that my mom made me change schools even though the conciliator made the decision after examining the facts, what would I think, how would I act?

- If I was a teen and got in trouble at school and my dad supported my harassing behavior toward another teen girl by taking my side and joining in on the name calling, what would I think, how would I act?

- If I was a teen mouthing off and swearing and my step mom told my father not to scold me because she said, "that is how she was raised," what would I think, how would I act?

- If I was a teen who witnessed my stepmother run her body into my mom then screams at my mom saying that my mom hit my stepmother, what would I think?

- If I was driving age and about to enter college and in order to have my car I had to do what my father and stepmother wanted me to do, how would I act?

- If I were this child I would be totally aligned with my father and his family. No matter what, they have given me everything and stuck up for me despite my behavior. I would believe them, especially because not only my father and stepmother know my mom is unfit, so do their other family members, even though several have never even met my mom.

- o If I were this child, I would focus on all the bad things I have been told about my mom by my step mother, father and their family. I would suppress all good memories, even though my mom has proof that we had many happy times together. In order to prove my loyalty, I would make sure my defenses against a relationship with my mom were strong. The defenses I would use would be hatred, anger and extreme disrespect and entitlement. She would get so angry with me that she would just want to give up, and then I would live where I belong full time, never having to put up with her crap.

- o If I were this child, my entitled behavior would begin to alienate others. I would not have very many friends, but would not care either, because I have my father and stepmother. Not being able to love my mom hurts, so I will remain angry and hateful. I don't have the coping skills to deal with this mess and either way I lose!

Cindy Smith
Administrator, Parental Alienation Awareness Organization (PAAO), contact through: Cindyfcst7@aol.com

WHAT IS THE BEST COURSE OF ACTION

What is the best course of therapeutic action to deal with this mess? There is no one perfect way, but one thing is absolutely clear when it comes to counseling, an improperly or untrained therapist will actually do more harm than good. Therapists grounded in other theories could serve to do additional damage to the child and rejected parent, while empowering the alienating parent. And it is important for the therapist to look at many things such as shared delusional disorder as a diagnosis as well as narcissism on the alienating parent's part.

Probably one of the best possible therapeutic intervention that does not require removal of the child from

Where Did I Go Wrong? How Did I Miss The Signs?

the aggressor would be Strategic Family Therapy, *(Dr. Craig Childress, drcraigchildress@gmail.com, http://www.drcachildress.org)*

THE HUMAN HIERARCHY OF NEEDS

For the child who is controlled and manipulated, especially in the last scenario, their ability to actually become an independent and self-actualized individual is impossible. Self-actualizing is a concept equated with Henry Maslow. (Maslow, A. H. Toward a Psychology of Being. New York, Norstand, 1962)

As previously explained, Maslow speaks about a hierarchy of needs to keep us alive. He depicts these needs as a triangle starting with our most basic "deficiency needs". (See Figure 1) The first of which are the physiological needs of food and water, thus making up the base of the triangle. Without food and water, we will surely die.

Once these needs are met, the next most important need for our survival is safety and security. As we progress in our endurance to live on, our need for love and devotion to and by someone else becomes important to our happiness. With love, we learn and need to develop self-esteem, which helps us to be proud of who we are and where we come from.

At the top two levels of the triangle are the needs for Self-Actualization and Spirituality that are not necessary to our physical survival as much as our emotional growth and psychological survival. Self-actualization is our ability to see ourselves honestly and openly, while continuing to grow and develop to the best of our ability. Self-Actualization enables sacrifice without guilt or worry, unconditionally.

At the spiritual level, there is transcendence to being an individual who is part of the whole of this universe. There is no better or worse, there just is. As we acquire all of these needs in a progression upward in the triangle, we develop into a stronger and stronger individual "able to leap tall building in a single bound".

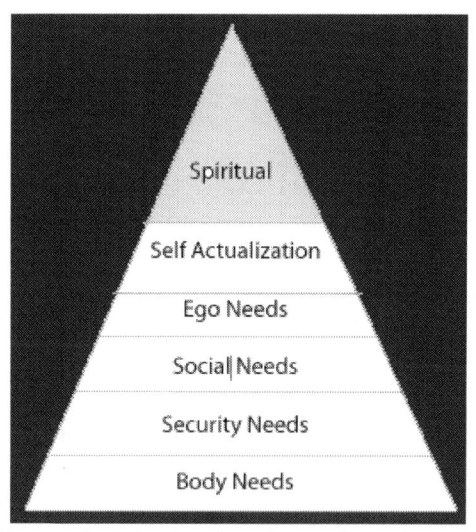

Figure 1. Maslow's Hierarchy of Needs

When this hierarchy of needs is interrupted or not allowed to progress completely in each stage, especially in the four earlier stages, physical and psychological dysfunction occurs. If development is stunted in any of the stages, a person cannot fully progress to the next stage of development. No food and water, we die. No safety and security, we could die or grow up very afraid and wary of all around us. No love or belonging, and we miss the nurturing of our souls to be good, kind and considerate. No self-esteem and we never believe we can succeed and be anything, so we never strive to be our best and instead just settle.

In PAS children who are denied these needs, it is apparent that if they make it to the love and belonging stage, but do not get the appropriate response and reaction, They never learn how to give and receive love either. They are left wondering if they are truly loveable, which in turn, lowers their self-esteem. Children caught at this level can never truly understand their true potential or capabilities as a human being. They are left stunted in their emotional growth to develop fully functioning and stable relationships with others. And if they do not have these skills, how can they possibly pass it on to their children. Thus, the vicious circle of multigenerational maladjusted relationships continues to spiral through these families, sending them down a road of self-destruction.

Where Did I Go Wrong? How Did I Miss The Signs?

RAISING CAIN
All parents have a choice as to how they will raise and guide their children, whether they are influenced by family heredity of learned behavior patterns or not. As humans, we still have the freedom to make a change in the way we operate and behave in our lives. Part of this has to do with how we teach our children to moderate behaviors in relation to the obstacles or stresses and crises in life. It is more than just how one punishes or disciplines their children because this, in itself, has much to do with the relationship between the parent and the child. It is more about helping them be in charge of their actions and reactions. It is about being able to trust them. It is about teaching them to not blame others, but accept their part in the problem. And it is about being able to put on another person's shoes and consider what that person feels, needs or thinks.

Another way that a parent can have a strong impact is on social skills passed onto the children. A parent can either be 'controlling or supportive'. (Stinnett, P. 304)   A Controlling Parent attempts to teach their children right from wrong by using intimidation, conditional love or supplying consequences for thoughtful decisions a child has outside of the Controlling Parent's wishes. A Controlling Parent does not allow the child to have their own thoughts until they are exactly like theirs. And depending on the children's age, the control mechanisms will also vary in their severity.

A Supportive Parent shows how to care and be receptive to others by becoming role models that nurture and are warm and accepting. (Stinnett, P. 304). A Supportive Parent might tell their child, "I will love you no matter whose home you decide to live in". They are accepting of apologies, listening attentively and responding with love and care. The children know there are no war games here, just honest to goodness open arms, loving them.

On the other hand, parents who use too much control can easily fail to socialize their children appropriately. This happens all too often in cases of PAS where a parent threatens their child with harm or the child witnesses the harm hurled at the Targeted Parent, (especially if the child shows any interest in the other parent). For example, a 5 year old son tells his mother that he wants to be a baseball player just like his Dad and therefore must go play ball with him right now. The mother might say, "Oh, you are just like your father, thinking you can do what ever you want whenever you want. He is such a rotten, no good.......... I wish I had never married him." Here the child learns that if he says anything associated with his father, it makes the child no good and rotten. Using the same scenario, a mother using conditional love or love withdrawal might say, "Well, if you want to go play ball with your father, that's fine, but don't expect me to be there to pick you up." In both cases, the child is demeaned and degraded for loving his father and wishing to be with him or like him. He learns very quickly, that in order to keep his mother's love, he must hate anything and everything having to do with his father.

On the other hand, had the mother used induction instead of these methods to teach her child proper social skills and etiquette, she might have said something more like, "Honey, that is wonderful that you want to go play ball with your father. I know how much this means to you. I also know that you would like to spend at least an hour or two with your father doing this, but I am not sure if there is enough time today. How about you call your father and ask him when he can set aside a few hours to play ball with you and I will make sure that we get this done together." In this case, the child is allowed to love and cherish his time with his father. He is allowed to be himself and not controlled by his mother's hostile and aggressive emotions and feelings. He also learns that there is a proper sequence to planning a get-together. One cannot just jump in the car and expect someone to be there to play ball. This little boy would have been taught to love, honor and cherish both his parents equally.

The previous two control methods of behavior, coercion and love withdrawal, have serious long-term affects on children. They are severe examples of psychological abuse and hostile aggressive parenting techniques, which ultimately lead to Parental Alienation and then Parental Alienation Syndrome in the children.

Where Did I Go Wrong? How Did I Miss The Signs?

One of the tragic problems with this type of psychological abuse is that it can have a "sleeper effect". (Stinnett, P. 313 from Belsky, 1980) What this means is that the child holds in all of his anger and feelings, never being allowed to express them and just stuff them inside. Ultimately, the child bursts, imploding or exploding, becoming both aggressive and violent toward themselves or others. Because they have not learned love, respect and compassion, they have no way to modulate their reactions and actions in a socially acceptable way. And chances are they will pass this trait on to their children if help is not received to replace the lack of love, belonging and respect that is missing from their life.

This brings us back to Maslow's hierarchy of needs. Without the first four basic needs, (physical body, security, social and ego) being properly met, a child will have a significantly harder time growing up and adjusting to the world. But teaching PAS perpetrators about how damaging their irrational emotional reactions are is almost impossible. They are stuck in their ways. And the only way out for their children is to get into counseling and reunification therapy with the ousted parent, as soon as possible. Time is of the essence. The longer the children are left to fend on their own, the worse the emotional trauma and chance of multigenerational passing on of this poor level of differentiation is likely to occur. The saddest part of all is that the courts are reluctant to sanction the non-compliant parent and force the children into counseling, which is much like saying the children do not have to be forced to go to school or the doctor's. These children are left to suffer for the rest of their lives, never understanding the true identity of their mixed up feelings, emotions and thoughts.

EMOTIONAL TRAUMA AND THE OVER DIAGNOSIS OF ADD AND ADHD

One of the most interesting observations I have made with children of PAS is the high preponderance of over diagnosis of ADD and ADHD in high conflict divorce cases. Below is an excerpt of a conversation from my support group:

GL writes:
My wife is a teacher and she says that all of the kids today are on medication for attention deficit disorder. She read what my old teachers had written under comments on my report cards and said, "that's what you have!" I replied that when I was in school they just called it "dumb!". hahaha....

The Author writes:
ADD and ADHD are overly diagnosed problems. Quite often the true cause of this behavior is emotional upset that a child cannot voice or does not know how to explain, such as a nasty divorce.

GL writes:
By the criteria they use today to diagnose ADDHD I'm sure that my wife's diagnosis is right. I daydreamed through school, and all of my teachers sounded just like Charlie Browns'. Wa-wa wa wa... I bounced off the walls. I was a teachers' nightmare. I wasn't at all a bad kid, and I made good grades, except for grammar tests I assume! haha..

I know that I've always had ADDHD. I started taking salmon oil fish supplements five years ago for my cholesterol. It helped with the cholesterol, but it helped even more with my mood and my ability to focus. My wife can really tell a difference when I've taken them as well. I don't go a day without taking them anymore! About a year ago I read in a magazine I think is called Neurology Today that fish oil boosts peoples moods. Better still, there's no nasty side effects.

The Author Writes:
First look at what was going on in your life as a child emotionally, then see what I have recently written about ADHD and emotional trauma. Then decide if it applies before you assume that you had ADHD. Some kids truly have ADHD, but when you are talking high conflict

Where Did I Go Wrong? How Did I Miss The Signs?

divorce or other emotional traumas, those need to be looked at and dealt with first before any medication is applied.

GL writes:

There was a lot of turmoil in my home when I was growing up. My parents divorced, I was the youngest of four, and one of my older brothers is manic-depressive (undiagnosed). Anyway, I don't know if this had anything to do with my condition or not. I just know that when I was at school when I wasn't bouncing off the walls that I was daydreaming. I swear by the fish oil personally. I wish I had known the benefits while I was a kid! I'm sure my teachers would have liked for me to have been on "something".

The Author writes:

The situation going on in your home absolutely had something to do with your behavior. Some kids are more immune to it, in that their systems are not so vulnerable, in other words, we all have a preponderance for things, in your situation, the stress at home reduced your defenses and triggered your weakest link, i.e. the emotional overload response, which may or may not have been actually ADHD and could have just been your emotional overload being expressed. And the fact that fish oil is used to stabilize moods, that tells me right there, that it is the emotional overload that we are talking about, which is a mood disorder in itself.

C & G writes:

Interesting G's daughter was just diagnosed with ADD by her therapist and she wants to medicate her. Do you have or point me in a direction to find more about this as a cause. This is alarming how his daughter is JUST diagnosed with in 4 weeks of no longer having visits with her dad.

The reality is that children are not mentally or emotionally mature. They do not know how to properly regulate feelings, emotions nor especially handle such adult things as divorce. In most cases, they do not have the vocabulary to describe it to someone, let alone be able to figure out what it is that truly makes them upset. They are in complete emotional overload. It is like a bottle of soda that you have shook up and it needs to be released. If they have nowhere to release these feelings, they become bottled up and explode.

To deal with these pent up emotions, feelings and hurt, the children will respond in several different ways.

1) They can completely shut down and go into a daydream type mode where they seem to be unable to focus in school. This is because they are so emotionally overloaded that they can no longer concentrate as, all this other stuff in their heads is getting in the way, and they have no one to express it too. They cannot tell the alienator how they feel or they will risk their wrath. They cannot tell the targeted parent because quite often they do not even see the targeted parent and, if they tell the target parent, they feel they are betraying the alienator. They cannot tell their friends or others, because they feel like a freak.

2) They can become very overactive trying to release all the emotional overload that is weighing them down. Again, because they cannot express it and it is being bottled up inside, it explodes like a bottle of soda that has been shook. Their behaviors become uncontrollable, just like how their emotions and feelings are at the time. Having nowhere to express things and talk to someone about it, so that they can let the fizz slowly out of the soda, it builds up and they act out instead. They do not know where to put all this bottled up emotion that is making them feel overwhelmed and so, instead, it comes out in hyperactivity, inability to sit still, inability to concentrate and so much more.

Where Did I Go Wrong? How Did I Miss The Signs?

It is no wonder that there are so many cases of ADD and ADHD diagnosed in young kids of divorce. They are like ticking time bombs of emotions and fears and feelings that have nowhere to be expressed and they do not have the mental maturity to deal with it properly. Like finding someone to talk to, or learning how to think in critical abstract ways about it and so on.

As far as this diagnosis goes, contact the physician who diagnosed this and explain the chain of events that has transpired and how you believe that this is not ADHD but instead an emotional overload caused by the divorce and inability to see the other parent. Then show the counselor this information above and any other professional documentation that you can find on the over diagnosis of ADHD in relation to severe emotional trauma.

My advice is DO NOT LET THEM MEDICATE YOUR CHILD until all of the facts have been disclosed, such as emotional trauma that the family or your child is going through. Tell them you want to make sure that the child's diagnosis is true ADHD and not an emotional overload from the situation going on at home. If you can clearly equate the change in behavior to the cessation of visitation with you, then give them this time line. That should be enough evidence to make them dig a little deeper before screwing your kid up permanently. Also, ask for alternative mood stabilizing suggestions such as fish oil. Below is just some of the information I found on fish oil, which is far less toxic than most meds.

In defense of fish oils, taken from www.psycheducation.org. (http://www.psycheducation.org/depression/meds/Omega-3.htm)

Omega-3 Fatty Acids (including Fish Oil)
(revised 11/2006)

Omega-3 fatty acids, given in the form of fish oil tablets, were shown in a 1999-controlled trial to maintain mood stability far better than an olive oil placebo. This was a very exciting result, especially as the trial was inspired by "bench chemistry" -- omega-3 fatty acids were recognized to have intracellular effects similar to lithium and valproate. Now some other small studies are beginning to be reported.

There are two "omega-3" fatty acids in fish oil: EPA (eicosapentaenoic) and DHA (docusahexaenoic). Some studies in people with depression or bipolar disorder have used EPA alone, including one of the most recent with the strongest positive results; but one of the larger earlier studies using EPA alone showed no benefit. Many of the other studies shown below, including the first one from Harvard, used fish oil tablets which provided both EPA and DHA. For now it seems safe to conclude that having both does not interfere with the antidepressant and mood stabilizing actions; and that EPA alone *might* be sufficient.

Conclusions (reviewed as of 3/2006; still seem to hold):
- the evidence is piling up that omega-3 fatty acids do *something*, at least in some people;
- the dose to use is not at all clear, as some studies suggest you can go too high and lose benefits (Nevets, Sagduyu), whereas many of the individual glowing results come with the higher doses;
- even at higher doses, the risks seem minimal, and there may actually be additional benefits (on cholesterol, perhaps arthritis);
- however, it's a large number of pills, though a minimal-moderate expense;
- fish burps can be managed easily
- it's not clear how long you have to wait to see benefits but, especially with the smaller doses, they may take 1-2 months to show up. So if you take them, prepare yourself for a period of taking a lot of pills with no benefits.

For more information on fish oils, please speak with your doctor or go to: http://www.psycheducation.org/depression/meds/Omega-3.htm. There is a list of resources and research as well as other important information there.

Where Did I Go Wrong? How Did I Miss The Signs?

    The point here is that do not just take any one's word for it that your child has ADD or ADHD until you have gone over the entire family history, including the high conflict affects of the divorce.

CHAPTER 11

PARENTAL ALIENATION: IT CAN HAPPEN AT ANY AGE

Don't believe what they say: that Parental Alienation cannot happen to older children, that it's just an oxymoron. Parental Alienation is the act of one parent deliberately undermining the relationship between the children and the other parent to the point of creating a hostile relationship and thus alienation of the children from the other parent. Another way to look at this is alienation of affection, which is one of the basic human needs discussed at length by Maslow in his Hierarchy of Needs. It is a serious form of psychological abuse, and it is very dangerous because it occurs internally and, thus, is harder to treat. Unlike physical abuse where the scars and wounds are on the outside, Parental Alienation Syndrome (PAS) is so deep inside that unlocking the key to it takes years of treatment and unconditional love.

Though PAS is primarily seen in high-conflict divorces, it also occurs in intact families. And though it usually begins in early childhood, this is not always the case, and does not mean that older children and even adults cannot be alienated from their other parent. In fact, PAS is often described as a cult form of control over others. In this respect, we can say that the perpetrator or alienator brainwashes and programs the innocent victims to hate their other parent/family members. In much the same way as the leaders of cults, like Jonestown, these perpetrators are able to take a person and convert him or her into the alienator's way of thinking and to renounce all ties with the victim's families and friends. If a cult leader can do this to adult

Where Did I Go Wrong? How Did I Miss The Signs?

strangers who have no familial ties to them, then it is safe to say that it would be that much easier for a parent to do this to his or her children, no matter what age they are.

Parents and family have a much stronger bond or hold on the children. In fact, a child, no matter what age, would be more likely to listen to and believe his or her parent than a total stranger. Therefore, any judge, counselor, agency or attorney who claims that an older child could not be alienated from his or her other parent, is actually stating that cults, like the Branch Davidians, could not possibly happen. In these non-believers' minds, only children can be brainwashed and programmed. This defies logic, as it is a proven fact that cults do brainwash people and program them, and most of these cult followers are adults. In other words, if a total stranger can turn a person against his or her family, then a parent can do it even more easily, no matter the age of the child.

Furthermore, as Amy J. L. Baker points out in her book, *Adult Children of Parental Alienation Syndrome – Breaking the Ties that Bind*, adolescents are just as vulnerable to the tactics used to impede a relationship with the other parent. These young adults are at a point in their lives where they are allowed more responsibility to make their own decisions and, one of those is custody and visitation. Baker feels that alienators are probably quite aware of this and utilize this idea as they intensify their tactics to distance the children from the other parent. In addition to this issue, young adults are struggling for their independence from their parents and if one parent, the alienator, offers them more freedom and thus are more liberal with them, the children will be swayed easily to side with this parent. Alienators know this very well, and actually use this same technique when bribing their children monetarily with gifts and toys. (Baker, p. 182-183) Alienators are good exploiters of weaknesses in people. They will go after the weakest link to break the chain and command control of the other links in the chain. What better way to do this than with bribery and offerings?

Case in point: two children from an intact family are raised since birth to hate their father's side of his family. The children are repeatedly told that relatives from their father's side of the family are no good and crazy and that the children are never to spend time alone with them. Their mother even tries to convince their father that his side of the family is not good and rarely lets the kids visit their paternal grandparents, niece, or nephew. Fast-forward 15 years, to a failed marriage. Though the children have spent very positive and rewarding times with their father and his family, especially during the holiday seasons, in the back of their minds they have been programmed to not trust them. So when the father initiates a divorce, instantly the mother begins to denigrate and berate the father. The children, though 14 and 16, are easily turned against their father and refuse to spend time with him, and when they do, they are disrespectful and rude. Despite the judge's orders, these two teenagers are too enmeshed with their mother's hatred, anger, and faulty beliefs that their relationship with their father is near non-existent. Despite 15 years of positive good memories that they could draw upon, the years of programming and brainwashing have taken their toll.

PAS does not differentiate between ages. PAS does not prejudice only the very young. PAS is real and can affect anyone of any age and gender. It is ageless, genderless and most of all, the most painful form of psychological abuse a guardian can inflict upon another human being. Until the judges, counselors, agencies and attorneys accept the fact that PAS has no preferences and can occur to anyone at any time in his or her life, this form of Domestic Violence will continue to grow and destroy families.

AND WHAT ARE THOSE EFFECTS ON THE CHILDREN AT ANY AGE?

Child Maltreatment is classified as actions that harm children physically, sexually or psychologically. Victims often use a defense mechanism to protect themselves called Abuse-Related Accommodation, which has 3-stages of adjustment. The first stage, "Initial Reaction" finds a victim who is so traumatized that their natural coping mechanisms do not operate. Overwhelmed by the abuse and separated from family and friends, these victims are completely defenseless from the perpetrator. In the second stage, known as "Accommodation to Ongoing Abuse", the victim attempts to stay neutral, keeping the

Where Did I Go Wrong? How Did I Miss The Signs?

peace at any cost, just to preserve their safety, sanity, security and to prevent further harm. The third stage," Long-Term Elaboration and Secondary Accommodation", is characterized by the extension of time that the abuse has occurred. The abuse becomes so ingrained into how the person sees and deals with their world, it is hard for them to separate themselves from the abuse. Their entire world is changed to fit the abusers' requirements for them to adapt and change, including how they cope and behave. (Kemp, P.239-240) This model, which was created by J. Briere, explains how a psychologically abused individual of PAS's handles life. With their entire normal coping response faculties disrupted, personal family contacts broken off and their safety and security in jeopardy, these children have no other choice but to side with their captor.

Furthermore, in psychological abuse, such as PAS, the fear of rejection and abandonment by their parent, coupled with the verbal abuse, can cause severe emotional damages, which often do not surface until much later in the child's life. By constantly degrading a very important figure in the children's lives, their own self-concept and self-worth is devalued. (Baron and Byrne, P. 160) This is especially true, if the children see themselves as similar to the opposed parent. Therefore, a change in the children's self-concept, such as a lowering of self-esteem in identifying with their parent and believing that if the parent is no good, they are no good, can affect their own self-esteem. (Baron and Byrne, P. 168-169)

According to Kemp, in order to protect themselves (P. 239), many of these victims use dissociation, avoidance, and end up developing distorted thinking patterns, becoming highly sensitive in their reactions. Because children do not have the emotional and mental maturity to place the abusive behavior into perspective, they have few choices to protect themselves. The stronger ones will function in exaggeration to compensate for their believed shortcomings, while those that are weaker are more in jeopardy of developing personality issues, such as multiple personalities.

Over time, as they begin to believe that the Target Parent does not love them or accept them, they acquire feelings of inadequacy, loneliness and depression. (Baron and Byrne, P.

173) When you include the fact that the Alienating Parent rewards the children with positive reinforcement for disliking the TP, the children become too confused to separate the truth from reality, let alone their own perceptions of themselves. And since they are cut-off from the TP and their extended family, the children have no way to confirm or disprove what they are being told. If the child's coping mechanism is completely depleted, this situation could pull the children into a deep depression, which later in life may have devastating affects. (Baron and Byrne, P. 175) The AP's action causes more harm because the AP has negated the necessary nurturing required to raise emotionally sound, independent and secure children who will go on to have normal family lives.

Carl Rogers, a clinical psychologist, made great strides in the field of personality psychology and self-concept that is used today by social psychologists. (Baron & Byrne, P. 174-175) His research demonstrates that the self is the key to our world and so it is important to maintain and boost the image of the self by seeking "positive regard". He further describes this as our need for love and affection that comes primarily from our parents. This is also part of Abraham Maslow's Hierarchy of human needs for love and belonging. So if a parent disregards this nurturing need and even prevents its occurrence with the other parent, it can only lead to personality conflicts and issues related to our personal safety zone. The child can never be sure of what true love and security mean. In addition, emotional comfort zone problems arise when the child is not given the proper positive cues, especially when what the child feels and what the child is taught to feel, do not correlate. Improper positive cues, give rise to low self-esteem and distrust of others, while inconsistency in feelings leads to a distortion of oneself image and an unbalanced perception of ones-self. (Baron and Byrne, P, 174) Thus, in the long run, these are children who are deeply depressed and confused about who they are, how they are supposed to feel, who to trust and become just like the AP.

In addition to their distorted views of themselves, they have very warped views of the other parent and extended family. They believe, no matter how many times it may be disproved, that the Targeted parent hates them. A stigmatization of the TP is

Where Did I Go Wrong? How Did I Miss The Signs?

then passed on to his extended new family, from new spouse to the children to grandparents, aunts and uncles. In fact, the children's own anger is fueled by jealousy and the thought that they are no longer needed and are being replaced, even though it is their own choosing to not have a relationship with the Targeted Parent. Again, this is the child's inability to see a linear relationship between the cause and their reaction based on their own mixed up feelings.

The negative issues toward the TP indirectly affected the children's self-esteem and desire to pursue any love from that parent. In the end, it will have a profound effect on their well-being. It is documented that the mortality rate of children from divorces is increased because they are less likely to take care of themselves, i.e. they tend to substance abuse more and are more likely to divorce, thus finding similar warped relationships as adults. (Baron and Byrne, P. 343) As well, the children's interpersonal trust and self-esteem is directly related to their attachment style. This attachment style is developed in infancy by the type of attention the parents give to the children. In other words, children who are given positive attention and unconditional love, are more secure and confident in themselves and the choices they make versus children who were deprived positive emotions and instead reinforced with negativity, anger and hatred. The emotionally deprived children tend to grown up untrusting, scared and angry at the world. (Baron and Byrne, P. 306-309) In fact, one of my classmates described her husband, who is a victim of PAS abuse, as follows: "He does not trust, does not believe and does not care about things that are family oriented." It is a reminder of how important it is to have the unconditional love and support that we as humans need to survive.

Baker, Amy J. L. (2007) Adult Children of Parental Alienation Syndrome – Breaking the Ties that Bind. NY, NY. W.W. Norton & Company.
Maslow, A. H. (1968) The Farther Reaches of Human Nature. NY: Esalen Books, Viking Press.
Maslow, A. H. (1968) Toward a Psychology of Being. NY: D.Vant Nostrand Company.

The following pages contain information and ideas for determining if a child is being abused. It is not the definitive word, but just an example of some of the kinds of questions that might elicit a more clearer picture of what the child(ren) are or are not going through.

DETERMINING TRUE CHILD ABUSE AND SPECIFICALLY PSYCHOLOGICAL ABUSE

The following Chart was created from research and questionnaires distributed to over 200 victimized parents and children. Though this list includes physical abuse signs, the more important ones are those that cannot be readily seen by the human eye but are internal. A user-friendly version of this chart can be found at www.KlothConsulting.com, then scrolling down to the Articles or Charts, Tests & Tools. There will be a link to an excel sheet that will automatically calculate your responses to these questions. It will be found as an article link entitled Signs of Child Abuse.

SIGNS OF PHYSICAL ABUSE	*Yes Column*	*No Column*
Burns, bite marks, cuts, bruises, or welts in the shape of an object		
Resistance to going home		
Fear of adults		
Anti-social Behavior		
Problems in School		
Total		
SIGNS OF CHILD EMOTIONAL/PSYCHOLOGICAL ABUSE INCLUDING PAS		
Excessive Allegations of abuse		
Apathy, depression.		
Hostility		
Difficulty concentrating		
Intimidation		
Belittling or shaming		
Lack of affection and warmth		

Where Did I Go Wrong? How Did I Miss The Signs?

Habitual blaming		
Ignoring or rejecting		
Extreme punishment		
Exposure to violence		
Child exploitation		
Child abduction		
Rejecting (spurning)		
Terrorizing		
Corrupting		
Denying essential stimulation, emotional responsiveness, or availability		
Unreliable and inconsistent parenting		
Mental health, medical, or educational neglect		
Degrading/devaluing (spurning)		
Isolating		
Exploiting		
Total		
SIGNS OF CHILD SEXUAL ABUSE		
Inappropriate interest in or knowledge of sexual acts.		
Seductiveness.		
Avoidance of things related to sexuality, or rejection of own genitals or body.		
Either over compliance or excessive aggression.		
Fear of a particular person or family member.		
Pain or irritation to the genital area, Soreness, redness, chaffing around genitals		
Vaginal or penile discharge		
Difficulty with urination.		

Behavioral changes		
Nervous or aggressive behavior toward adults,		
Sexual provocative-behavior before an appropriate age		
Use of alcohol and other drugs Boys		
Specific Comments such as "My mother's boyfriend does things to me when she's not there," or "I'm afraid to go home tonight."		
Nightmares and bed wetting		
Drastic changes in appetite		
Precocious behavior		
Sexual knowledge, through language or behavior, that is beyond what is normal for their age		
Copying adult sexual behavior		
Inappropriate sexual behavior such as kissing on the mouth and/or attempting to insert tongue in your mouth		
Habitual sleeping with parent of opposite sex in pre-teen or older		
Reluctance or outright refusal to let you wash or dry those parts of the body		
Persistent sexual play with other children, themselves, toys or pets		
Total		
SOME SIGNS OF NEGLECT		
1. Unsuitable clothing for weather		
2. Dirty or un-bathed		
3. Extreme hunger		
4. Apparent lack of supervision		
Total		

Where Did I Go Wrong? How Did I Miss The Signs?

Total All Responses		
COMPARISON OF YES/NO RESPONSES	**DIFFERNCE** **Positive=Abuse** **Negative=No Abuse**	
Physical Abuse		
Emotional Abuse		
Sexual Abuse		
Neglect		
Total differences		

CHAPTER 12

STATISTICAL INFORMATION FROM MASSACHUSETTS GENERAL HOSPITAL

RESEARCH, DR. AMY J. BAKER AND DR. LOWENSTEIN, DR. KRUK OF CANADA
March 2009

Recently, Massachusetts General Hospital (MGH) conducted a research project on the effects of High Conflict Divorce on the children. What they discovered was an overwhelming and profound impact on the emotional wellbeing of the children. The age of the child did not matter. The anxiety of the high conflict divorce was devastating. In their minds, no matter the age, they think, "If Mommy and Daddy no longer love each other, then will they stop loving me too?" This fear ultimately leads to anxiety, which invariably can cause an emotional meltdown at various levels. MGH also discovered that the more the parents fought or were at odds with each other, the more intense or disturbed the children became mentally and emotionally. And the more disturbed and upset the children became, the more their emotional well-being was affected. The following are the statistical results from MGH's project on the Impact of High Conflict Divorce on Children:

- 65% had anxiety severe enough to require therapy
- 56% Developed Attachment disorder;
- 48% had abnormal fears and phobias;
- 44% of both boys and girls became physically aggressive;

Where Did I Go Wrong? How Did I Miss The Signs?

- 31% had sleep disorders
- 29% withdrew from activities including ones that they loved to do
- 24% developed opposition defiant behavior, including temper tantrums and uncontrolled outbursts
- 21% prematurely became involved in sexual activity
- 13% began bed wetting
- 10% developed dissociative personality disorders (once known as multiple personality disorders)

Amy J. Baker, Ph.D backs this up with her research in her article, *The Cult of Parenthood: A Qualitative Study of Parental Alienation, Cultic Studies Review* and in her book, *Adult Children of Parental Alienation Syndrome – Breaking the Ties that Bind (2007)*. Dr. Baker's research and interviews of 38 adults who were victims of PAS as children revealed seven (7) precedents about the effects of PAS. Furthermore, as Baker points out, these abused interviewees suffered lifelong pain as a result of being alienated from a once loved parent (36). Ms. Baker's results from her interviews are as follows:

- High rates of low self-esteem to a point of self-hatred
- 70 % of the adults suffered with serious depression episodes in their adult life.
- 30% had substance abuse problems with drugs and alcohol
- 42% had trust issues with themselves and/or others
- 50% were alienated from their own children, thus proving that PAS is multigenerational
- 66% had been divorced and of those, 25% were divorced more than once
- And the last pattern was Identity issues

Dr. F. L. Lowenstein of Southern England Psychology Services also describes the problems that the child of PAS suffers. His list includes:
- Anger

- Loss or lack of impulse control in conduct
- Loss of self confidence and self esteem
- Clinging in separation anxiety
- Developing fears and phobias
- Depression and suicidal ideation
- Sleep disorders
- Eating disorders
- Educational problems
- Enuresis
- Encopresis
- Drug abuse
- Self destructive behavior
- Obsessive compulsive behavior
- Anxiety and panic attacks
- Damaged sexual identity problems
- Poor peer relationships
- Excessive feelings of quilt.

According to Dr. Edward Kruk, associate professor of social work at the University of British Columbia, whose three-year study is now in the hands of Canada's justice minister, "Some 85 per cent of youth in prison are fatherless; 71 per cent of high school dropouts grew up without fathers, as did 90 per cent of runaway children. Fatherless youth are also more prone to depression, suicide, delinquency, promiscuity, drug abuse, behavioral problems and teen pregnancy", warns the 84-page report, which is a compilation of dozens of studies about divorce and custody, including some of his own research over the past 20 years. I believe that this statistic about the Harm of Fatherless Families will soon include Motherless families where PAS is concerned, thus making these statistics ominous and of serious concern. Though the stats on Motherless families related to PAS have not had a chance to be studied, I can almost guarantee that the stats would be quite similar where PAS is involved. It is not just the lack of a father or mother, (think families where a father or mother has passed away in an intact family), but instead think about the psychological abuse from PAS which pushes these kids to react so horribly.

Where Did I Go Wrong? How Did I Miss The Signs?

What this means is that these children are losing the battle to have a normal life. Because of the anxiety disorder, which leads to attachment disorders, they never learn how to have a normal emotional relationship with others. If the fighting continues, the child has no choice but to spiral out of control, becoming more and more anti-social in their behavior and responses. Ultimately, if the war is not ended, the weaker of these children can and will end up with personal and mental problems for the rest of their lives. This is why it is so important for parents to put aside their differences, angers and need for retaliation/revenge. This is why a program like PIPI, Prevention and Intervention Program Initiative is so important. If we can get to these parents before this happens, then we can stop the ravages of high conflict divorce on the children.

For more information go to the following websites:
http://paao-us.com/StatsandCharts.asp
http://www.prevent-abuse-now.com/stats.htm

Citations:
Ayob, C., Deutch, R. Andronicki, M. (1999) Emotional Distress in Children of High Conflict Divorce; Impact of Marital Conflict and Violence. Family & Conciliation Courts Review, Vol. 37, No. 3. P. 297-315

Baker, A. Accessed March 2005) The Cult of Parenthood: A Qualitative Study of Parental Alienation, Cultic Studies Review, Vol. 4, No. 1 http://f4.grp.yahoofs.com/v1/kGNgQpS2btksTX7hfl_BAGMbqPtY tOeMa4RdGXV1vXRdH4R58xD3bmeG0R6ObDPj_bvMvSaYayJ czdsEcTxu/CultofParenthood%20final%20version.doc

Baker, Amy J. L. (2007) Adult Children of Parental Alienation Syndrome – Breaking the Ties that Bind. NY, NY. W.W. Norton & Company.

Kruk, E. Children harmed by sole custody, report says. Canadian judges rarely use voluntary arrangements in which kids live with each parent roughly equally Apr 03, 2009 04:30 Am. http://www.thestar.com/article/612728

Lowenstein L F: The Psychological Effects and Treatment of Parental Alienation Syndrome. Justice of the Peace Vol. 163. No... 3 January 16, 1999 p 47-50.

CHAPTER 13

BLASTING THROUGH THE MOUNTAIN: MAKING IN ROADS TO THE VICTIMS OF PAS WHILE PUTTING THE EX IN THEIR PLACE.

The first thing to do is NOT Constantly Defend and Argue with the Ex or the children. It gives them ammunition and fuels their engines to come after you. In addition, you are just giving them more to use against you. In particular, the best part about not defending yourself and arguing with the ex is…that it will piss them off, because you refuse to interact with them. The one thing that AP's cannot deal with is abandonment and so they will try to force you and antagonize you to continue contact with them, even if it means in a negative way. It is a way for them to continue to control you and keep you still attached to them. To do this they need complete domination, but if you do not respond, then they have nothing to use to fight with you about, leaving them standing there with their mouths wide open. If you take back the control and refuse to fight back, they have no way to keep engaging you in their lives and in the fight. They have lost the control. As Amy J. L. Baker says in her interview on WABC with Ken Rosato (http://vimeo.com/7169377), "Don't take the Bait. Be empathetic."

Below is an excerpt from one of my support groups involving a grandmother who keeps trying to reach out to her daughter and grandson. Her daughter's boyfriend's father is a corrupt Mayor of a town, where he has bought his son out of numerous criminal charges. This is the guidance that came through.

KLD writes:

I don't know why you're still keeping communication lines open with him (the Mayor/Father of the Boyfriend). If there's anything I've learned from G's run-ins with his ex, A, it's that you don't feed the troll. The more you contact them to explain things or attempt to justify yourself to them, the more opportunities and ammunition you give them to hurt you. You're hurting enough as it is without handing them more opportunities on a golden platter. Better to just limit contact with Mayor Worthless to business and necessity-only correspondence, and pretend that he's just some guy on another planet the rest of the time.

The Author writes:

I agree 100% about constantly contacting Mayor W., the less he knows, the better, This allows you to work in the background undetected. Your daughter is being backed up by Mayor "Worthless" and he is probably telling her that you are crazy and no good and to stay away from you. Stop communicating with Mayor Worthless and let the authorities deal with him. You are just harming yourself by constantly re-opening those nasty wounds. I am going to again post something called the Festering Wound and it goes like this.

It first starts as a red rash that itches, so you scratch it. But it just itches more and more. So you scratch it more and more. You scratch it so much that it starts to get raw. Soon you are scratching it so much that it starts to bleed. Pretty soon, it is not just bleeding but infected and oozing. In fact, it is a festering open wound. And the only way for it to heal is to cover it with a bandage and ointment and just leave it alone for a while, so that eventually, you can reach out and touch again. That is to say, we must move forward and come back to this when the time is right and the healing has begun or been done.

Where Did I Go Wrong? How Did I Miss The Signs?

KF writes:

I used to be the WORST at calling and explaining myself to my ex, or still reaching out to him like he was human. I didn't realize that I was "feeding the troll"; it's only been this past year that I've just stopped all together. I'll email him information he needs or call him if I need to speak to him in regards to the kids. He now tries to "goat" me in emails brings up things that happened 7 years ago or insinuates things that aren't true to try and get me to justify or explain myself. It's been hard stopping my "turrets" but when I feel the need I'll respond a nice lengthy FU letter just to get it out of my system and then I delete it. He has now recruited his new wife to send me emails in hopes that I will respond to her, but "I've held strong". It drives them CRAZY, in fact 2 weeks ago when she was at my house (when she called the police), as she was yelling at me telling me that I had to answer her questions, as I was walking away, she just got louder and louder, made herself look like an idiot. I finally realized that I was the one looking stupid by arguing with my ex in emails about, trying to call out his lies or explain myself when he was twisting everything around. I feel better too, because now he has NOTHING, when before he was taking everything out of context and using it against me...even if it was volunteering at the homeless shelter, it didn't matter what it was. It's hard, and truthfully, now that the wounds have healed, I don't even want to know what type of scar is left. I caused a lot of damage when I was trying to communicate. These people are not normal, they are mean and hateful and they prey on us, because we are good-natured and we want to do what is right by everyone. But we can't if we keep selling ourselves out to these people. We have to protect ourselves.

The Author writes:

You are right. Responding to them just fuels their fire and keeps them attached to us. One of my relative's ex's would do anything to get him to notice her, even if it required using bad attention, such as dragging him into court on bogus claims of being in the arrearages. The less we communicate with them, the more it pisses them off and takes the controls out of their hands. When we respond, it just gives them more ammunition and allows them to still be close to us, even if in a negative way. As well, when we stop responding, sometimes it helps to get the alienator to back off on the psychological abuse of the kids, because they do not know what to tell them, as there is no response or fight from us, so they start to back off of the kids.

HOW TO DEAL WITH A LONG AWAITED MEETING WITH YOUR CHILDREN. WHAT TO DO IF THE EX INSISTS ON BEING PRESENT.

So it has been awhile since you saw your child(ren), and you are finally set to have a meeting with them. But what do you say? What do you do? How do you respond? What if the ex is in the room? Below are responses to one parents quarry as to what to do.

C & P writes:

I try to keep up to date with everyone's situation and have gained a lot of helpful info reading all the emails. Most of you are residents in the USA but we are fighting PAS over here in the UK, where it is termed 'Hostile Parenting'.

It took a while to realize what was happening as the situation developed, then trying to deal with the contact issues without going to court, and then finally applying to the Courts. Of course we are now the bad guys! Despite now having a contact Order, my partner has not had direct contact with his (8yr) daughter for nearly 2 years (since she was 6yr). We live a fair distance away from where his daughter now lives with her mum. There is also my own 8yr old son, (same age), plus two half-siblings (1yr and nearly 3yrs). In fact, the ex's

Where Did I Go Wrong? How Did I Miss The Signs?

Hostile behavior seemed to start after the birth of the first half-sibling.

He has had fairly regular telephone contact with his daughter, (usually met with a negative response) but his ex has kept coming up with excuses each time there was suppose to be direct contact, (i.e.; doesn't want to go, not well, too tired, gone horse riding, etc.) The courts then issued a 'Penal Order' on his ex, that she must comply with the Contact Order, but she did not even bother turning up in court. Finally the courts have Ordered us all to attend 'Family Group Mediation'. He (my husband/the father) was supposed to have direct/staying contact over the October school holiday. The first mediation session is at the start of the holidays, on 26th October. I suspect that the ex will find another excuse for just not turning up with the daughter and we would have travelled a fair distance to attend this.

But it has been so long since he has actually seen his daughter that he just doesn't know how to handle this first meeting - if it takes place!

We are preparing to take things along to remind her of some of the good times such as photos. He doesn't want to 'demand' that she comes to stay with him, but on the other hand this is probably the only way he is going to have any positive influence on her about future contact, without her mum being present. Obviously the qualified mediator must have some recommendations, and she has been very positive that it is very important for contact between father and daughter to be resumed as soon as possible in a positive way.

Please can you offer any advise as to how he should approach this? He is so frightened that he will do something wrong, but is so desperate to let her know that he loves her and misses her very much. He also feels that this is his first, and maybe only, chance to try to encourage her to have positive attitude to re-establishing direct contact. It tears me up each time he is expecting to have some contact, and then it just doesn't happen. He goes off on a long walk, and I know he has been crying when he gets back.

I know that many of you have faced far greater hostility, but we are hoping to catch this before it just gets too out of hand. Any suggestions about how to handle this will be really appreciated.

AB writes:

I hope things go well with you when you do see her. I only had two experiences with seeing my daughter after PA had started occurring. The first time she was 3 (one year no physical contact), I sat down and started playing with the things I had brought for her (she hadn't wanted to approach me). This sounds funny, but I handled it like I would with a scared animal. I got really interested in something, didn't make eye contact and basically, pretended she wasn't there. First she got out of her dad's arms and just wanted from there. She then slowly approached me, when she was very close, I then directly addressed her, but still didn't use her name or make eye contact, but only showed her the object. That was enough and she crawled in my lap and I was able to hug her, tell her I loved her, etc.

The second time, she was 6. I did the same thing; even through her dad/stepmom had already started avoiding my calls, so we'd had very little phone contact on top of no physical contact. In addition, the stepmother had 'hidden' her upstairs and her dad had to call them several times before they came out. At first, I said, "hi" but then the 'adults' talked and I just watched. The stepmother had her the whole time, so I went to her toys and started playing with them. She watched me for about 10 minutes then came over and started to play with another toy, but very close to me. I think that approach would have worked and we would have had a much better over all visit (we were there for a week), BUT, the step mother, in a tone of voice that said, "danger", called her back (she did have to call her twice), then held her between her legs in a protective hug and didn't let go of

Where Did I Go Wrong? How Did I Miss The Signs?

her for the rest of that visit. J (my daughter) never loosened up and the stepmother continued to do stuff like that...address me as "A...", took her out of my arms, refused to let her hug me good bye, never let her spend the night, etc. My warning to your husband is to make sure none of that happens. If necessary, I would go so far as to have a court representative, an evaluator, or some other third party to witness, and report, if any of that happens. In addition, just her refusals will start speaking volumes. All the ones you mentioned are not considered valid excused in the US, it sounds like the courts there don't like them any better as excuses either.

Author writes:
   First, you are doing the right thing by bringing old photos to spark her memory to this meeting. It will start to help her to uncover past memories that she has been forced to repress. Next, he definitely has to tell her how much he loves her and misses her at this meeting, but not so much that she gets overwhelmed. Also, make sure that she knows your phone numbers, all of them. If you have business cards, use them to give her something solid to hold onto. Try not to bribe her to come, but help her to want to come to visit, using things such as family time and spending time with her siblings. If you have a weekly routine that you do, such as going bowling, tell her that you would love to have her come along.
   Also, your husband should be honest about the fact that when she refuses to come, that it hurts very much and that he actually goes for a walk, during which time he cries about missing her. Or something to this affect, so that she knows this is a real emotion and not just words. Actions speak louder than words as well, so a huge hug or even a gentle brush of the hand across her cheek or through her hair will feel comforting to her. If she likes to have her hair brushed, hubby can offer to do that while they talk or something. Just little gestures sometimes make the biggest impact on them. (If you are worried about false allegations of abuse, please discuss this with

the Mediator and let them know that as a parent, you have a right to hug your child etc. but that you have no problem with holding back. But that you believe actions speak far louder than words.) Also, see if the mediator will allow daddy and daughter to go for a walk outside, with the mediator in tow or whatever. Sometimes, the fresh open air, can help to release and ease the tension.

LM writes:

I know how hard it is to watch your partner go through these feelings of rejection and hurt, and to feel helpless. At least he has your support and sympathy. I'm certainly no expert with PAS, only a survivor of being a 2nd wife, but being on the OTHER side of PAS where the damage has been done and at the moment, seems unfixable, (from our standpoint) I can only suggest that your partner starts NOW to develop a certain mindset that will help him gain the confidence he needs now and in the future to SAVE and PRESERVE whatever relationship he and his daughter DESERVE to have!

I know he is nervous, and because of all the games the ex has played, you both probably EXPECT the worst, etc.... But he cannot let that DETER HIS determination and perseverance of fighting for the bond that every decent parent is entitled to. If this ex does NOT participate in this mediation, it will look extremely bad for her. But if she does show up and the opportunity is there for the Father to talk to his daughter, then I would encourage him to have and plan on SPECIFIC things he wants his daughter to know and think about. Such as: Every child is born with a Mommy & Daddy. Every child deserves and needs to be loved and cared for by BOTH parents, (even if they do not live together) Because of the daughters age, I suppose some things have to be said in the context that she will understand.

I don't know if the parents and the daughter will all be in the same room at the same time or what, but if they are, and I was the Father, I would be posing questions to the Mother that put her on the spot and in a

Where Did I Go Wrong? How Did I Miss The Signs?

position that she has to either AGREE with what is being said or DEFEND what she has been doing with the alienating. Example: Father to EX: "You believe that it is important that our daughter knows and feels that BOTH of us love her dearly?" and "You agree that it is important that our daughter has a GOOD relationship with me, her Father?" also, You would NEVER want to make our daughter feel like she has to CHOOSE between loving her Mother OR her Father, correct?" Do you see what I mean?

This EX who is exhibiting PAS is the one who needs to be nailed to the wall. Not the other way around. If you can get your partner to even start to slightly change those feelings of being a victim, to being the LEADER and CHAMPION of TRUTH and INTEGRITY, then maybe, just maybe, he will dig deeper and find the courage to stand up for himself and his daughter; to figure out and use all of the reasons and opportunities he has to TEACH and SHOW his daughter what is RIGHT behavior, and WHY it means so much to him and for her to understand these things.

I know it's much easier for me to say these things versus your partner and you having to deal with the actual circumstances, but I hope at least ONE thing I said made sense and you can use it in a positive way for the benefit of the Father and his daughter's future relationship. Best wishes. Keep us updated.

Again, here is another example of a father who is hopeful for a positive reunion with his son and ideas of how to handle it.

PG writes:

Hi everyone. I have some news to share. Whether it is good or bad, I'm not sure yet, but the possibilities are obviously good.

My son from the two kids who were alienated from me 22 years ago has told me he wants to reconnect with me and wants to try to establish some form of father-son relationship.

Now, although this all sounds well and good, I have to say that he did this in mid 2008 also. After a lengthy conversation with me on the phone in August 2008, we had made plans for him to come and spend time with me. Well, two weeks later he phones me and tells me how he had been to see his mother and told her what he wanted to do. But to his amazement, she was so nice to him and for the two days he was staying with her, they didn't have one argument. Apparently, they fight like cat and dog, which has something to do with her betraying him when he left home. Not sure!

I asked him if he was still going to come see me and he said yes, but he will need to try to fit it in with his work and would get back to me. I didn't hear from him again for about 4 months, when I got a phone call for Christmas. I asked him then about spending time with me and he said he just can't fit it in. This is the same old bullshit I always got from him. So, it is obvious the abuser, his mother, had gotten to him to stop him reconnecting with me.

Well here we are now just over a year later and I have him committed to travelling the 3.5 hour journey to my home town on Sunday afternoon, the 27th of December and then returning to Perth on the 30th of December so he can see in the New Year with his mates.

He had already committed himself to spend Christmas Day with his mother as he always has done for the last 22 years, but at least he apologized for not seeing me on that day.

Anyway, that is where I am at with him at the present. I do not have any hopes at all, because he has done this before and never turned up, but also, 22 years of pain is a long time and I am not prepared to allow myself or him to take me up then crash down again, especially when I have 4 other children who desperately rely on me to be there for them, because their mother is only there for herself. I have to remain aloof of any emotional extremes for the time being and just wait and see if he turns up.

Where Did I Go Wrong? How Did I Miss The Signs?

Now, if he does turn up, this will open a Pandora's Box for sure. There is a lot he and I have to deal with and I have allotted a whole day for him and I to spend together on our own, without the other children around. But, he will then need to be prepared for the fall-out he will face from the "b" that did this to him and his sister. This woman is like all the rest of these abusers, she is a narcissist and she will do what she can to de-rail any attempt made by my son to reconnect with me. Let's hope he now has the strength and maturity to stand on his own two feet and tell his mother that he needs to do this and that she has no right to stop him.

That's the news everyone. As I said, I am not getting my hopes up and won't really believe anything until he is at my front door. And if that day comes, I will mark that day on my permanent calendar as a day to celebrate and be thankful to God for. Unfortunately, his sister is controlled by her mother far too much and will probably never do anymore than she already does.

The Author writes:

First, PG, I have my fingers crossed that he comes. Second, I would NOT be going into any of this stuff that happened with his narcissistic mom. What he needs to see is a happy, healthy and successful Dad. This is what is going to attract him to come back. This is what is going to prove to him that you are the better parent. This is what is going to allow him to think critically. If you sit down and spend a day discussing all of this crap, it is only going to make you look like the nasty evil parent that she has portrayed you as. If you can show him that you have moved forward in a healthy positive way in your life, he will only want to be around you more and more. This does not mean that you tolerate any abuse, what it means is that you take the high road and show him who is the better parent.

Now, if he comes to you and starts apologizing and saying he knows that his mother is wacked, and then you can nicely say, I love you and have always loved you no matter what. That your mother may not have handled things appropriately, but she is still your mother and that the door is always open for him with you. If he wants to discuss things further about stuff his Mom has said, you can say, yes, I would like to do that, but it is not as important as us getting to know each other first. I think once we do that, then many of your questions will be answered about what you have been told. You can further say, but if you want me to, I will answer one question a day that you have, so long as we can move forward from there.

He needs to see that you are not still harboring all sorts of anger and resentment. He needs to see a mature Dad who has moved forward with his life and has helped raise 4 more awesome children and is nothing like what his mother has described all of these years to him.

EB writes:

Good luck and prayers to help Peter. The emotional roller coaster is a ride many don't want to keep taking for good reasons, yet it is tough to stop and get on solid ground. That feeling becomes foreign. It sounds like he maybe ready to try one more time, with you bracing for the unknown. The loss of a child is the worst fear of any caring parent, a living loss is no less hurtful, even if we do our best to toughen ourselves working toward solutions.

Driving for 3.5 hours is a lot of time to think. Would it help any if you could provide him with a Christmas CD to listen to as he is driving your way? People used to provide mixed tapes to help the long drives.

When I drove long distances I used to listen to Jonathan Livingston Seagull, and John Denver, I worked in the Canadian Rocky Mountains, an interesting mix of a philosophy to consider life including pensive music that made me feel good, in a melancholy yet positive way.

Just a thought, I don't know if recording some of your favorite music, with a short dialogue from you might

Where Did I Go Wrong? How Did I Miss The Signs?

help him get closer, positively thinking over that 3.5 hour drive or help him turn around? I wonder what Joan and others might think about that? Is there some benefit to talking about something important to you and your son, in a non-threatening way on a CD a good idea?

Narcissistic people, wives (husbands too), focus on themselves, and only what's best for them. The CD, focusing on your son combined with even older yet positive memories you have about him and some light hopes you have for the present and future might be something to consider for him to change his focus too? It's just a thought, and one I talk to my younger children about, hoping their week with me will provide them something positive and tangible to hold onto while they are with their alienating mother.

I have not tried the CD or MP3 player Idea to add to his iPod.... an idea that I respectfully offer for consideration, not knowing if there might be a benefit, hoping their might be.

Take care Peter. Your kind words earlier in my time along this road did help me. The struggle is no less, having ideas to consider and support helped me move and look for ways to move along, and help my children, looking for a way to improve our new family structure. Caught up within the old one.

The Author Writes:

Interesting idea with this CD/iPod thing. I can see the positive and negative sides to it.

Positive: He hears good and wonderful things about how his father feels about him. Possibly helps him to not feel stressed and nervous about coming to see his Dad.

Negative: It might make him think his father is too sentimental and warped and thus proving his mother right that he is crazy. Feelings and Emotions and Sentimental stuff can be easily turned around to make us look mentally ill.

If one gets the chance to reunify with their child(ren), here is an idea that Kathy Turesky came up with when a member said that was discussing his new tattoo of his daughter's name on his shoulder and how to tell her about it but still keeping it a positive thing. *Create a father/daughter pack going. Ask K if you two can come up with a list of how he can be part of her life. You could start the list with*
1. Having her named tattooed on him (a dedication of sorts)
2. Dad writing a letter to her once a week and then K reading it in the session.
3. K writing a letter to her Dad once a week and then her Dad reading it in the session.
4. Thinking of each other once a day and coming up with a good thought about that person.

KNOWING IF THE THERAPIST OR A SITUATION IS THE RIGHT THING TO PROCEED WITH:

Often we are faced with situations that send up huge red flags on one end but might be the opening of a door at the other end. Below is an example of such a situations and the advice and ideas that transpired on this subject.

ABA writes:

Last week my son called me, the first time in 18 months. At that time he agreed to have lunch with me this week, but he said that he would call and let me know when. He called today and asked me to go with him to see a therapist on Monday. Of course I agreed, but then I heard his dad in the back ground coaching him. Now I am suspicious. I lost my cell phone signal and the call dropped off. I saw that my son tried to call me again, but my cell phone would not let me pick up the call. The call went to voice mail and my son left a message that he was having his final scuba dive this Sunday and that I should come watch and bring my parents with me. I know my ex

Where Did I Go Wrong? How Did I Miss The Signs?

will be there and I heard him orchestrating this whole thing.

As I was trying to digest this information, the doorbell rang and it was my son! He said that he tried to call me and he wanted to let me know about the scuba dive and that I should bring my parents. I was holding my dog and he asked If it was the same dog that I had before. I told him that it was and asked if he wanted to come in. He declined, but when I asked if he wanted to see the cat he came in and left the door slightly open. He visited with the pets for a couple of minutes. I asked if I could have a hug and he said "sure". He said he would email me with the location of the beach dive. I said "I love you and I miss you". He said, "I miss you to" and started to go. He again said he would email me with directions. As he left I said "love you" and he said "love you to". When I opened the door to let him go, I saw that his dad was waiting at the curb. My gut feeling is that I am being set up. What do you think???

SZ writes

I think it's easy for us to default into the notion that every transaction has a sinister intent lurking behind it somewhere. You might be right, perhaps you are getting set-up (for what, who knows?). Despite such a possibility you have to view this as an opportunity to connect with your son. Get the info, go to the dive session and bring your parents along. Regardless of what the ex does - no matter how anger provoking, idiotic or whatever his behavior or intentions might be - you need to go and remain even keeled no matter what anyone else does or says. Your only mission is to be there to support your son. Be civil to your ex and ensure your parents are as well - no discussions of the divorce or other issues... just be there out of pure love for your son and put the notion of being set up to bed. In the end, even if you are being framed - if your motives are pure, anyone else's agenda will be irrelevant.

Author Writes:
    I think you are right to be suspicious. I think you need to bring a witness with you along with a tape recorder that runs through out the scuba test. I also think you need to find out if he has a specific therapist in mind, or if he would go to one that you found that specializes in high conflict divorce and relationships, i.e. a PAS specialist. If he says he has one in mind, then I would get the name and number and have an initial meeting with this therapist and explain that you are bit suspicious as your son has refused communication with your for 18 months and whatever you need to tell her about the ex. See if she knows why your son wants to see a therapist with you.

ABA writes:
    My sister, mother, and boyfriend think that I should not go to the scubadive on Sunday. They think that my ex is setting me up for something. Also, they said that after all that has happened (threats, blackmail, falseallegations of child abuse, and just being mean) that I should not jumpthrough hoops to do what they want and when they want it. They think thatany meetings with B should be on my terms, with structure andlimitations and should not include his father. I can see their point. Myfirst reaction is that I don't want B to feel rejected, but this isthe same child who lied to CPS, the Sheriff, and tried to have me arrested.My sister suggested that I call him and tell him that I would love to be athis dive, but after all that has happened we should take things slowly. Shethinks that I should go to the therapy session (it is with a therapist thathis father picked and I have met her once over a year ago. I was notimpressed.), but only if I know who will be

Where Did I Go Wrong? How Did I Miss The Signs?

there and what the topic of discussion will be. The ex has a new girlfriend that has little kids. I pay $1,050.00 a month in child support and I only have 4 ½ more payments to make. I think my ex might be done with my son and wants to move in with his girlfriend after B graduates. I welcome any thoughts and advice.

BC writes:
What could they possibly be setting you up for? Something physical? Take a camcorder and have your mother record everything from the time you step out of the car or hire a sheriff deputy @ $15 an hour to go with you. I would think there's a bigger risk by NOT showing. Then they can say you don't care enough to see your own son, to go to an event like this that HE invited you too, blah, blah, blah. Seriously, what's everyone afraid of? And yes, go to the therapy session! Again, let the therapist know you're going to record the session. If she doesn't like it, kindly remove yourself and suggest to your son that you go the following week, you'll let him know where. But being "not impressed" with the therapist is a pretty lame reason not to spend time with your son and work on the relationship with him.

GL writes:
Hi ABA. I think that you should attend your sons scuba diving event. I can understand your reluctance to go to see a therapist the alienator hand picked for you. I doubt I would feel thrilled by the prospect of having my ex dictate to me where (or even if) I should go to spend time with a therapist. How about a therapy for your ex! :) Did your son say why he wanted you both to go to therapy? Was it to help the two of you re-build a healthy relationship? Who's supposed to pay for this...your ex? I would be wary too, although I have no idea what they could be setting you up for. I hope that you'll go to his event, and take someone with you. I liked the suggestion that you take a camcorder if you can.

Author writes:

First, why don't you have your sister and mother and boyfriend go to B's scuba thing and video record it for you? You can then tell him exactly what you have said about taking it slowly and putting the responsibility on him to own what he did. As for the therapist, I would be setting up a pre-appointment with her before the group appointment. She needs to know what has and is going on. As for ex wanting to move in with his girlfriend, you might be very right on this and he is trying to shove B off on you now.

Not being impressed with the therapist to me is a heads up that this therapist does NOT know anything about PAS. And that is something that needs to be discussed prior to this meeting. If she goes into this session with a therapist who is NOT versed in PAS, it could actually make the situation worse. As for the Scuba thing, though I do agree that she should go, and I do like your idea of paying a sheriff or someone of that caliber to go as well as tape record the entire event, I also think that she should tell her son that if she comes, it will be with a sheriff to protect her and a tape recorder, because of what he has done in the past with false allegations. Her son needs to hear and know that because of his behavior, there are consequences, such as his mother no longer trusting him. He is going to have to own up to some of this stuff before his mother will ever trust him again and he needs to hear this loud and clear. Right now, his father has NOT talked to him about responsibility for his actions.

ABA writes:

I called the therapist. She knew that I was coming on Monday. She said that the ex is not going to be in the session. I told her I felt a little whip-lashed with all of his. Just Thanksgiving he wanted me the "F" out of his life and now I am being invited to scuba lessons? She said

Where Did I Go Wrong? How Did I Miss The Signs?

that she could not (would not) tell me what they want to discuss in the session. She just said, "B is now ready for this" .... I still have that icky feeling about all of it. I want to be happy about this, but my instincts tell me not to be.

Author writes:
You need to point blank ask her if she knows what Parental Alienation is. If she does not, I would advise either not going to this meeting or not putting too much stock in it, until she has read up on this form of psychological abuse. The sad reality is that if she does not know about PAS or believe that it exists, she will only make the situation drastically worse.

ABA writes:
When I met with her about a year ago, she did not seem willing to consider that the father had anything to do with, as she put it, my son's complete hatred of me. She said that he and his father had a good relationship, that he was doing well in school, and that he had many friends. She said the only negative thing in his life was his intense hatred of me, for which he could not give a reason for having. I am not expecting much - other than when the other shoe drops. Do you think I should print out some information on PAS, put it in an envelope, and leave it for the therapist?

Author writes:
No, you need to point blank call her and ask her if she knows what PAS is? And if she does not, ask her if she is willing to read some information on it. If not, tell her thank you very much but that you will NOT be attending this meeting, unless you can have another therapist there who specializes or understands what PAS is. Do NOT go to this session without either of these conditions being met as it will just be a disaster and you will loose your son forever. I know this is NOT what you want to hear, but this is exactly what happened in my husband's case and all the other cases I have worked with

where they saw a counselor who did not either know about PAS or did not believe in PAS.

SZ writes:
The evidence of an impending disaster has already been placed squarely in your face. If you've met with this therapist in the past and the outcome was that you were the problem and that PAS didn't exist, you are in for trouble. The only thing that will be accomplished is another session where the outcome will reinforce that you are the issue to the complete exclusion of other root causes, re; PAS... You'll be taking 100 steps backwards if you go to this meeting without preconditions. Pardon my French as they say, but the fact that your son has friends and does well in school is a bullshit response as grounds for determining that PAS is not in play. The reason kids might continue to do well in school and have friends is because their PAS behavior has become so ingrained that's it's normalized. In my lay opinion the fact that he does well in school and has friends while at the same time hating you, should be a waving red flag for any therapist worth their salt. The act, or extreme feelings of hatred are not a child's or adolescent's normal response and a child harboring such feelings would be in a state of disequilibrium. The fact that he can profess this hatred and carry on normally in most other respects in my mind is very disturbing because the hatred is now ok and it has been validated hence normalized. Please, please, if you go to this session do all you can to protect yourself as outlined by J, (the author).

Author writes:
SZ, this is so "spot on" about the kids seeming normal, when in reality how can hating the other parent be normal. Most truly abused kids go running to their abuser for fear of them not loving them. They defend them to the hilt. They believe that it is their fault they are being abused because they did something wrong in many

cases, as well. Very complicated mind set on this one. My husband's kid's are a prime example of having friends and doing basically well in school. But this does not mean they were NOT PAS victims. The reality is that they did well on and off in school depending on how the situation with court orders, i.e. if they were in court again or not or what was being said to them at home. It depends also how the Alienating Parent projects things, i.e. that if their schoolwork drops they will be sent to live with their father or other types of threats. With my husband's kids, when we would back off, the kids' grades would fluctuate at first. And then when the time had been long enough without the festering wounds being reopened by their Mom, they would do well again in school. I think in their case, it was an emotional roller coaster and they could not concentrate on school. So if we backed off, at first, they were upset because they thought we did not love them and their mother would be badmouthing their father left and right. But after a while, if we were not in the picture, their mom would back off and they would calm down emotionally and be able to focus again on school.

It is important to remember that these kids all have positive memories locked away in the recess of their mind. The Alienators objective is to erase any and all memories of the Targeted parent and their family, even if it means changing that perception to fit this need. If we can help the children to unlock these memories, then we can help them to think critically and heal. We can help them to move forward and get back the warm fuzzy feelings they had to begin or should have had about the Targeted parent and their families.

To follow is a narrative written by a high school student from a topic called 'I celebrate myself'. This child has been alienated from her two step-siblings for many years. Her story shows that kids do hold on to positive memories, even if they are associated with painful thoughts such a missing their step-siblings. It also shows the effects on the other children in the family who are not alienated.

"Perpetual Youth"
By JAKZ
Nov. 2009

It was kindergarten, maybe the start of first grade, when my stepbrother and sister and I found the giant rock in my back yard. It was hidden in the woods covered with leaves. It was the perfect rock for a fort. For days and days we cleared out all the leaves, pretending that deep inside the huge crack of the rock lived a family of snakes, so we had to be careful and not walk on the crack. We found brooms and rakes, and worked hours on end as if we were professional landscapers working hard on the job. When the rock was finally cleared of leaves, it was time to collect the sticks.

My brother wanted huge, long sticks; he had a plan. We must have found at least thirty of the biggest sticks I could carry at that time. I had no idea what my brother was going to do with them; all I knew was that it was going to be great. For days and days he strategically set up the sticks, leaning each one against the rock so that they began to form a circle. As he worked on his project my sister and I began examining the secrets hidden within our new fort.

The rock was slightly separated in one part, with a crack the perfect size for me to sit on without falling through. My brother handed me an extra stick and told me to do what I'd like with it. My sister and I sat in the crack holding the stick trying to find the perfect thing to do with it, when she began singing, "row, row, row, your boat, gently down the stream..." as she moved the stick around pretending to paddle a boat. Since that day, every time we went to the fort we pretended to get into the canoe and row into a land of unknown.

About a week went by when my brother finally finished his masterpiece, he had made the greatest, most spectacular tepee I'd ever seen. It fit each of us inside perfectly, if we went one at a time. After the tepee, the fort really began to take shape. We found an old rope in my dad's workshop and an unused piece of wood, which soon became the impossibly dangerous swing. It started with rope, yellow as the sun, one side tied around a tree and the other side connected to the rock. Then came the wood, rectangular, no more than a foot or two long, and no wider than maybe six inches. We attached it to the rope, I can't even remember how, all I remember was it was completely unstable. My brother got the hang of it pretty quick, he was able to balance on the wood and swing back and forth ever so slightly, while my sister and I fell backwards tumbling down

Where Did I Go Wrong? How Did I Miss The Signs?

the little hill of leaves, dirt and rocks, every time. Eventually, my sister and I gave up on the swing, and stuck with our "canoe."

The fort was fun, and we had put so much work into it, but there was so much more to be found within those woods. So one day, we took a walk, which was when we found the tree. The tree that had fallen in between two trees and was perfectly horizontal between them. My brother of course, the monkey he was back then, climbed it immediately, showing just how great he was being able to get up there and walk around. I was only six or seven at the time, but I had guts, and I wasn't too far behind him climbing up to that tree.

My favorite part of the tree-fort was the dangling vine. It hung from a tree way up, and looked just like a vine that Tarzan would swing from. We used to hang onto it, swinging back and forth, pretending to be in the jungle, with all the elephants and gorillas, just like Tarzan. Back then; Tarzan was my dad's favorite thing to watch, so we had all the necessary background to figure out just how Tarzan would swing on this vine.

Every time my step-brother and sister would come over we'd play in the woods, running back and forth between our two forts that we had so perfectly put together. However, time had begun to pass and I began seeing them less and less.

The tree-fort was cut down, along with the Tarzan vine. A little while later, a few storms had past and the tepee had past with them. Sometimes I still go out into the woods, just to sit on top that rock that brings back so many good memories. Memories that prove, "In the woods is perpetual youth." If I close my eyes, I can see us sitting in the crack pretending to row the boat, and hear us singing as if we were sailing across the Atlantic. I can see the vine swinging from the tree, with my brother holding on for dear life calling out sounds only Tarzan would be able to understand. I remember having the most difficult time climbing up that rock, that now takes me no more than two seconds to climb.

The tepee is there, in pieces, no longer standing, but the sticks lay silently, reminding you of its presence. Reminding me of the time I spent that summer, the last summer, I saw my stepbrother and sister.

INTERACTING WITH THE CHILD AND TEACHING THEM CRITICAL THINKING

One of the most important things that we can do for the children is to teach them to critically think so that they can abdicate for themselves. What is critical thinking? It is the ability to look at things from an outside perspective and realize what is truth or fiction, what is right or wrong, what is good or bad. It is the ability to think decisively about what is being told to them and know when they are being lied to. Critical thinking allows children to think for themselves and thus be there own advocate without feeling guilty. The following are excerpts from members of my support groups' conversations about helping the children and other individuals, to think critically about what is really going on.

> *LL writes:*
> *I didn't even realize it but I guess I've been practicing a lot of critical thinking myself in the past months because that's exactly how I've been approaching W (new wife of ex-husband). Example: The day before yesterday she was asking me if I had attended the WWE Wrestle Mania with G (ex-husband) and N (son); and I said yes I did. She then told me that G told her I wasn't there. I asked her to look at the pictures from this event, which I had on my computer and sent to her; and still G said he had gotten someone else to take those. I then asked W (stepmom) how do you suppose these pictures ended up on my computer and how do you suppose the picture of N sitting in the front seat of the van, looking at someone in the back got taken? Maybe a hitchhiker took it? What do you think?*
> *Anyway, she did manage to confirm that I was there through N who told her I was and caught G in yet another lie. That's when she wrote me that letter. I guess it was too painful for her to realize just how many lies he's been telling her. Who knows!*

> *The Author writes:*
> *I think you just hit the nail on the head, it is extremely painful to realize that the man she married may actually not be the man he portrayed himself to be. She is possibly in shock and trying to figure out how to deal with this very painful truth. And if she, as an adult, is having*

Where Did I Go Wrong? How Did I Miss The Signs?

major issues dealing with this, then you can imagine how N, your son is having a horrific time trying to deal with this, when he is lacking the emotional maturity or years of experience dealing with dysfunctional people.

AJM writes:

I agree with the view/strategy of helping our kids develop their own critical thinking skills. When I was first separated, and was still seeing my sons on a regular basis, our family was also involved with CAS(CPS or Child Protective Services) at the time. My sons were caught in a whirlwind of "Dad says" vs. "Mom says" vs. "the CAS worker says". While the tempting path would have been to say "I'm telling you the truth, and they're not", I decided instead to give my sons a message of "listen to what people say, watch what they do, and make your own decisions. You have the power to make a difference. You are very smart boys, and I have confidence in your judgment." I have been consistent with that message ever since.

The funny thing is I have no idea why or how I thought of it at the time. It was just one of those moments of unexplained brilliance that we all have on occasion -- i.e. "I'm not going to make you choose between Dad and Mom. I'm going to empower you to make your own decision, and reaffirm your self-confidence by letting you know that I believe in you". I believe that being consistent with the message will also pay off one day, i.e. "Dad never changed his story, so perhaps he was telling us the truth all along".

Even if it never plays out that way, my conscience tells me that my response was sincerely made in my sons' best interest and not my own.

AB writes:

A critical thought to try to get across: The divorce didn't affect the child's relationship with the alienator so why should it have affected the relationship with the target parent.

These are just some examples of the dent one can make on the roadway into PAS. A good visual image of this is to imagine there is this huge mountain of rock in front of you and you need to cut a road through it to get to the other side. It takes more than just dynamite and explosives to get through. You also have to make sure that everyone on either side is safe and secure and that in blasting through this mountain, you are not going to also permanently destroy something else that depends on the strength and power of this mountain.

Part of this process of helping the other person or people to think critically about what they hear and see, is to do it with caution. Critical thinking is one of the strongest tools available to us to convert victims of Parental Alienation to realizing that what they have been led to believe all this time, may not be as it seems. But this also can leave a wake of destruction if not done properly. But how do you teach critical thinking, especially when you have no contact.

Well, first, yes, having contact is a crucial element. With contact, you can subtly point out discrepancies between what is being told to them and what they actually witness or hear. It is for sure a very slow moving process, but with each new revelation by the person being brainwashed, the closer they get to understanding and knowing the truth. When teaching critical thinking, we never come right out and say, the other person is lying or try to defend ourselves outright, because, first, it makes us look bad and second, it puts us on the defensive. And we do not want to be in either of those places as it boxes us in.

Instead, we carefully pick examples of things that contradict what is being said. For example, if the ex has told the children that we do not love them. Then we show them with our actions that this is false, by telling them we love them, by showing them we love them and without having to buy their love to prove it. Love can be expressed in many ways, such as doing things together as a family, helping out with homework, going to the children's events and so on.

Another example might be if the ex claims we are not paying the child support. In this case, we start with empathy by saying that must hurt very much to hear something like this.

Where Did I Go Wrong? How Did I Miss The Signs?

Then we can explain that though you feel it is inappropriate for the children to be involved in any of the aspects of the divorce decree itself, that you are more than willing to show them all the cancelled check stubs signed by the other parent or CS to prove that child support has been paid and accepted. You can also explain that if this were true, then Child Support services would have contacted you and dragged you into court and locked you up in jail. And that if this was true, then how was your other parent able to purchase x,y and z for you if she has no child support, and this would be especially true if the child just received a brand new jacket or toy or other luxury item? Subtly try to pick out things that would prove what the child is being told and what is really going on do not match.

In addition, if this is a matter of financial problems and you are slow paying the CS, then explain that to them, but that just because you are having financial problems does not mean that you do not love them. You can also use the analogy of an intact family who is struggling financially. Explain that even in intact families, sometimes, things get financially tight and they all have to do a little give and take to make sure that everyone is okay. That it does not mean the parents do not love their kids because they cannot buy them the latest toy. That in fact, the parents are showing they love their kids very much by having to make sacrifices to ensure they have food, shelter and clothes.

If the children are complaining that the other parent has no money to buy them this thing or that. Then you explain that this is what the child support payments are for and that it is not their job to come to you when the other parent is having financial problems. It is the responsibility of the other parent to come to you and see if there is someway to work things out financially. That you appreciate them letting you know that the other parent is struggling, and that you will try to help out, but that things are difficult for you as well. And again, that in an intact family, they all do what they have to do to survive the financial crisis, including forgoing certain luxuries or shopping only when things are on sale.

If the Alienating parent is claiming poverty but has just gone out and purchased something expensive or gone and had their hair and nails done, you could subtly bring this up by saying, that if they are so poor why was money just spent to purchase x, y and z. In other words, try to point out the discrepancies between what they are being told and what is really going on.

In another case scenario, a member's child realized that they really wanted to live with the other parent after going through some pretty awful psychological abuse. They told this member that they were going to tell the other parent that they wanted to try living with the target parent. Within one week, the child received a brand new moped. The child called the member explaining that they knew this was a bribe but that they did not want to loose it and had agreed to finish out their school year with the alienating parent. The targeted parent knew darn well, that the coming year would be no different when the child tried to move and instead was bribed again with a car. This was one member's response to this situation:

> *KL writes:*
>
> *I should've known!! I'm so sorry to hear about this set back. :(I don't know if the conversation will ever come up again, but if the situation arises again, and your child tells you that they know they are miserable with your ex because xyz, but they are still going to stay with your ex because the ex is giving them a totally awesome new [insert bribe here], you might want to ask your child something similar to: "What price is your soul?"*
>
> *Of course, you will want to reword it... The above sounds really blunt and accusatory, but it's not meant to be. You want to ask your child in a way that will spur their thinking not just about rewards, but about consequences. Sure, (for example) they'll get a wonderful new car to drive, but will that solve the problems they feel they have living with the other parent now? Does he/she remember why they wanted to move back in with you in the first place? Will getting the new car really solve all the issues that they have living with the other parent now? If so, how?*
>
> *One mantra I learned a little while ago was, "Everything has a price. It's just a matter of whether*

Where Did I Go Wrong? How Did I Miss The Signs?

> *you're willing to pay it." In fact, I could give you a perfect example from my own life of how the acceptance of a "gift" similar to your child's and then finding out the price was too high, kind of blew up in my face. Mind you, it has nothing to do with PAS or any of the topics at hand, so I won't bore you with the details...*
>
> *One way or another, they'll figure it out. Sure, they are going to learn the hard way, and the price may be very steep indeed unless they figure out a way to take their own life in their own hands and make a few hard decisions, but they'll figure it out.*
>
> *At the very least though, you can be glad that they don't seem to be buying into the lies about you anymore and that they are willing to talk to you about everything. Even if they have decided to stay with the other parent for the time being, there is some progress. Hugs, and stay strong!*

In this example, the parent is able to teach the child critical thinking about the consequences of making a deal with someone that is going to keep them in an uncomfortable situation. The child can take this information, mulling it around in their heads, and hopefully come to a critically thought out decision that they can live with or that helps them to move forward in a healthy manner with their lives.

Another chance to teach critical thinking is when the children make unrealistic demands upon us. For example, many alienated parents find themselves in a position with the kids demanding money and claiming that it is owed to them, while in the next breath they are telling the alienated parent to leave them alone and never talk to them again. A beautiful suggestion came through one of my support groups and I think it could be applied to so many situations to teach children critical thinking. In this particular exchange, the child wants the money but refuses to meet personally with the alienated parent because the alienator has told them that it would turn out very badly. The child further states that if they were to meet that the alienated/targeted parent was not allowed to hug the child and that they would only think about shaking hands. Here is what was recommended to her by another member as to how to respond to this demand:

"Thank you for getting in touch with me. I am very sad to learn that you think any meeting with me, would turn out badly. I will hold the bond/money from your grandmother for you, until you are ready for me to give it to you in person. On that occasion, I will respect any constraints you may wish to place on the extent or depth of our contact, but I will also expect equal respect and courtesy from you. For example, addressing me appropriately as "Mom", or "Mother". Hopefully soon, we will have another time to talk about what is obviously troubling you. I look forward to working with you on any problems that prevent us from having a positive mother/grown-up son relationship. I miss you. Love, Mom." The sender of this comment further pointed out that, "Being positive to my son and non-judgmental was, in my opinion, key to having a good meeting."

As it turned out this mother never had to send this email/letter to her son. He agreed to meet with her and they even hugged. As soon as he saw his mother, his emotions just came flooding back. I think in this case, the son knew in his heart what was right and wrong, but had to play his father's game. So many of these children suffer beyond the psychological abuse because they become the alienating parents emotional support. The alienator actually depends on the children when they are down and out. As one child voiced to his father, "Mom is an emotional wreck after she gets off the phone with you. All she does is cry and scream and yell at us. We are responsible for her emotional well-being and it is just too overwhelming."

Another example is the filing of false allegations of abuse. If a child claims they have been abused and this is truly false, it is important for them to understand the consequences of such actions. One way is to turn the situation around so that it makes them think about what is right or wrong. For example, you could say to the child, what if your best friend decided to cheat off your test paper in school and you both got caught, but your friend lied and told the teacher that it was you who was cheating off of her. And because of this you were given an "F" on the test and an "F" for the entire marking period, how would that make you feel? Would this be fair?

Where Did I Go Wrong? How Did I Miss The Signs?

Or you could use the example of plagiarism and being accused of copying someone else's paper when in fact they copied yours and because of this you were thrown out of school, i.e. expelled. Would this be okay? By using examples such as these, it helps the child to see the consequences of their actions and take responsibility for the lie.

The above examples are not set in stone and may or may not work. The point is to try to diffuse the situation and help the kids to start thinking critically about what is being told to them and what is actually the truth. And sometimes that does require giving them hard facts such as paperwork as proof. But the key is NOT to bad mouth the other parent. But to let the kids figure it out for themselves by slowly blasting through the mountain that has been put in front of them.

CHAPTER 14

COMBATING THE NEGATIVE RESPONSES – PUTTING YOUR FOOT DOWN

WHAT IS THE WORST THING YOU CAN DO FOR YOUR KIDS? ALLOWING THEM TO DISRESPECT YOU AND ABUSE YOU!!

Conversation on Putting your Foot Down with Tough Love
SMR writes:

I'm in this same situation. I cannot believe I've asked the daughter that lives with me to move. I cannot take the constant mean, ugly way she talks and treats me. I've cut her slack for the last few years because I feel I cannot abandon her the way her dad did back when she was 17. The way he has dismissed her a non-existent is something I could never do. But she is now a 24 y.o. young woman and has a full time job. Now I feel she's just using me. I cannot stand the negativity in my home. Am I wrong for taking a stand against the abuse and disrespect?

The Author Writes:

Actually, S, you are doing exactly what you need to do. If you expect respect, then you need to demand respect or they will never respect you. When you allow these kids to walk all over you and disrespect you, you are in effect giving them permission to do this. You are telling them it is okay. The hardest part is putting our foot down and standing up for ourselves, because we deserve better than this and because we are afraid the kids will cut us off permanently. Most target parents deep down inside have been so brainwashed by the abuse from the alienator, that some how we actually believe we deserve to be treated like crap. Until you stand up for your human rights to be respected and treated properly, how can these kids or even the alienators ever take us seriously, when they know they can step all over us. As well, if we do not start showing these kids that their behavior is inappropriate and not going to be tolerated, they may never learn it, or learn it too late.

And in keeping with this topic is also the fact that we cannot make the alienator or the kids change. But we can change our own behaviors so that we are not taken advantage of and abused. This is a choice we have and we need to start standing up to that choice and realize that through our own change in behavior, we may be able to influence the outcome of things and maybe even influence how the other party treats us and reacts. Sometimes the changes we make in our own reactions and responses are a catalyst for positive change in the children and the alienator.

G Writes:

I agree! Asking my daughter to leave my house after having waited fourteen agonizing years to reunite was the hardest thing I've ever had to do! I second-guessed myself every day for months until she returned. I felt I would be doing her as well as myself a disservice if I were to allow her to run roughshod over me. How could I expect her to respect me when I didn't respect myself enough to draw some boundaries? When she finally came back I could tell that she finally respected me. She respected that I wouldn't allow her to do whatever she pleased just to keep her in my life. In reality, I would've done almost anything! It may take every bit of strength you have left, but you must not allow them to treat you the way they are. I know that it's easier to say than it is to practice, but you deserve so much better than that.

The Author Writes:
G, this is so important what you have said here. If we want respect, we need to respect ourselves and command that respect. And if we do not, then we will continue to be abused and walked all over. So many of us have had our self-esteem hog-tied and whipped, that we forget that we deserve better than this. Time for a new mantra, "I will not allow anyone, not even my children to abuse me and disrespect me."

It is never okay to allow your children to treat you poorly or abuse you. You need to put your foot down or send them packing back to the other parent. I know the biggest fear is that if you tell them to stop or send them packing that it will mean the other parent is correct and that you do not love them. The reality is, their behavior is unacceptable and wrong. And this is always the reason why parents do not put their foot down. They think the kids will believe they do not love them. But that is exactly why the kids get away with it. The kids know they can pull that card.

When you take that card out of the deck, they see that they cannot win that game and use that excuse because it's not going to work. And if they are that screwed up and decide to go with the other parent, there really is not much you can do except protect yourself from their abuse. And in the end, they will either realize that they really miss you and need you (like in one of my group member's case) or they are too far gone to be helped right now and it is a matter of your own sanity and safety to stay away.

Our responsibility as parents is to teach them right from wrong. But, if we allow them to continue to be disrespectful and abuse us, then we are teaching them that it's okay to treat people this way. We are teaching them the wrong lesson.

In addition to the wrong lesson, we are putting our own lives, and the lives of others who live with us in danger. And that sends the wrong message to those innocent victims because they see that the abusive kids can get away with whatever they want. These innocent victims, especially the children, think that you

Where Did I Go Wrong? How Did I Miss The Signs?

have to let others abuse you if you want them to love you. Sometimes these innocent victims might even think that they are not as special as the alienated kids because they cannot get away with this stuff.

By putting your foot down and not letting these kids walk all over you, you are sending a clear message that you will not tolerate their behavior, it's inappropriate and if they want your love and respect, they will have to treat you with respect.

I have a case with a mother who had two sons that were extremely destructive, both verbally and physically. She let this go on for a long time until finally, she listened, and sent the boys back to their father's house every time they acted out of control. We are not talking about typical teenage stuff (like rolling the eyes or saying whatever), but telling her to drop dead, that they wish she were dead, breaking things, physically harming her, etc. Well, it took about 7 months before the boys started to "get it". They realized that if they wanted to see their mom and spend time with her, they had to treat her with respect and stop the abuse. Now, they call her and come over as much as they can. They open up to her and tell her things about what is really going on in their father's home and how scared or mad they are. Their relationship is now back on track as mother and teenage sons should be.

No, it is not easy to put your foot down or send them packing. But it's the only way to send a loud and clear message that you will NOT tolerate their behavior and that it's wrong. If you allow them to continue, you are putting you and everyone else in danger, including the alienated kids who will grow up believing that it is okay to treat people this way.

To follow are some other thoughts on things to say or do when your children say hurtful and mean things. One of my members' children used to say nasty things related to the relationship between the member and her dog. Here is an idea of how to handle it which is taken from an excerpt of that conversation:

> *Author writes:*
> *As for the dog, in my mind I am thinking, the reason the dog is so happy to see you, is because he*

> senses your pain and your daughter is jealous because the dog does not jump up and down and lick her all over. The dog knows that your daughter does not care about him. But the next time your daughter says something about the dog, maybe say something like, "Dogs know whom they can trust; those who will always be there for them." Dogs have not had their natural instincts warped by others who want to control them. They love faithfully, truthfully and always, so long as someone is not hurting them.'
>
> And maybe the happy medium in some cases is to just accept that the children cannot say anything positive or nice right now in their life and that it really is not about you, but about the other parent. And though this is hard to always remember, when we are reading nasty words that flow off the paper at us, maybe there is a mantra we can repeat in our heads as we read this crap. Like, "My ex sucks" or "Words cannot hurt" or "Her pain is her pain" or "Let the pain go" or "Breathe and let her vent". These mantras are not meant to be said to the child, but more to be thought in our own heads to help us calm down and not react in an inappropriate way. And when we have cleared our heads long enough, then put your foot down and tell them you will not tolerate this kind of behavior. We discussed earlier in this chapter that abuse of any kind is inappropriate and teaches our children the wrong lessons. And as parents, part of our job is to teach our children right from wrong.

So what happens when the alienated child who has moved out, now wants to move back in but only under their conditions? This is never an easy thing to deal with because we want them back in our lives so badly, but we should not give them all of the control. Tough love is hardest thing to do, but setting those boundaries is a necessity or we will be back where we started. Below is another excerpt from a conversation on my support group and what was recommended.

Where Did I Go Wrong? How Did I Miss The Signs?

KD writes:

My 15-year-old son left to go live with his father almost 2 years ago (this is what he REALLY wanted and was making life a living hell in order to go). He would not come visit during Summer Visitation and has been more than distant the past 2 years. Yesterday I picked him up for my birthday. He handed me a list, the list contained things he wanted to move back home (home schooled, bird, karate). At first I told him I would think about his requests...then I told him that if he wanted to move back home he would have to do so because he wanted to, not because I would do things for him...he has mentioned in recent visits how his Father has not held to the promises that he has made and I think he is starting to realize that life is not as GRAND as he thought it would be. So, do I give in to the bribes to bring my son home to rebuild our relationship (although then I'm playing my ex's game) or do I hold firm on why my son should return. Part of me thinks I should cave, as I do feel like we are in a game and the next step is mine...I would teach him a very bad lesson in life, but maybe it could be reversed later.

Penny Threlfall, Counselor, B.A., Grad. dip. Psychology writes:

Hi. Having been there and done that . . . . I can only advise that you do NOT give in to your son's demands. Instead turn it around and advise him of your conditions for him to return to live with you.

My now 20 yo SS tried that one when he was 15 too. Instead we stuck to our guns and practiced tough love. It was hard, it broke our hearts and we knew we were risking loosing him forever. But as Children's Services pointed out to us . . sometimes you have to let them go before they realize they want to be with you that we wouldn't succeed in rebuilding our relationship by giving in to him. Instead if we stand firm with our decision that for him to return to our home he would have to do so according to the household rules (same ones we used for the older 2 kids) we may succeed in getting him to return to us permanently. We were one of the lucky ones, after his bio M abducted him (for 4 days), FS removed him and placed him in foster care as he refused to return to us, he returned 9 months later. At 19 he finally returned to his mum and less than 6 months later he's living independently and calls us regularly.

The Author writes:

Exactly, sometimes you have to let go to get it back in totality. If you love something, set it free. If it comes back, it was always there, if not then move forward and see what life brings. Just because I bring something I think is wonderful into this world, does not mean that it will not betray me at some point in time. And no matter how hard it is to do tough love, it sometimes is the only way to teach the right lessons.

MH writes:

Lots of factors to consider here:
1. Why does he want to be home schooled? Is he being home schooled now? Are you even able to do this?
2. As for the bird and karate, would these be things you would do for him anyway?
Maybe, use this as an opportunity to talk. Sit him down and explain to him about divorce and custody and how he shouldn't have to choose between his parents, #1 and #2, that he doesn't GET to choose one parent over the other just because he's not getting what he wants at one home. Let him know that you love him and want more than anything for him to be back in your life. Let him know that these things he asks for are not out of the question (unless they are) and as time goes on, he may be getting them, but you will not accept a bribe to have him in your home.
Thinking about my 14 y/o step son, giving in to that bribe would give him a continual sense of power over my husband and if his "conditions" aren't met all the time,

Where Did I Go Wrong? How Did I Miss The Signs?

he will tell us that we suck and he's going back to his mother's. If that were our situation, I would consider giving a bird/karate as Christmas or Birthday presents. And we would not be in the position to home school...and if that was what he wanted, then I would be trying to find out why. But, that's because in our situation, if N asked to home school, it would be a red flag....don't know if that's the case in your situation.

This is such a tough age. So tough. And I hear more and more how the AP's choose 11 to BEGIN the hard-core alienation tactics. Truly shows how little they care about these children. Tweens and teens have enough emotional crap to deal with without being thrown into the custody blender. Hope this helps.

KL writes:

Add my voice to Joani and Penny's saying, don't give in. He needs boundaries, and giving into his bribes teaches him that adults will cave to him to get what they want. Also, if you accept his list and then cannot honor some aspect of it for whatever reason, it would take longer to rebuild the relationship because he won't trust you any longer either.

As you can see from the support groups' answers, there are many ways to look at things and handle them. But one of the most important things they all agree on is NOT letting the children step all over us and take advantage. Parents are not doormats. They deserve to be treated with respect. And every time we let them use and abuse us, we are teaching them that this is okay and that we willing accept this treatment because we deserve it. In addition, the children then think that this is appropriate behavior and continue to treat others with this same indifference. Thus learning a very bad lesson about life and communication. We need to be the positive role model and example by putting our foot down and stopping the abuse and disrespect starting with us.

CHAPTER 15

HELPING CHILDREN TO UNDERSTAND AND LEARN COMPASSION

Email Transmission between Group Owner and Member who's daughter moved in with her father and is continuously rude and demanding, along with her ex husband who constantly puts her down around the children:

> *The Author writes:*
> *There really is no right or wrong answer sometimes. It is just what is in our hearts or minds that we need to deal with or say.*
>
> *Anonymous (Names & Events Altered to Protect Innocent) writes:*
> *One of my kids called today asking if I can help with transporting a bike and a few other items to a new place. My ex is screaming and yelling in the background. I said to come get the truck. My child wanted to know if I am going to help them out with this move. I respond that I still am trying to clean up the mess you left in your room here, for which I needed your help. So no I cannot help you. It is just more than I am willing to deal with. My child responds it is not true and I can certainly handle this. I responded that though in the past I may have taken a lot more, but that this is not one I am willing to negotiate on.*

Where Did I Go Wrong? How Did I Miss The Signs?

The Author writes:
You were honest and open, that is the best you can do, right now with your child. They still do not understand how much you struggle to do the right thing with the limited situation you have. See if you can find a way to give your child an analogy that they will understand. For example, their belief that you can handle more than you think you can. Is there something in your child's life that you know was hard to handle and then the pain or suffering was too much for them to handle it anymore? Maybe a physical injury and the pain was excruciating. Maybe a relationship break up and the pain of it was so unbearable they could not be around the other person. Maybe a friend they really trusted or believed in did something so horrible that they could never speak to them again or not for a very long time. If you can draw on one of these type examples, it might help them to step into your shoes and understand how you feel.

HOW TO SPEAK TO THE CHILDREN ABOUT THE OTHER PARENTS ACTIONS: WHAT IS OKAY AND NOT OKAY TO SAY OR DO WHILE TEACHING CRITICAL THINKING.

Is it okay to tell children the truth about what the alienator has done and is doing, versus letting them find out on their own over time as they mature?

Okay, this is a tough question, because the problem is that if you directly tell the children what the other parent has done is wrong, you are in effect bad mouthing the other parent. However, if you do not say anything, how are they ever going to find out the truth? If you can find a way to help the child to critically think about the issues and come to the correct conclusion that the other parent has done wrong by them, then they are drawing their own critical conclusion to the situation. For example, bringing up past memories of things that would contradict what they have been told as they recall the event.

Next is the recap of an excerpt from two members of my support groups:

AJM writes:
I agree with the view/strategy of helping our kids develop their own critical thinking skills. When I was first separated, and still seeing my sons on a regular basis, our family was also involved with CAS(CPS) at the time. My sons were caught in a whirlwind of "Dad says" vs. "Mom says" vs. "the CAS worker says". While the tempting path would have been to say, "I'm telling you the truth, and they're not", I decided instead to give my sons a message of "listen to what people say, watch what they do, and make your own decisions. You have the power to make a difference. You are very smart boys, and I have confidence in your judgment." I have been consistent with that message ever since. The funny thing is I have no idea why or how I thought of it at the time. It was just one of those moments of unexplained brilliance that we all have on occasion – i.e. "I'm not going to make you choose between Dad and Mom. I'm going to empower you to make your own decision, and reaffirm your self confidence by letting you know that I believe in you". I believe that being consistent with the message will also pay off one day, i.e. "Dad never changed his story, so perhaps he was telling us the truth all along". Even if it never plays out that way, my conscience tells me that my response was sincerely made in my sons' best interest and not my own.

AB writes:
The divorce didn't affect the child's relationship with the alienator so why should it have affected the relationship with the target parent.

In other words, in the above comment by AB, if you say to the child, do you think it is appropriate for a parent to get upset when their child tries to speak to their other parent on the phone? Or you could say, do you have any other friends, whose parents

Where Did I Go Wrong? How Did I Miss The Signs?

are divorced? What happens when they get on the phone with their father/mother who they do not live with? Putting things in question form that make the child think about what is happening to them and deciding on their own whether it is normal and okay are better than you telling or dictating to the child what is right or wrong. And there is a better chance that they will learn something from this lesson and it will then stick with them for life. Also, you have created a visual image for them and this too tends to stay with them longer.

Another idea is to ask them to pretend that this situation is not happening to them but to someone very close to them, like a best friend, or family member. Ask them how they would see the situation from that point of view and what would their advice be to that person. This technique can also be used for many other situations, as it makes the person stand on the outside and look in, which gives them an entirely different perspective. Often I use this technique with a parent to help them figure out what their next step should be.

This all leads us to the concept of teaching critical thinking to help a person see how ones actions affect others. One example that I like to use is based on a story of a teacher helping her students to learn about the permanent damages of bullying. In the original, it is a teacher who is helping her students to understand the true extent of the damages that bullying causes. I have adapted it to two different PAS situations, one with a therapist and one as a parent.

TEACHING CRITICAL THINKING USING THE BULLY STORY AND A PIECE OF PAPER:

Therapist Version:
I want you to take this piece of paper and crumple it up, stomp on it and really mess it up but do not rip it. (After the child(ren) have done this). Now I want you to unfold the paper, smooth it out and look at how scarred and dirty it is. Now I want you to tell it you are sorry and try to fix it. As you can see, you have left a lot of scars behind. Those scars will never go away no matter how hard you try to fix them. This is what happens when you bully another person. You may say your sorry but the scars are

there forever. When you do this to your (targeted) your mother/father, well, they are special, in that they love you unconditionally, and have a small supply of clean paper that they will let you start fresh with. (Therapist hands the child(ren) a fresh piece of clean paper from a very small pile). But this pile as you can see is only so big and eventually, they run out of paper and are like the original piece scarred and hurt forever.

The Parents Version:
Parent: (Pulling from a small pile of about a dozen pieces of paper. If this is not being done in person, describe the small pile of paper or direct the child to take 12 pieces of paper and put them in front of them)

I know you will think this is odd but I want you to do something silly for me. Take a piece of paper and crumple it up. Now I want you to stomp on it, yell at it, call it names and tell it you hate it. Now, I want you try to unfold the paper, smooth it out. Look at how scarred and dirty it is. Now I want you to tell it you are sorry and try to fix it.

As you can see, you have left a lot of scars behind. This is what happens when are mean, nasty and hateful to another person. You may say your sorry but the scars are there forever. When you do this to me or your "other parent", well, we are special in that we love you. In my case, I love you unconditionally. But we only have a small supply of fresh clean paper to give you to start all over with again. (Parent hands the child a fresh piece of paper or tell the child to take a fresh piece of paper from their small pile). But this pile of paper as you can see is only so big and eventually, it will run out and all you will be left with is the scars and hurt forever.

CHAPTER 16

BORDERLESS BOUNDARIES: ALTERNATIVE TERMS TO USE IN COURT
January 23, 2009

I have been sitting here thinking about the next topic to write about. It dawned on me that finding appropriate terminology to use in the courts is of upmost importance. The terminology would give us the tool to present Parental Alienation to the courts. As we all know, most courts will not even listen to, let alone tolerate, the use of the term Parental Alienation Syndrome. Thus, until the DSM and APA accept it as a bona fide diagnosis, we must come up with other means of "outing" this tragic form of abuse.

We all know what PAS is, the systematic ritual of destroying the relationship between the children and the other parent. But what does that really entail? It entails a hostile and aggressive approach to parenting a child. It involves a relationship that is so unceasingly enmeshed between the children and the offending parent, to the point of bordering on overprotective. The relationship that develops between the offending parent and the child or children is relentlessly enmeshed with borderless boundaries.

What do I mean by borderless boundaries? Basically, the offending parent does not see any difference between themselves and their children. They see their relationship as one entity and not two different and separate beings with individual thoughts and feelings. The normal boundaries that should be present between a parent and child are borderless. That is, they meld together and it is difficult to see where one starts and the other begins. In other words, the parent and the child/children are almost as one and there is no differentiation (Bowen) between the two.

This is most notable when a child parrots the offending parent's comments, thoughts and actions. The child does not differentiate from this offending/aggressive parent or themselves. Whatever this offending parent is or how they believe, is exactly what the child is and believes. If one were to draw a picture representing this relationship, it would look like two exact images of each other, just one is a smaller version of the other. And, in this mental state, the child believes they are an independent thinker and that all these thoughts are their own, because they cannot distinguish between their thoughts and the thoughts of the offending parent.

This independent thinker idea is used often in court to claim a child knows what they want. And, according to Dr. Baker, empirical evidence shows that individuals do not become completely independent thinkers until they are in their 20's, because they are still influenced by their peers and family. (Baker, A.J. , Adult Children of PAS) For some, this independent thinker ability never happens, because they always need to follow someone else who can be their leader, (i.e. Jonestown and all those adults who willingly poisoned themselves because the cult leader told them to.) But a trained specialist should be able to see all sorts of red flags if the child's words, thoughts and feelings precisely parallel the offending parent's words, thoughts and feelings. In fact, if the child has no thoughts of his own regarding the Targeted Parent and parrots all of the opinions of the offending parent, it should be a huge red flag. This also applies to the child's opinions of the TP's extended family. Unfortunately, in this case, the child is not an independent thinker and is depending on the offending parent to tell them how to live, love and be in the world.

So how do we break through this and get the courts to understand that any relationship between a parent and child that seems too close, too controlled, or too enmeshed is probably too good to be true? First, try to expose that the child is a parrot or puppet of the offending parent. This requires a developmentally

Where Did I Go Wrong? How Did I Miss The Signs?

appropriate approach. Children, usually from age's toddler to 8 or 9, have limited understanding of complex scenarios pertaining to why parents hate each other. In these small children, this is much easier to diagnose as they are considered too young to be independent thinkers. These children will literally parrot the exact words that the offending parent uses. They do this because, quite often, they do not totally understand what they are truly saying and thus cannot translate it into their own speech. A teenager or older child, who is more articulate, might be able to do so. Obviously, there are exceptions with young children who are more precocious and aware and can articulate things. Child Protective Services has, in many cases, actually determined that in cases with younger children, the offending parent has fed everything the young child knows or says to them. CPS can do this by using phrases and questions designed that are age appropriate for the children.

For teenagers, this might be accomplished by asking and posing the proper questions that determine whether the child has any personal thoughts or ideas of their own that are different from the offending parent's (i.e. not similar to the offending parent.) For example, a normal teenage child's musical tastes should not be exactly like their parent's, nor should their clothing tastes. In addition, a normal teenage child's choice of television shows and games should not be exactly like the offending parents. In both these cases, 9/10 year olds and up should be beginning to emulate peers and idols they have in the outside world. They should have different opinions and experiences about the TP and their family, which are different from the AP's. If every commentary made by the child about the Targeted Parent seems similar, if not exactly the same as the offending parent's commentary, this should be suspect. This is especially true if these thoughts, feelings and behaviors are inappropriate for their age or experience.

Also, and very important, is their negative statements. If they sound exactly like the offending parent, that should be a red flag, especially with no real reason or motive for this hatred and negativity toward the Targeted Parent. Maybe asking the child if there is anything that the AP, offending parent, and the child disagree on; or asking the child if they ever have a difference of opinion with the AP, like they do with the TP. Normal teenagers, in particular, should have many ideas and opinions, if not a book of ideas and opinions that express disagreement with both parents on many issues. If the child, insists, instead, that they and the AP never fight and always get along, no matter what, you are looking at a red flag.

For a smaller child, this might mean watching the words that they use. Are the words too big for them or are their statements too mature? Is the subject matter something way over their heads? The point is, if a child seems to mimic the offending parent to a point that their similarities are uncanny then brainwashing and programming or an unhealthy enmeshed relationship should be suspected. This is a sign that the parent has crossed over the boundary between child and parent and now it is borderless with no division between the child and the parent's personality and self.

A child who emulates inappropriate thoughts, feelings and behaviors that seem to be similar, if not exactly like the offending parent, should not be considered an independent thinker but instead, a follower in a cult of hatred toward the Targeted Parent. Think Stockholm Syndrome, also known as the Patty Hearst Syndrome. These children are identifying with the aggressor to protect themselves from the same wrath that the offending parent enacts against the Targeted Parent. The same thing occurs in families of physical abuse. The abused will defend and protect the abuser, because they fear losing the abuser's love and fear being harmed again.

Once the enmeshed and borderless boundaries of the relationship between the offending parent and child are established, then the evidence can be presented to the courts to show how unhealthy the relationship is to the point that the child does not even have a pure thought or feeling of his own. It will be quite apparent that the only thoughts coming from the child/teenager will be the ones that the parent has programmed into them and the child has been brainwashed to believe that these are their thoughts and feelings, not the offending parent's thoughts and feelings. This does not make an independent thinker but one controlled by a cult leader or Alienating Parent. This should show how the parents have violated the normal and natural boundaries that make a parent a parent and a child a child. When this boundary knows no border, we have proved that the parent has programmed and brainwashed the child.

I know this is not a perfect science and has to be presented by a competent attorney or pro-se, with the help of a professional who specializes in Parental Alienation, but I think this is a start to proving and providing an alternative term to get this type of psychological abuse noticed and reacted to by the courts.

Some other alternative names and diagnoses are as follows:

Alternative Names
Children:
- Overburdened Children, especially emotionally and with adult matters
- Chronically Enmeshed Relationships
- Vulnerable Children's maladaptive reaction

Parents:
- Hostile Aggressive Parenting
- Borderless Boundaries
- Medea Syndrome – based on the Greek myth of Medea avenges her husband's leaving her for another women through the gods
- High Conflict Model
- Unholy Alliances
- Extreme forms of parental alienation
- Sabotage
- Estrangement

DSM Diagnosis
Children:
- Acute Distress Disorder (308.3)
- Reactive Attachment Disorder (313.89)
- Posttraumatic Stress Disorder (309.81), which includes estrangement
- Projective Identification (DSM-IV 301.83) Part of Borderline Personality Disorder

- ☼ Splitting (DSM-IV 301.83 Part of Borderline Personality Disorder

Alienating Parents:
- ☼ Narcissistic Personality Disorder (301.81)
- ☼ Borderline Personality Disorder (301.83)
- ☼ Adjustment Disorders with Mixed Disturbance of Emotions and Conduct (309.4)
- ☼ Antisocial Personality Disorder (301.7)
- ☼ Personality Disorder NOS (301.9) such as Passive Aggressive Personality Disorder
- ☼ Phase of Life Problems (V62.82)
- ☼ Relational Problems (V61.9: Relational Problems related to a mental disorder or General Medical Condition, V61.20: Parent-Child Relational Problem, V61.81: Relational Problem NOS,
- ☼ Problems Related to Abuse (V61.21)

CHAPTER 17

ETHICAL AND LEGAL CHALLENGES IN CONTEMPORARY FAMILY THERAPY
NOVEMBER 23, 2007

Parental Alienation is one of the most challenging forms of psychological abuse. Often the perpetrator is such a good con artist and manipulator, that the therapist is easily drawn into their tales of supposed woe. An inexperienced and unaware therapist could easily be caught up and become a co-conspirator to the Alienator's web of deceit to destroy their ex-spouse. In fact, Alienators will deliberately pick therapists that they know they can manipulate because they have no understanding of Parental Alienation. And, if the Alienator is forced or accidentally becomes involved with a therapist who is well-versed in this form of psychological abuse, the perpetrator will immediately find an excuse for why they can no longer attend counseling with the therapist.

Even more important is the fact that the minute a therapist allows these manipulators to dominate and control what the therapist thinks about the other parent, the therapist becomes a party to the psychological abuse of the children and the other parent. And once the therapist allows this to happen, any positive treatment and renewal of a relationship between the Targeted Parent and the children becomes impossible.

The same can be said for psychological evaluations that are administered by a therapist with no comprehension of the psychological abuse that is being perpetrated or the ability of an Alienator to actually fool these tests. Manipulators, like

Narcissist's and Parental Alienators, can actually complete these tests creating the appearance of normalcy. Narcissists are so good at passing these tests that psych evaluations need to also include behavior tests and other evaluations that diagnosis narcissism. In addition, a Targeted Parent can come up as paranoid, and have other signs and symptoms that are typical of an abused spouse, which are then misinterpreted by the evaluator. This is especially true when the evaluator has been influenced by the Alienator and believes that the Alienator is the victim and that the Targeted ex-spouse is the problem. Unless the therapist understands the disease process of Parental Alienation, they can easily be persuaded to be a willing partner in the destruction of the other parent.

In both these scenarios, if the therapist/evaluator does not give equal time and weight to what the Targeted Parent says, both in session, and during the evaluation (as an abused spouse), they will cause irreparable damage by joining with the abuser and violating their code of ethics to be impartial.

According to Dean Tong's article, "Unfounded Child Sex Abuse Charge is a Form of Parental Alienation":

> *The child sex abuse charge is a very effective weapon to both start and continue the process of parental alienation. A very common strategy by parents in the midst of contentious divorces and child custody battles today is the unfounded child sexual abuse card. Oftentimes referred to as Sexual Allegations In Divorce or SAID, the "timing" of the accusation coupled with the brewing acrimony of ongoing court litigation provides ample opportunity for the alienator to coach alleged child victims of abuse and shop the same to area "experts" who are all to eager to treat.*
>
> *These therapies, which almost always begin before a court has made a finding of fact and conclusion of law on the validity of the child's outcry of abuse, exacerbate the alienation process. Typically in these cases, masters level counselors employ unscientific methodologies with little reliability and validity such as play therapy, which includes anatomical dolls, puppets*

Where Did I Go Wrong? How Did I Miss The Signs?

and drawings, abuse focused and trauma focused cognitive behavioral therapy, psycho education, and Eye Movement Desensitization and Reprocessing or EMDR.

When professionals treat a child for a condition such as sexual abuse that has yet to be medically, psychologically, or legally grounded in fact, it can cause the "victim" to believe s/he experienced bad or secret touches. And it reinforces the alienating parent behind the scenes of the litigation to further denigrate and vilify the accused. The Trier-of-fact, or court, in family and juvenile cases, is required to rule in the child's best interest and will oftentimes keep the therapeutic fire lit in order to err on the side of caution, on the side of the child. (Tong, Dean (2002).Elusive Innocence: Survival guide for the falsely accused. Lafayette, LA: Huntington House Publishers)

With more and more evidence that Parental Alienation causes horrific damages in children and their families, the more corroboration there is that when a therapist sides with the aggressor, (whether willingly or unwittingly), they violate their moral and ethical oaths. For this reason, it is imperative that Therapists and Evaluators become experts in the field of Parental Alienation and its subsequent syndrome so they can prevent and preserve their reputation and practice as well as refrain from causing more harm.

The most important point of this chapter is to make sure you choose a therapist or evaluator who is well versed in Hostile Aggressive Parenting and Parental Alienation Syndrome. Ask point blank questions of the prospective therapist. Do you know about PAS? What are your thoughts on PAS?. How do you treat PAS? What will you do to prevent PAS? If they say they have never heard of PAS, say, "Thank You" and hang up. If they say they do not believe in PAS, say, "Thank You" and hang up. Make sure that you find a therapist who really does understand.

CHAPTER 18

PROACTIVE APPROACH TO DIVORCE COURT

NOTE: I am not a lawyer. I relate all my statements to my personal experience and research. Please consult an attorney for proper legal information. This is only just a general guide as found on most websites and in most law libraries.

So your ex has just violated one of the court orders, such as visitation, or counseling or something else. Do NOT wait for them to do it again. You must be proactive immediately. This means filing immediately and every time they violate the court orders. It is the only way to show a pattern of behavior to the judge so that they deal with it. It is also why it is so important to include penalties in the court orders to make sure that there are consequences for not complying. In every case, where the parent did not deal with the contempt of court orders immediately, the ex-spouse was able to maintain complete control of the situation and continue their attack because by the time the contempt charges were filed, the brainwashing and programming had already begun. If you do not take action at the first contempt of court orders, the situation will snowball out of control and neither the courts nor a therapist will be able to stop the avalanche from creating a huge path of destruction.

As MH, one of our members writes:
Mistake #1 and #2 when dealing with AP's.....do not wait to file contempt charges against them....and DO NOT back down on those charges because you feel compassion for their situation. The AP will not hesitate

Where Did I Go Wrong? How Did I Miss The Signs?

> *to file bogus contempt charges on you at the drop of a hat, based on lies, and trust me- they will not EVER back down. Joani, can you note that somewhere? LOL....I want people to learn from our mistakes.*

NOW YOU ARE THINKING YOU HAVE HAD ENOUGH AND IT IS TIME TO GO TO COURT TO DEAL WITH ALL THIS CRAP. WHERE TO BEGIN?

The courts have been slow to get what is going on when one parent impedes the relationship between the children and the other parent. The major reason for this is a lack of proper education in Hostile Aggressive Parenting and Parental Alienation Syndrome and because a pattern of behavior has not been clearly established to determine the signs and symptoms of this type of psychological abuse. And it does not help that PAS is still waiting to be included in the DSM or Diagnostic And Statistical Manual of Mental Disorders. But even with that education, the court does not follow through and uphold it's own orders for various violations by a parent such as contempt of visitation orders and so on. Below are just some ideas for things to put into court orders for divorce, custody and programs that could be used to prevent all of this from snowballing out of control through the court system.

Before going into this battle in court, make sure you have a clear picture of what you want to accomplish and how you are going to get there. In other words, create a reasonable, attainable set of goals for stopping PAS and restoring relationships. Goals are usually set out along a time continuum as listed below, but could be altered to fit any situation.

- ☼ Short Term Goal – to be accomplished within the first 1st 6 months
- ☼ Medium Term Goal – to be accomplished within the 1st year.
- ☼ Long Term Goal – to be accomplished within the first 4 to 5 years.

Next, to stop disparaging remarks the following could be included into the courts orders:

> *"Each of the parties and any third party in the presence of the children shall take all measures deemed advisable to foster a feeling of affection between the children and the other party. Neither party shall do nor shall either parent permit any third person to do or say anything which may estrange a child from the other parent, their spouse or relatives, or injure a child's opinion of the other party or which may hamper the free and natural development of a child's love and respect for the other parent and this includes comments within hearing distance of said children."*

Now, of course this inclusion in the court orders does not mean that the other parent will comply. And thus adding the following list of penalties could also be included in court orders, so they can be enacted if parent violates any court order involving the children and the other parent's relationship. Please note that these are not necessarily the order that they need to be utilized in.

PENALTIES TO INCLUDE IN THE COURT ORDERS TO HELP PREVENT PAS/HAP

Below is a list of penalties taken from the experiences and comments of Victims that can be included when creating court orders during a divorce and custody hearing. Each case is different so prioritizing which penalty is less or more valuable to utilize will be up to you and those assisting you. Also, you might consider the following idea from AS, a member of one of my groups:

In addition to the below-mentioned penalties, the idea of 3-strikes law and you are out should be applied. In other words, 3 violations of the visitation orders, with police documentation, and that parent looses custody of the children. If a parent violates the court orders related to the child/parent relationship, there are the possible penalties to use with the 3 strikes and you are out.

1. A warning is issued that they will risk forfeit of custody of the children and the children will be turned over to the

Where Did I Go Wrong? How Did I Miss The Signs?

non-alienating parent for residential and possibly sole custody.

2. If a parent continues their attempts to impede the relationship, i.e. badmouthing, denigrating, instigating or running away, they can, and will be, ordered to perform community service appropriate to the situation. If the parent continues to impede, the parent may be denied one–on-one contact with the children and all visitation will be supervised and tape recorded. This information will be presented to the judge who will decide whether improvements, if any, have been attained in the behavior of the Alienator and the Alienator's family. All phone contact will be strictly monitored and not permitted outside of the monitoring system.

3. Mandatory counseling shall be established with a professional counselor well versed in PAS and HAP, for all family members. The counselor will report all findings, advancements or refusal to correct behavior to the courts, attorneys, other counselors, agencies and GALs on a bi-weekly basis.

4. During all visits or stays with the Targeted Parent, if telephone contact becomes an issue with excessive calls to the children or the children start to behave irrationally after the calls, all phone contact with the Alienating Parent will be reduced to once a day but could be limited to one phone contact every 2 days. All phone contact henceforth, will need to be on speakerphone and recorded to ensure that the Alienator is not continuing his disruptive tactics.

5. If the parent, who is receiving child support payments, is the one impeding with visitation, the child support payments will cease after the first report of obstruction. This money will be paid into an escrow account in the children's names and will not be released until the perpetrating custodial parent, who is destroying the

relationship, shows a clear reversal of their Hostile Aggressive Parenting tactics. In addition, the children's behavior must revert to a healthy relationship with the other parent. If the Alienating Parent's impeding behavior does not cease, the money will continue to accrue interest and be available to the children when they turn 18.

6. If violence and "out of control" behavior are being exhibited by the children toward the non-custodial parent (or the parent who feels they are being pushed out of the children's lives), the following process should be enacted:
   a. Full primary custody is given to the Targeted Parent and the Alienator's visitation is limited to supervised visitation for one to two hours per week . This will be recorded and reported to the courts, counselors, attorneys and other agencies involved.
   b. During the next 4-6 months/or at the end of the school year, the children will attend a twice a week anger/behavioral management class, which the Aggressor/Alienator must pay for.
   c. If, during the school year, the children's behavior is deemed as a danger to themselves or others, the children will be removed and placed into a Behavioral Health Center at the Alienating/Offending parent's expense.
   d. If the behavior does NOT improve or becomes worse, all communication with the Alienating Parent will be terminated in order to get the children back into a healthy mental state.

7. If a parent files allegations of abuse, the burden of proof will be on that parent to prove, beyond a shadow of a doubt, that such abuse exists. If the charges turn out to be false, the filing parent shall be charged with fraud, slander, defamation and filing of false information for the purposes of harming another innocent person. Punishment will be according to criminal law and said

Where Did I Go Wrong? How Did I Miss The Signs?

parent will be brought up on these charges in a separate criminal court.

8. If custody is removed from either parent due to alienating tactics, all communication, including supervised visitation, will be removed. No outside phone contact via any other route will be permitted until such time that the offending parent can prove that they will not interfere and psychologically abuse the children or other parent. If either of these situations is violated (That is, the alienator is found communicating with the children in any way), serious financial penalties will be charged and possible jail time issued.

These penalties are designed as a safety net for you and make it impossible for a judge to ignore the penalties because they are written into the court orders and consequently, give the judge a means of preventing PAS and HAP.

AN EXAMPLE OF COURT ORDER LANGUAGE FOR PREVENTING ALIENATION

In addition to the above penalties, a member of one of my support groups recently forwarded what their attorney, David Karabinus of CA, had included in their court orders to help deter interference. It is listed below:

- Should either parent fail to pick up or return the child in accordance of this agreement without immediately notifying the other parent as to the reasons for nonconformance, it shall be considered that the nonconforming parent is not acting in the best interests for the child, and such nonconformance shall be the basis for the modification of this order, including to return to mediation for evaluation of a change in this parenting plan.
- Should either parent engage in conduct, which sabotages the shared parenting agreement or attempts to alienate the other parent, it shall be considered that the parent is not acting in the best interests of the child, and such

nonconformance may be the basis for modification of this order.
- Each parent shall exert every effort to maintain free access and unhampered contact between the minor child and the other parent and to foster a feeling of affection between the minor child and the other parent. Neither parent shall do anything, which would estrange the minor child from the other parent, injure the opinion of the minor child's mother or father, or impair the natural development of the minor child's love and respect for the other parent.
- Telephone Communication: The noncustodial parent shall be entitled to reasonable telephone communication with the Minor child. The noncustodial parent shall initiate the phone call to the Minor child. Reasonable is defined as every….. The parent shall not place Minor child on speak phone and shall leave the room so as to give Minor privacy. Each parent is restrained from interfering with the Minor's right to privacy during such conversations. The Minor child must be given the message by the custodial parent that the other parent has called and assist the Minor in returning the telephone call. Neither parent shall block the telephone number of the other parent at any time or deny access to the child by any means or methods. Minor may call either parent at will.

Now, believe it or not, in some states, there is a law for interference of custody. I would suspect that most states have some version of this law but for purposes of this book, I am copying New Jersey's law as an example. This law might help a parent who has custody, joint custody or no custody but has parental rights to fight for their legal right to uninterrupted visitation with their children.

Where Did I Go Wrong? How Did I Miss The Signs?

2C:13-4 Interference with Custody
a. Custody of children. *A person, including a parent, guardian or other lawful custodian, is guilty of interference with custody if he:*
  1) *Takes or detains a minor child with the purpose of concealing the minor child and thereby depriving the child's other parent of custody or parenting time with the minor child; or*

  2) *After being served with process or having actual knowledge of an action affecting marriage or custody but prior to the issuance of a temporary or final order determining custody and parenting time rights to a minor child, takes, detains, entices or conceals the child within or outside the State for the purpose of depriving the child's other parent of custody or parenting time, or to evade the jurisdiction of the courts of this State; or*

  3) *After being served with process or having actual knowledge of an action affecting the protective services needs of a child pursuant to Title 9 of the Revised Statutes in an action affecting custody, but prior to the issuance of a temporary or final order determining custody rights of a minor child, takes, detains, entices or conceals the child within or outside the State for the purpose of evading the jurisdiction of the courts of this State; or*

  4) *After the issuance of a temporary or final order specifying custody, joint custody rights or parenting time, takes, detains, entices or conceals a minor child from the other parent in violation of the custody or parenting time order.*

  Interference with custody is a crime of the second degree if the child is taken, detained, enticed or concealed: (i) outside the United States or (ii) for more than 24 hours. Otherwise, interference with custody is a crime of the third degree but the presumption of non-imprisonment set forth in subsection e. of N.J.S.2C:44-1 for a first offense of a crime of the third degree shall not apply.

b. *Custody of committed persons.* A person is guilty of a crime of the fourth degree if he knowingly takes or entices any committed person away from lawful custody when he is not privileged to do so. "Committed person" means, in addition to anyone committed under judicial warrant, any orphan, neglected or delinquent child, mentally defective or insane person, or other dependent or incompetent person entrusted to another's custody by or through a recognized social agency or otherwise by authority of law.

c. It is an affirmative defense to a prosecution under subsection a. of this section, which must be proved by clear and convincing evidence, that:

1) The actor reasonably believed that the action was necessary to preserve the child from imminent danger to his welfare. However, no defense shall be available pursuant to this subsection if the actor does not, as soon as reasonably practicable but in no event more than 24 hours after taking a child under his protection, give notice of the child's location to the police department of the municipality where the child resided, the office of the county prosecutor in the county where the child resided, or the Division of Youth and Family Services in the Department of Children and Families;

2) The actor reasonably believed that the taking or detaining of the minor child was consented to by the other parent, or by an authorized State agency; or

Where Did I Go Wrong? How Did I Miss The Signs?

        3) *The child, being at the time of the taking or concealment not less than 14 years old, was taken away at his own volition and without purpose to commit a criminal offense with or against the child.*

   d. *It is an affirmative defense to a prosecution under subsection a. of this section that a parent having the right of custody reasonably believed he was fleeing from imminent physical danger from the other parent, provided that the parent having custody, as soon as reasonably practicable:*

        1) *Gives notice of the child's location to the police department of the municipality where the child resided, the office of the county prosecutor in the county where the child resided, or the Division of Youth and Family Services in the Department of Children and Families; or*

        2) *Commences an action affecting custody in an appropriate court.*

   e. *The offenses enumerated in this section are continuous in nature and continue for so long as the child is concealed or detained.*

   f. *As listed below:*

        1) *In addition to any other disposition provided by law, a person convicted under subsection a. of this section shall make restitution of all reasonable expenses and costs, including reasonable counsel fees, incurred by the other parent in securing the child's return.*

        2) *In imposing sentence under subsection a. of this section the court shall consider, in addition to the*

> *factors enumerated in chapter 44 of Title 2C of the New Jersey Statutes:*
>
>> *a) Whether the person returned the child voluntarily; and*
>> *b) The length of time the child was concealed or detained.*
>
> *g. As used in this section, "parent" means a parent, guardian or other lawful custodian of a minor child.*

Dr. Reena Sommer suggests the following ideas to catch the Alienating Parent in their own deceptions and then be used in court to establish the lies.

1. *Establish for the record the AP's position (i.e., the child is afraid of their parent; the parent is inappropriate with the child; the parent hurt the child - whatever)*
2. *Get the AP to make admissions on what constitutes a "good" and healthy relationship between parent and child*
3. *Get the AP to make admissions concerning under "normal" circumstances it is beneficial for children to maintain a relationship with both their parents*
4. *Get the AP to make admissions concerning the circumstances under which a child <u>should not maintain</u> a relationship with their parent post separation.*
5. *Get the AP to make admissions concerning the damage associated with getting any child to make a false allegation of abuse etc.*
6. *Present the AP with evidence that prior to the separation/divorce proceedings, the child had a positive and healthy relationship with the parent. etc.*

The following are court rulings from NJ that may or may not be useable in your own state but are worth looking into and trying to use as a precedent in your state if necessary.

In Smith v. Smith, Hud-L-1837-08, Superior Court Judge Maurice Gallipoli ruled on Nov. 21 that a man can sue his ex-

Where Did I Go Wrong? How Did I Miss The Signs?

wife and her parents for allegedly turning his children against him by making false accusations of sexual misconduct." Smith v. Smith, Hud-L-1837-08--New Jersey Law Journal; Dec. 1, 2008. The plaintiff in this case claimed that the defendants' alienating conduct has caused him emotional distress.
http://www.helenglassesq.com/new-jersey-divorce-news.htm

    Though, in this case, damages for Intentional Infliction of Emotional Distress were allowed as a possible remedy for parents whose relationship with their children has been damaged or destroyed by ex-spouses. (Smith v. Smith [Hud-L-1837-08]), there is a conflicting case, (Segal v. Lunch [MRS-L-3076-07) where the Morris County Superior Court came to the opposite conclusion. http://www.njicle.com/seminar.aspx?sid=663

    For the Smith v. Smith case to succeed, it was backed up with professionals and tons of counseling sessions. There were mountains of evidence that proved that the deceptive and significant actions of the Alienating Parent were at the heart of the damages to this father and in reality, the children. What this means is, it might be worth a shot to sue for these type damages, even if damages are not awarded, in order to prove a point, and make a statement that PAS harms and causes serious life-long psychological damages to all involved.

    Another thought to consider when going into court is to have a line of questions for the Alienator that will force them to disclose their motives and create doubt in the mind of the judge that the Alienating Parent is actually behaving in a manner that is in the best interest of the children. In fact, these questions probably could be used in a deposition to lay out a case for Hostile Aggressive Parenting (HAP) and Parental Alienation.

    The following is a set of 74 questions developed by Douglas Darnall to assist in proving that the other parent is not behaving in the children's best interest. They are not written in stone and of course, you or your attorney may come up with even more questions to ask. However, this is a great start to "outing" the Alienator publicly and in the courts.

AGAIN PLEASE NOTE: I am not a lawyer. I relate all my statements to my personal experience and research. Please consult an attorney for all legal matters.

QUESTIONS FROM DOUGLAS DARNALL AUTHOR OF "PARENTAL ALIENATION: NOT IN THE BEST INTEREST OF THE CHILDREN.

Questions to Ask the Alienator:
1. How would you describe your children's relationship with Parent prior to the divorce?
2. Have you had occasions since the divorce when you felt angry towards Parent?
3. Could you explain to the court the various reasons for your anger? (This line of questioning helps assess the Parent's possible motivations for parental alienation).
4. Since the date of the divorce have you ever made negative comments to your kids about Parent?
5. What type of comments have you made about Parent to your kids?
6. Since the date of the divorce, have you ever argued with Parent about visitation?
7. (If yes) Could you explain your reasons for arguing or why the arguments about visitation occurred? What were the issues?
8. What have you been doing to help encourage the relationship between Parent and Child?
9. Have you ever talked with your children or asked your children about Parent's personal life?
10. Have you failed to return the children from a visit? Why?
11. Have you ever commented to your children since the date of the divorce concerning any lack of money that was a result of the divorce?
12. Have you ever asked your children since the date of the divorce any questions regarding with which parent they want to live?
13. Since Child has been living with you, has Child ever talked to you on the telephone complaining about their time with Parent?
14. (If yes) After hearing Child's complaints, have you felt a need to pick him up from their Parent's home without Parent's consent?

Where Did I Go Wrong? How Did I Miss The Signs?

15. Have you shown either of your children any of the legal documents associated with this case? What documents have you shown? Why did you show them?
16. Do you believe that Parent exaggerates Child's medical, psychological or health problems?
17. (If yes) Could you explain these exaggerations to the court?
18. Do you perceive yourself as having a very different parenting style than Parent?
19. Do you believe that Parent should follow your recommendations or beliefs about rules and discipline?
20. (If yes) Have you tried to communicate to Parent your beliefs about rules and discipline?
21. Do you believe that you have good reason for being critical of Parent's parenting skills? Why?
22. Has Child ever suggested to you that he had a good time with Parent?
23. Have you ever heard any complaints from the children about their safety?
24. (If yes) When you heard the children complain, what did you do to communicate with Parent the complaints?
25. Have you ever expressed your anger toward Parent in the presence of your children?
26. What do you think Parent's role as a divorced parent should be with the children?
27. What do you think the relationship should be with their stepparent?
28. Have you heard Child make allegations of abuse by Parent?
29. Have you ever known Child to exaggerate or lie to get what he or she wants?
30. What do you believe should be the Child's relationship with Parent's family?
31. (If negative) Would you explain your reasons why your Child's should not have a relationship with Parent's extended family?
32. Do you believe that Child has good reasons for not wanting to live with Parent? Why?

33. Do you believe that the Child is old enough or is sufficiently mature enough to decide for themselves whether or not they should visit the Parent?
34. Have you suggested to Child since the date of the divorce that they have the right to choose for themselves whether or not to visit their Parent?
35. Since the date of the divorce would you say that there are occasions when Child is too busy to visit his Parent?
36. What have you done to help strengthen the relationship between Child and Parent?
37. Do you believe you have any responsibility to help strengthen the relationship?
38. (If no) Why not?
39. (If yes) Would you explain the steps you have taken to help strengthen the relationship between Child and Parent?
40. Do you believe that you know better than Parent as to what is best for Child?
41. (If yes) Could you explain the reasons for your belief?
42. Do you believe that Parent does not discipline Child?
43. Are you ever concerned that Parent is excessively punitive with Child? Why?
44. Since the date of the divorce, have you personally witnessed Parent being excessive with discipline?
45. Have you ever filed a complaint with the local Children's Service Board (your jurisdiction may have a different name for the investigative agency)?
46. Could you explain the reasons for your report? (This line of questioning may offer some insight into a parent's motivations for alienation, but at the same time it could open up a can of worms that will require a lot more testimony.)
47. Do you believe that Parent should follow your rules when it comes to how visitation is to be accomplished?
48. Do you believe that Parent should follow your rules or suggestions about how Child should be raised?
49. Do you believe that there are aspects of your private life that Parent has no business knowing?

Where Did I Go Wrong? How Did I Miss The Signs?

50. Have you conveyed to your Child that they should not share any information or activities to Parent about your private life?
51. (If yes) Could you explain how you have communicated to Child that they should not share certain information with Parent?
52. What information about your life did you not want Parent to know?
53. Have you had any discussions with Child about your plans to gain his custody?
54. (If no) You mean to tell me that Child doesn't even know you are going to court to seek his custody?
55. (If yes) Then please explain what you and Child have discussed about how you are going to get custody?
56. Would you explain what those plans are?
57. Have you ever listened in on phone calls between Child and Parent?
58. Have you ever asked Child to get information for you or report for you on any of Parent's behavior since the date of the divorce?
59. Do you believe that the court has any right to tell you what to do with respect to your children and their relationship with Parent?
60. Would you describe Parent as a good parent or a poor parent?
61. Could you explain your reasons for your opinion?
62. Who initiated the divorce between you and Parent?
63. Could you explain the reasons for the divorce? (This line of questioning again is to assess possible motivation for parental alienation. The question is looking for continued bitterness, a sense of betrayal or anger.)
64. Do you blame Parent for the divorce?
65. Are you and Parent able to talk with each other without arguing?
66. (If no) Could you explain why you are not able to communicate?
67. Is Child presently having visits with Parent?
68. (If no) Could you explain to the court the reasons?

69. What is Child's attitude about seeing his Parent?
70. (If the child has resisted visitation) How long have you observed these behaviors?
71. What have you done personally to help Child overcome these feelings and encourage visitation with his Parent?
72. Do you believe that whatever problems have occurred between yourself, Child and Parent that these problems should be worked out?
73. Do you believe that working out these problems is in Child's best interest? Why or why not?
74. What do you see as your role in helping work out any problems that exist between Child and Parent?

Douglas Darnall, Ph.D.,
PsyCare
2980 Belmont Ave.
Youngstown, OH. 44505
Wk 330-759-2310
Fax 330-759-0018
douglas900@com.

WHAT IF YOU CANNOT AFFORD AN ATTORNEY? FILING AS A PRO-SE

It is without saying that Court is one of the worst experiences we have in our lives, especially, when we are on the end, which is getting slammed. But, making it more palatable or at the least more friendly, is something I can only attempt to do. Since I am not an attorney, I cannot give you true legal advice about Divorce or courts. However, I can provide an example of what a Motion might look like. On the following pages you will see a sample of what a motion might look like if you needed to file one pro-se along with a certification of mailing that proves you have sent the defendant or their attorney this document to them. This is very important.

It is advised that if you plan to file things without an attorney, which is called Pro-se, that you contact your local courts to find out if they have any specific formats that they prefer you use or if they have specific forms. For example, there

Where Did I Go Wrong? How Did I Miss The Signs?

is a fee for filing in court, but there is also something called a fee waiver that you may also qualify for. In addition, once a case is filed and assigned a docket number, a pro-se can then make a motion to the court for a court appointed attorney to assist them. Every state is different. And for that matter, county to county within one state can be different. So please make sure if you plan to go pro-se in court, i.e. without attorney, that you get all the facts on how to file from your court clerk.

And one last note on this matter is that there are rights that protect pro-se litigants from being held to the same standards as an attorney when submitting and presenting their case. See below for an example of this ruling from one state.

Pro se litigants' court submissions are to be construed liberally and held to less stringent standards than submissions of lawyers. If the court can reasonably read the submissions, it should do so despite failure to cite proper legal authority, confusion of legal theories, poor syntax and sentence construction, or litigant's unfamiliarity with rule requirements. Boag v. MacDougall, 454 U.S. 364, 102 S.Ct. 700, 70 L.Ed.2d 551 (1982); Estelle v. Gamble, 429 U.S. 97, 106, 97 S.Ct. 285, 50 L.Ed.2d 251 (1976)(quoting Conley v. Gibson, 355 U.S. 41, 45-46, 78 S.Ct. 99, 2 L.Ed.2d 80 (1957)); Haines v. Kerner, 404 U.S. 519, 92 S.Ct. 594, 30 L.Ed.2d 652 (1972); McDowell v. Delaware State Police, 88 F.3d 188, 189 (3rd Cir. 1996); United States v. Day, 969 F.2d 39, 42 (3rd Cir. 1992)(holding pro se petition cannot be held to same standard as pleadings drafted by attorneys); Then v. I.N.S., 58 F.Supp.2d 422, 429 (D.N.J. 1999).

The courts provide pro se parties wide latitude when construing their pleadings and papers. When interpreting pro se papers, the Court should use common sense to determine what relief the party desires. S.E.C. v. Elliott, 953 F.2d 1560, 1582 (11th Cir. 1992). See also, United States v. Miller, 197 F.3d 644, 648 (3rd Cir. 1999) (Court has special obligation to construe pro se litigants' pleadings liberally); Poling v. K.Hovnanian Enterprises, 99 F.Supp.2d 502, 506-07 (D.N.J. 2000).

Defendant has the right to submit pro se briefs on appeal, even though they may be in-artfully drawn but the court can reasonably read and understand them. See, Vega v. Johnson, 149 F.3d 354 (5th Cir. 1998). Courts will go to particular pains to protect pro se litigants against consequences of technical errors if injustice would otherwise result. U.S. v. Sanchez, 88 F.3d 1243 (D.C.Cir. 1996). http://www.zorza.net/JudicalTech.JJWi03.pdf

On the following pages is the sample motion and certifications that you might see used to file an order in courts.

Where Did I Go Wrong? How Did I Miss The Signs?

Name of District/Other Court
Additional Name of Court
Street Address of Court
City/Town, State ZipCode

Plaintiff's Name
PLAINTIFF
Vs.   CASE NO.(insert if known)
Defendant's Name
DEFENDANTS

MOTION TO FILE CONTEMPT OF COURT ORDERS FOR VIOLATION OF VISITATION, CUSTODY, CHILD SUPPORT...

The Plaintiff, (insert full name), a resident of (insert county), and residing at (insert full address), in the referenced matter respectfully requests the filing of a (insert complaint) against the named Defendant

1. On Insert Date, the court granted/ordered joint custody of the minor children of (Your name and Your ex spouse's name)
2. This court order included the following:
    a. Example, Not allowed to leave state
    b. Example: All medical and Educational Info.
    c. Example: Visitation every other weekend and on Wednesday evenings for which ever parent it is.
3. On Date or on or about such and such date, If you are the plaintiff in the case, put Plaintiff, if you are the defendant in the case, defendant, saw the minor children.
4. On Date or on or about such and such date, Plaintiff/Defendant, attempted to contact/pick-up/whatever it is, the children but they did not respond.
5. Plaintiff/Defendant found out that
6. Plaintiff/Defendant has not seen or heard from children since (Date)

WHEREFORE, the Plaintiff/Defendant respectfully requests that the Court find the Plaintiff/Defendant in contempt of court orders. Furthermore, Plaintiff requests this Court order the Defendant to pay all costs, including court costs, attorney's fees for the bringing of this motion.

Respectfully submitted:

_____

Plaintiff/Defendant
Your Street Address
City, State ZipCode

Where Did I Go Wrong? How Did I Miss The Signs?

CERTIFICATION of MAILING

This is to certify that a copy of the foregoing was sent on this _____ day of _____, 200_____ to all defendants as follows:

(State the name and address of the defendant/Alienating Parent or their attorney here.)

_____

Plaintiff's Name/Target Parents Name

Defendant/Plaintiff, Pro-Se

NOTE: I am not a lawyer. I relate all my statements to my personal experience and research. Please consult an attorney for proper legal advice.

CHAPTER 19

CHOOSING WHICH BATTLES TO FIGHT

Sometimes it is hard to take the high road and know if it is the right thing to do. Below is an Email from a parent whose child was not being permitted to bring an important medical apparatus with them that they needed for their overall health.

> *Anonymous writes:*
> *I picked up my child last night and now have learned that they are not allowed to bring medically necessary prosthesis for vision to my house. My child is forced to wear a very old broken, fragile prosthesis. This is abuse!!!! I am just so angry. How can these people continue to abuse my children like this. They are denying this child the right to see just so that they can live in their make believe world. My child is suffering from pain from not having the proper prosthesis. How is this not abuse? I can't call CPS because it will only bring more pain to my children. I gave my child the option of do I tell on your other parent or do I buy you a new prosthesis. My child has chosen that I buy it new. I am going to honor this decision but believe me that I will teach my child at a more appropriate time that some things you just have to tell. I have worked so hard to teach my child how to live drama free and they always find a way to turn the knife. I am so sick of this. They are refusing a prosthesis!!!*

This is just one of many examples of times when we must decide which battles to fight. In D's case above, asking her daughter's opinion helped her daughter to understand that her

Where Did I Go Wrong? How Did I Miss The Signs?

mother trusted her. She further showed her respect by agreeing to buy her glasses to use at her home. Furthermore, when caught in one of these situations, always document it and keep all receipts. Other examples of things that a parent will use to control the children and your relationship with them include clothing, toys, cars, game schedules, and of course, visitation.

But these are not the only battles that we are up against and must fight. But of all these battles one of the most important ones that we should fight to stop, is the abuse that is directed at us. Allowing our children or others to abuse us, sends a very clear message that we will not fight back and that we will continue to take this abuse, just to have our children in our lives.

We have to set a good example by standing up for ourselves, and not taking abuse. If the children see us doing it, then they know that they can do it to, and stop someone from abusing them. This also works in the reverse in that if the alienator is allowed to abuse us and get away with it, the alienator sees this as an example of something they can do and get away with and the children will follow suit. So by us making a stand and putting our foot down, we are showing that we control our own lives and will not tolerate abuse. If we do not stand up, we look weak; just like the alienator has portrayed us.

Unfortunately, as many have stated to me during sessions and emails, it means that the alienator will step up their alienating tactics. But in doing so, the alienator usually goes over-board to such an out of control extent that the kids start to see the bigger picture. And if the kids do not get it, hopefully the court, judge, attorney and agencies due.   Hopefully by helping the judges, courts, attorneys and agencies to see this bizarre behavior from the alienating parent, all because the targeted parent refuses to take their abuse and insists on being a part of their child's life, the game will be up and intervention can begin immediately. It is only a problem for the kids, when the court, GAL and so on do NOT put down their foot and stop the alienator.

DO NOT CONSTANTLY DEFEND AND ARGUE WITH THE EX IT JUST GIVES THEM MORE FUEL FOR THEIR FIRE OR AMMUNITION TO USE AGAINST YOU. AND WORSE IT KEEPS THE CONFLICT GOING AND THUS YOU EMBROILED WITH THEM.

Below, again, is a recap of an excerpt from one of my support groups involving a grandmother who keeps trying to reach out to her daughter and grandson, though her daughter's boyfriend's father is the Mayor of a town. This is the advice that came through.

KL writes:

I don't know why you're still keeping communication lines open with him. If there's anything I've learned from G's run-ins with his ex A, it's that you don't feed the troll. The more you contact them to explain things or attempt to justify yourself to them, the more opportunities and ammunition you give them to hurt you. You're hurting enough as it is without handing them more opportunities on a golden platter. Better to just limit contact with Mayor Worthless to business and necessity-only correspondence, and pretend that he's just some guy on another planet the rest of the time.

The Author writes:

I agree 100% about this constantly contacting Mayor W. The less he knows, the better, because the more you can work in the background undetected. Your Daughter is being backed up by Mayor W., who is probably telling her that you are crazy and no good and to stay away from you. Stop communicating with W. and let the authorities deal with him. You are just harming yourself by constantly re-opening those nasty wounds. I am going to again post something called the Festering Wound. It first starts as a red rash that itches, so you scratch it. But it just itches more and more. So you scratch it more and more. You scratch it so much that it

Where Did I Go Wrong? How Did I Miss The Signs?

starts to get raw. Soon you are scratching it so much that it starts to bleed. Pretty soon, it is not just bleeding but infected and oozing. In fact, it is a festering open wound. And the only way for it to heal is to cover it with a bandage and ointment and just leave it alone for a while, so that eventually, you can reach out and touch it again. That is to say, we must move forward and come back to this when the time is right and the healing has begun or been done.

KF writes:

I use to be the WORST at calling and explaining myself to my ex, or still reaching out to him like he was human. I didn't realize that I was "feeding the troll", it's only been this past year that I've just stopped all together. I'll email him information he needs or call him if I need to speak to him in regards to the kids. He now tries to "goat" me in emails brings up things that happen 7 years ago or insinuates things that aren't true to try and get me to justify or explain myself. It's been hard stopping my "turrets" but when I feel the need I'll respond a nice lengthy FU letter just to get it out of my system and then I delete it. He has now recruited his new wife to send me emails in hopes that I will respond to her, but "I've held strong". It drives them CRAZY, in fact 2 weeks ago when she was at my house (when she called the police), as she was yelling at me telling me that I had to answer her questions I was walking away she just got louder and louder made herself look like an idiot. I finally realized that I was the one looking stupid by arguing with my ex in emails about, trying to call out his lies or explain myself when he was twisting everything around. I feel better too, because now he has NOTHING, when before he was taken everything out of context and using it against me...even if it was volunteering at the homeless shelter, it didn't matter what it was. It's hard, and truthfully, now that the wounds have healed, I don't even want to know what type of scar is left, I caused a lot of damage when I was trying to communicate. These people are not normal, they are mean and hateful and they prey on us, because we are good-natured and we want to do what is right by everyone. But we can't if we keep selling ourselves out to these people. We have to protect ourselves.

The Author writes:
You are right. Responding to them just fuels their fire and keeps them attached to us. My relative's ex would do anything to get him to notice her, even if it required using bad attention such as dragging him into court on bogus claims of being in the arrearages. The less we communicate with them, the more it pisses them off and takes the controls out of their hands. When we respond, it just gives them more ammunition and allows them to still be close to us, even if in a negative way.

Every time we defend ourselves or argue with the ex, we are giving the alienator and the children more excuses to fight with us. Every time we defend ourselves and argue, we are continuing to engage in tit for tat controversy. Every time we defend ourselves and argue, we are playing right into the alienator's hands and allowing them to continue to control us. Every time we defend and argue, we are letting the alienator know that they have pushed our buttons and we are mad. And every time we do this, we are setting ourselves up for failure because the ex and the children know that they have got us running in circles, chasing our tails to try and regain control of our lives and the situation.

So what should you do? Do not stand there and defend or argue trying to prove you are right and they are wrong, because they really do not care. It is a game to get your riled up and upset. It is a game to make you mad and piss you off. It is a game to show who has the control and who does not. Instead just look them in the eye and say, if that is what you believe, so be it and just hang up the phone or walk out the door.

If they are being rude and nasty, just smile and say when you can talk to me civilly and with respect I will listen. Until then, I am hanging up the phone or just walk out the door. Or if they are in your home, say I am now going to ask you to leave. If it is the kids, just tell them you will not tolerate this abuse. Then either walk away, hang up the phone or if it is bordering on a danger to you or someone else, call the police. And alternately, you can tell them to now call their other parent and have them pick them up, because they are not allowed to stay with you behaving like this. Don't worry about what they are going to think or say, it really does not matter as they think it already. But by putting your foot down, they will start to realize that you are not going to take their crap and that if they want to have a relationship of any kind with you, they will have to behave like they want one. It is not going to be easy. And it may take months of sending the kids home or hanging up on them or the ex to get the point across. But once they get it, they will start to treat you with respect.

Again, I want to bring up the Case example of one of my support groups members who had joint custody of her two sons, until the ex starting brainwashing the boys to hate her. These boys were not just verbally abusive but physically destructive. It got so bad, that finally the judge let the boys move permanently with their father. The boys still had bi-weekly visitation with their mother, but during this time they were continuously abusive. Finally taking advice, she started sending the boys back home to their father. It took about 6 months for the boys to get it, but finally, they realized that if they wanted their mother's attention, they had to treat her properly. It hurt for her to do this and she cried herself to sleep, praying that she was doing the right thing, but knowing she could not take their abuse anymore. And yes, it paid off and big time. She now has a strong relationship with her boys. They confide in her and ask to stay at her home every week, even when it is not their visitation week.

CHAPTER 20

HOW TO DEAL WITH EDUCATIONAL INSTITUTIONS & PARENTS RIGHTS KNOWN AS FERPA

In 1974, the Federal Government created an act to protect parents and students. What this act also did was entitle parents to any and all information in their child's educational file (with a few exceptions such as small side notes from staff) for children under the age of 18. What this means is that whether you have sole custody, joint custody or no custody but still have parental rights, you are entitled to a copy of this file along with and any all information that is sent home to the other parents house. Below is a brief summary of it from the Department of Education but you can also go to www.deltabravo.net for even more information by state including forms.

The Federal Educational Rights and Privacy Act (FERPA) (20 U.S.C. § 1232g; 34 CFR Part 99) is a Federal law that protects the privacy of student education records. The law applies to all schools that receive funds under an applicable program of the U.S. Department of Education.

FERPA gives parents certain rights with respect to their children's education records. These rights transfer to the student when they reach the age of 18 or attend a school beyond the high school level. Students to whom the rights have transferred are "eligible students."

1. Parents or eligible students have the right to inspect and review the student's education records maintained by the school. Schools are not required to provide copies of records unless, for reasons such as great

Where Did I Go Wrong? How Did I Miss The Signs?

distance, it is impossible for parents or eligible students to review the records. Schools may charge a fee for copies.

2. Parents or eligible students have the right to request that a school correct records, which they believe to be inaccurate or misleading. If the school decides not to amend the record, the parent or eligible student then has the right to a formal hearing. After the hearing, if the school still decides not to amend the record, the parent or eligible student has the right to place a statement with the record setting forth his or her view about the contested information.

3. Generally, schools must have written permission from the parent or eligible student in order to release any information from a student's education record. However, FERPA allows schools to disclose those records, without consent, to the following parties or under the following conditions (34 CFR § 99.31):
   a. School officials with legitimate educational interest;
   b. Other schools to which a student is transferring;
   c. Specified officials for audit or evaluation purposes;
   d. Appropriate parties in connection with financial aid to a student;
   e. Organizations conducting certain studies for or on behalf of the school;
   f. Accrediting organizations;
   g. To comply with a judicial order or lawfully issued subpoena;
   h. Appropriate officials in cases of health and safety emergencies; and
   i. State and local authorities, within a juvenile justice system, pursuant to specific State law.

Schools may disclose, without consent, "directory" information such as a student's name, address, telephone number, date and place of birth, honors and awards, and dates of attendance. However, schools must tell parents and eligible students about directory information and allow parents and eligible students a reasonable amount of time to request that the school not disclose directory information about them. Schools must notify parents and eligible students annually of their rights under FERPA. The actual means of notification (special letter, inclusion in a PTA bulletin, student handbook, or newspaper article) is left to the discretion of each school.

For additional information or technical assistance, call (202) 260-3887 (voice). Individuals who use TDD may call the Federal Information Relay Service at 1-800-877-8339. Or contact them at the following address: Family Policy Compliance OfficeU.S. Department of Education, 400 Maryland Avenue, SW, Washington, D.C. 20202-5920

Quite often the alienating spouse will abuse the school as a way to keep us from being involved in the children's lives. But the law is on our side with this one, so long as our parent rights have not been terminated, we have a right to the children's educational information, along with all the flyers and information that comes home with the kids. As well, all parents are entitled to copies of the children's school photos, class trips, having their name listed as one of the emergency contacts and so on. Key here is that if a parent impedes this it violates the laws and a judge will see this as clearly a problem. It would be a rare judge that would be hard pressed to not see the damage in not allowing the other parent the children's school pictures or to be listed on the emergency contact list. Just denial of this is a serious red flag for anyone.

CHAPTER 21

DOCUMENTING EVIDENCE INCLUDING TAPE RECORDING PROPERLY

When it comes to proving Parental Alienation, sometimes the best way is to the old fashioned way, that of documenting everything. Documenting your evidence of missed visitations and holidays creates Visual Aids for the Judge.

Penny Threlfall , Counselor, B.A., Grad. dip. Psychology writes:

Lay things out as far as scheduling on a Calendar starting either with last year, or the year before or even going back as far as the beginning when visitation began to be impeded, if you can. Show when the ex had the child(ren) for vacation, and when you had them. Also, show as many of the visitations that you can. Try to use a color code, like Red for her and Blue you. If you have a computer calendar program such as Outlook or iCal (Mac program) or some other computer calendar for setting up dates and things, this will be really easy to do and then you can print it out by the month and show when she had him and when you had him, and if color coded it will show the differences. This also might help you to focus anger and energy into a productive project that can help your case.

CREATING EXCEL SHEETS, PIE CHARTS AND GRAPHS TO SHOW A CLEAR PICTURE OF THINGS.

Write a journal or daily log that documents all visitations and confrontations as well as incidents. Include date, time, place and event. Use no emotions, just the facts. Provide any extra evidence, as needed such as phone logs both incoming and outgoing. The phone company will help you with incoming logs if you know the exact day and even better time.

In addition, I, the author, have created an excel sheet of 167 Red Flag Behaviors. This sheet lists 167 alienating behaviors that are used by alienators to impede relationships. On the left side of this sheet is a column that automatically tally's up the number in this column for how many times you put in that this has happened. In other words, if this red flag behavior happened 5 times, put a 5 in this column. The middle column lists the 167 Red Flag Behaviors used. On the right side of this sheet is a column for documenting dates, times, events and any other information pertaining to these transgressions. This helps to recall and prove that this is not just being made up but there are actually true times and places for these red flag behaviors. For a copy of the excel sheet go to www.KlothConsulting.com and click on the link for Divorce and Relationship Issues, then scroll down to find the link for 167 Red Flag Behaviors. Or go to www.PAS-Intervention.com and click the link at the top of the page or bottom for Charts, Tests & Tools. More will be discussed on this topic in the next chapter.

TAPE RECORDING:

Tape recording conversations is a great way to get evidence but it is NOT always accepted by the courts. That being said, it can be used to show a counselor, Guardian Ad Litem or other official what is really going on. The following information about proper ways to taper record comes from Diana Buffington of the Children's Rights Council of Texas.

Diana writes:
Most states allow tape recording without notification in family civil matters. With the CRCAK, now CRCTX procedure, courts have usually accepted taped

Where Did I Go Wrong? How Did I Miss The Signs?

recordings without notification because notification will make the custodial parent act and talk differently. (CRCTX's website is http://www.crckids.org/chapter-locations-texas.htm)

Notification is usually only required in criminal case recording, because the burden of proof is higher. Remember Monica Lewinsky that was a criminal case. If you want to be sure and comfortable, check your state's Rules of Civil Procedure of the Court at your local law library or ask an attorney.

You can also usually find Rules of Civil Procedure of the Court on your own state's website such as www.state.tx.us. However, persons outside of Texas should use their state's two initials CT, VA, NY, NM etc. Look for law or statutes. It may also be found under the judiciary, courts, legislature sections of the main website. (Also the author notes that www.DeltaBravo.net has a list of all states on their site.)

Once you find the statutes, then look for tape recordings under evidentiary rules. Moreover, I have actually had several courts rule the tape recordings admissible in states that prohibited recordings without notification in PAS/custodial interference cases, because the moms were so vicious and cruel on the tapes and in front of the children who overheard the conversation. Each mom's attorneys tried to file with the DAs in the counties, but the DAs refused to file due to hearing the tapes, and since the case was not a criminal case.

By the way Linda Tripp, was charged with illegal wiretapping but the charges were finally dropped because of the nature of the crime and tapes. The Trip defense was "I didn't know it was against the law to record without notification".

In the three cases, out-of-state moms lost custody to Texas dads. Each mom now has supervised visits at a local access sites chosen by the court, and their visits are video taped to assure the court no further PAS is continued. The videotapes have been used successfully to obtain sole custody to prevent one mom from *emotionally harming the children until the children are all 13. She has lost all appeals. As you can see, judges do give tape recordings done, the CRCTX way, a great deal of latitude.*

In another email, Diane goes into more detail as she writes:

Hi--I have been advised by three attorneys (not in Texas) that if a Targeted Parent (TP) plans to tape conversations over the phone or in person, where the state requires notification, here's is a way to get around the law and still pass evidentiary muster. Attorneys who have these state laws informed me to send a certified letter, with return receipt card, or deliver in person with a witness obtaining a signed receipt to the Alienating Parent (AP) who is interfering in custody or committing PAS.

In the letter the TP needs to make a list the times of specific dates, times and location of visit pick-up/drop-off, according to the TP's court order. Also do the same things with calls, whether specified by court order or not. The lists covering 6-12 months of visits and calls, and the TP should not be late and find no excuses for no shows. In the letter notify the AP that the TP may or may not be recording the visit pick-up/drop-off and telephone calls.

If the TP is under temporary orders and the AP has an attorney, send a certified letter to the AP attorney also. The TP should also include a copy of the access/visitation orders, and a copy of the state statute that covers interference of custodial periods by the AP or other parties, just in case the AP's attorney has stated that their attorney has advised them to interfere (this seems to become a trend in some areas of the country) in order to gain control by sole custody, supervised visits or incite inappropriate behavior on the TP's part (anger, threats, DV or kidnapping).

My information tells me that the AP and their attorney tend to forget that they might be recorded or really doubt that the TP really means to record

Where Did I Go Wrong? How Did I Miss The Signs?

conversations. With certified mail or in person delivery, the TP has given proper notification by due process for court to enter tapes into evidence at hearings, and the TP has shown the court that the TP implied, directly and indirectly, that the recording could take place and the TP probably intended to record <u>all</u> conversations.

At the hearings, the recordings are entered after proving that the AP received notification by certified mail or in person that their conversations may be recorded. A court has to presume that the TP's written notification was received and read; therefore, the AP either ignored or forgotten the notification, but recording notification had been served properly.

By sending the letter to the AP's attorney, by ethical standard he should have advised the AP to be careful in their interaction with the TP, since the calls or visits may be taped. Check it out with local attorneys in those states that require taping notification, to see if this is an acceptable alternative method. It has been used successfully in three states where recording notification is required. If your state requires that the notification must be done while on tape, these attorneys state the written notification can be done, with the verbal confirmation of the recording can be done at the end of the conversation by stating "AP, I just wanted to remind you of the written notification I sent you by certified mailed, with a return receipt concerning the possibility of my taping our conversation during visits and calls. I wanted to let you know this conversation has been recorded." Use this alternative as a last resort.

I think this may help those who need to get around the taping notification process. These three attorneys stated that most family courts waive verbal notification if written notification is delivered in a proper manner. However, check with you local courts or DA/state's attorney, or check the evidentiary Court Rules of Civil Procedure through your state's website at www.state.initials of state.us. [i.e. www.state.il.us]. One of these attorneys was from Illinois, who recommended

> CRCTX to a former client, whose ex is still in Illinois, where recording notification is required. Diana L. Buffington is the State Coordinator Children's Rights Council of Texas. Her site address is http://www.crckids.org/chapter-locations-texas.htm

> *The Author writes:*
> This is about as close to the truth re-tape recording telephone family issues, as one can get. The only thing I would add is that tape recording can be transcribed and this also will make them legally admissible in court.
> Family issues are a civil matter, not a criminal one. Just watch any TV civil court action (like Judge Judy). Tapes are used as evidence all the time.

> *N writes:*
> I did some research about tape recording and I believe it's a great idea to try so I want to pass along that Radio Shack carries a Telephone Cassette Recorder that will do what is intended. Another product is a Modular Telephone Jack that other stores should carry which is even better.

As far as Tape Recording goes, this is a state-by-state issue, but for the most part, so long as one person has knowledge they are being taped, it is okay. For example, CT is a 2 party state except where there is a 3rd party involved and then only one of the other parties needs to be notified. CT's state statute on tape recording reads like this:

> Conn. Gen. Stat. § 52-570d: It is an invasion of privacy to tape a telephone conversation in Connecticut without the consent of all parties. Consent should be in writing or should be given on the recording, or a verbal warning that the conversation is being taped should be included in the recording.
> Anyone who records a telephone conversation without the consent of all the parties is subject to liability for civil damages, as well as litigation costs and attorney fees. In

Where Did I Go Wrong? How Did I Miss The Signs?

addition, it is a felony punishable by imprisonment for one to five years for anyone who is not a party to a conversation to mechanically overhear or record that conversation, including telephonic and cellular or wireless communications and face-to-face discussions, without the consent of at least one party. Conn. Gen. Stat. § 53a-187, 189 (1999).

For states where tape recording requires both parties to be notified, you can either formally notify them with the note to follow that is also sent to the courts or if you feel that this will put them on their guard, a transcription of the tape (especially by a professional transcriptionist) is admissible as evidence. Again please check this with your attorney. To follow is an example of a notice that at any time communication could be tape recorded.

NOTICE

TO: _____   Date:

_____

_____

_____

      You are here by notified that _____ will be audio recording EVERY contact made through telephone and in person for the purposes of obtaining accurate documentation of conversations. This action will be taken regardless of whom the caller is. Also every visit with the children will be recorded as well.

      It is strongly urged that this notice be maintained in the front of my child's/ family's case file / record with your office/agency/school. There will be no additional notices given.

      Consider your office/agency notified that such recordings can and will be used in all judicial proceedings if necessary and are considered to be fully admissible as evidence in court.

      Copies can be obtained through trial discovery or upon request with reasonable notification of such request for copies and at a charge of $6.00 per tape.

      Transcripts can be obtained to accompany such recordings at the cost of $1.00 for the first page and $0.50 each additional page.

      Any such request must be submitted in writing at least 30 days in advance.

Signed: _____

Notary Seal:

Where Did I Go Wrong? How Did I Miss The Signs?

CHAPTER 22

RED FLAG BEHAVIORS AND CHILD BEHAVIOR INDICATOR

Behaviors Exhibited by Alienators
Red Flags Examples of Parental Alienation

Created by
Joan T. Kloth-Zanard, Life Coach/Counseling Consultant,
Penny Threlfall, Counselor, B.A., Grad. dip. Psychology,
Rebecca Gominger and the members of various support groups for Parental Alienation
December 31, 2003

The Alienating Parent will exhibit specific behaviors, signs and symptoms. These behaviors, signs and symptoms differ from those of the children and the Targeted Parent.. The following examples of alienating behaviors are called Red Flags. The more the Alienating Parent exhibits these behaviors, the higher the probability that PAS is occurring. To follow is a list of over 160 tactics used most often to alienate children from a parent. For a Microsoft Excel Automatic Calculating Sheet of this list, go to www.KlothConsulting.com and click on the Link for Divorce and Relationship Issues and then scroll down to the link to 167 Red Flag Behaviors or go to www.PAS-Intervention.com and click on the link at the top or bottom of the page for Charts, Tests & Tools. This excel sheet will automatically calculate the number of Red Flag Behaviors using the left hand column. For example, if the red flag behavior has occurred 5 times then put a 5 in this left column. A score of 10 or more is an indicator of PAS.

1. Impeding with visitation despite court orders
2. Denigrating the other parent in front of anyone who will listen, including the children. Calling the Target Parent or stepparent derogatory names in front of the children.
3. Filing allegations of abuse while constantly dragging the ex into court for child support or alimony. (Note: A truly abused individual wants to have nothing to do with the abuser. (Initiating face-to-face confrontations is out of the question.)
4. Stopping any contact between the children and the ex's extended family, friends or anybody who disagrees with them
5. Believing that they are above the law, and that all orders/laws were made for everyone else but them.
6. Impeding communication with the children, including blocking the Target Parent's access to school records, meetings and events.
7. Grilling the children about their visit and asking the children to spy or collect evidence.
8. Refusing visitation because the ex spouse has been unable to afford the child support or missed a payment.
9. Statements of constant hatred and vengeance about the ex-spouse.
10. Refusal to disclose their home address
11. Refusal to keep the other parent in the loop on medical issues, educational issues, and events pertaining to the children and so on.
12. Continually referring to the child as their own children and not the spouses.
13. Continually not enforcing the visitation with the other parent by claiming the children do not want to go (Barring no true abuse is truly going on) and using the excuse that they are not going to force the

Where Did I Go Wrong? How Did I Miss The Signs?

children to go see their other parent if they do not want to.
14. Impeding any court orders, including court orders for Counseling.
15. Moving the children away from a parent they once had a loving relationship with.(thus making visitation and a relationship next to impossible).
16. During visitation times, constantly calling the house, to speak with the children or leaving nasty disruptive messages.
17. On days that the Target Parent is in a public place the parent shows up to push, swear at or just intimidate the TP or the stepparent in front of the child.
18. Making the child feel emotionally responsible for the parent's happiness. (The child becomes the parent and the AP becomes the child.)
19. Lying or even involving the child in the divorce proceedings and custody or child support issues.
20. Making the child feel uneasy about talking to their therapist or another official person.
21. Having the child call his non-custodial parent by their first name; instead of Daddy or Mommy
22. Preventing the children from contacting their father by pulling the phone out of the wall, changing their phone number, refusing to allow them to accept calls, refusing to allow them to make phone calls or lying and claiming the children are not home or are asleep.
23. Discussing with and involving the children in court matters, child support and other legal matters, which they should not be involved in.
24. Insisting that the children call the new person in the AP's life "Mom" or Dad"
25. Escalating PASing behavior if the NCP commences a new relationship
26. Insisting that the children NEVER call a stepparent "Mom" or "Dad".

27. Hanging up the phone if discussions do not follow "their" agenda
28. When the child is allowed to speak to the Target Parent on the telephone the PASing parent will oversee the call, instructing the child on what to say and how to respond to the TP and force the end of the call if either the child or TP fails to conduct the call in a manner the PASing parent deems appropriate.
29. Deliberately pulling the children away if they meet the Target Parent when they are "out and about" or shopping.
30. Avoiding children's activities or school activities because the Target Parent may be there.
31. Previous evidence of anger management issues
32. Poor family support network or a family network that supports the PASing behavior
33. Refusing to communicate via fax, email or letter because to do so will provide evidence of their activities in the form of a paper trail.
- 34. Waiting until the last minute to inform the Target Parent of changes to visitation.
- 35. Feel it is their right to be late when the children are supposed to visit with the TP at a certain time or on a certain day but insist the children MUST be returned to them at the exact time the visitation is supposed to end.
- 36. Will not provide any information to the Target Parent about the children's day-to-day activities but will insist on a specific and exact schedule of activities when the TP has the children.
- 37. Will choose to pay others to provide childcare and not utilize the Target Parent even if it would be more suitable for all parties.
38. Will claim the child is too sick to visit the Target Parent.
- 39. Will claim the Target Parent is not capable of parenting the child "properly"

Where Did I Go Wrong? How Did I Miss The Signs?

- 40. Will make the child feel guilty if they want to see the other parent.
- 41. Will avoid, at all costs, a neutral drop off / pick up location
- 42. Will not permit the Target Parent to communicate with "professionals" who support the AP.
- 43. Will not allow the children to participate in activities where they might have contact with children who are associated with the TP.
- 44. Will instruct the school that the Target Parent is not to be trusted, inferring or clearly stating that the TP has lied to others about the PASing parent and children. This includes the insertion of notes in school files that prohibit contact or pick up by the Targeted Parent.
- 45. If cornered by Protective Services or any other official about providing the Target Parent's information for school records, the PASing parent will give false or misleading information.
- 46. PASing parent has removed pages from a child's classroom journal that fails to support the PASing parent's ideology or conversely, the child's support of the TP.
- 47. Totally controlling the children's social life
- 48. Becoming overly involved with the children's activities i.e. cub leader or parent support worker in order to be with the children constantly and discourage the other parent from attending these activities.
- 49. Lying to the children about the separation/divorce by giving details that are 'obviously' untrue which deliberately impede the child's ability to love the other parent (i.e. "Dad spends all his money on his girlfriends so I can't afford to send you to camp.")
- 50. Involving the children in all the aspects of the separation/divorce and legalities while claiming the child has the 'right' to know what is happening
- 51. Claiming the Target Parent is victimizing, stalking, abusing or harassing them. Repeatedly, filing false

allegations of abuse with the police and child protective agencies in order to constantly torment the Targeted Parent with investigations.
52. Encouraging the child to support the PASing parent and make false allegations against the Targeted Parent. This includes allegations of poor treatment during visitation even though there is no evidence of poor treatment and the reverse is actually true.
53. Encouraging the child to be defiant, "go on strike", or not comply with reasonable rules requested by the Target Parent during visitations.
54. The PASing parent deliberately organizes 'activities' for the children on the Target Parent's visitation days (i.e. parties, outings and social gatherings).
55. The PASing parent will use bribery and enticements to prevent a child from visiting with the Target Parent. The PASing parent may also plan an event at the same time that the child has visitation with the TP and make the child feel guilty if they go with the TP.
56. Not allowing the children to have photos of or objects provided by the Target Parent in the house. The PASing parent will destroy any gifts, photo's etc. if the child brings them home.
57. When the child receives gifts from the Target Parent and takes them home to show the PASing parent, the PASing parent refuses to allow the child to keep them or take them back to the TP's house.
58. PASing parent refuses gifts from the Target Parent and his family, actually making the children return them saying they are "no good", cheap or useless etc.
59. PASing parent will deliberately condemn the Target Parent's gifts or deliberately purchase them ahead of the TP in order to make the TP'S gift meaningless.
60. The PASing parent changes the child's surname to the 'new Dads' name without asking or notifying the birth father.

Where Did I Go Wrong? How Did I Miss The Signs?

61. PASing parent will attend the Target Parent's family functions without a prior invite despite 'knowing' that their behavior will be viewed negatively. The PASing parent will use this negativity to tell the children that the TP's family hates the PASing parent.
62. Refuses to pick up the telephone when the child is calling from the Target Parent's residence.
63. Insist that when the child is with the Target Parent they have the 'right' to excessive telephone contact with the child. However, when the child is with the PASing parent, the TP is not allowed to have telephone contact with the child.
64. Deliberately changes the telephone number and maintains a 'silent' number without notifying the Target Parent or providing the TP with the new number.
65. The PASing parent tells the child that "they hope they will be okay" when they visit the Target Parent and they "hope they don't end up in the hospital" during the visit. .
66. Telling the child that "something" may happen" to the PASing parent while the child is with the Target Parent.
67. Demanding the Target Parent pay for extra costs associated with child rearing, i.e. orthodontic work etc.
68. Informing the child that they cannot have braces or other essentials because the Target Parent won't pay for them.
69. Refusing a child's request to spend extra time with the Target Parent, even when this time is for a special occasion.
70. Refusing to send the child to school for events when the PASing parent becomes aware that the Target Parent will be attending.
71. Removing money placed in the child's bank account by the Target Parent and not allowing the child to spend it and/or not spending it on the child.

72. Telling the child in a deliberately malicious and vindictive manner that a certain behavior of the child's is similar to the Target Parent.
73. PASing parent will excessively emphasize the child's physical and facial features, which are similar to the PASing parent and associated family members but ignore or deny any physical/facial features associated with the Target Parent.
74. PASing parent refuses to allow the child to take a pet on visitation with the Target Parent even though the TP is happy and willing to accommodate the pet.
75. PASing parent has deliberately moved without providing the Target parent with details prior to the move.
76. PASing parent has deliberately moved and refuses to provide the Target Parent with appropriate details.
77. PASing parent allows the child to have contact with someone the Target Parent disapproves of, despite the fact that the TP has reasonable grounds for concern. (i.e. domestic violence and previously proven abuse, etc.)
78. The child undergoes or has undergone unnecessary surgical procedures without the prior knowledge or consent of the Target Parent. The PASing parent approves of the surgery even when there's evidence supporting the TP's objections.
79. The PASing parent attempts to bribe, extort or threaten the Target Parent into signing court documents that will exclude the TP from the child's life or enhance the PASing parent's position.
80. The PASing parent has expressed a desire for the Target Parent to be dead, die, killed, or severely injured.
81. The PASing parent has expressed a desire for the Target Parent and other family members / friends associated with the TP to suffer some major mishap or injury.
82. The PASing parent attempts or succeeds in changing the child's religion.

83. Told the child they can't see the other parent because they are behind in their child support payments.
84. Is unjustly rude and refuses to work cooperatively with the new partner of the other parent for the benefit of the child.
85. Has refused of failed to provide mental health support for the child when there is reasonable evidence to support that the child needs mental health intervention and would benefit from it.
86. Refusing to allow the child to participate in weekend sporting/developmental classes because the Target Parent would be present for some of the lessons.
87. Parent has attempted to bribe officials, specialists and professionals to carry on in favor of that parent even when there is evidence to the contrary.
88. Parent has deliberately mislead, lied or concealed information or evidence in order to advance his own case.
89. Parent has physically assaulted the Target Parent in the presence of the child.
90. Parent has forged, altered or tampered with official documentation to advance his own case.
91. The parent has submitted false, and misleading statements to the police about the Target Parent and his family. The false and misleading statements were premeditated.
92. Has displayed anger/verbal abuse concerning the Target Parent in front of the child or a third party.
93. Has attempted to or actually assisted the child to write letters /notes or to deliver same to the Target Parent
94. Encouraged the child to support them in their allegations against the Target Parent despite evidence to the contrary and despite past statements and actions by the custodial parent and child.
95. Coaching, threatening or intimidating the child to remain silent about incidents the child has witnessed that do not support the custodial parent.

96. Threatening or punishing the child for saying positive things about the Target Parent.
97. Refused to provide the child for DNA testing when requested to do so.
98. Deliberately causing alienation between siblings when one supports the Custodial Parent and the other the Target Parent.
99. Told the child that the other parent does not love him or her and that the other parent never wanted the child to be born.
100. Told the child about intimate details pertaining to the marriage, which are inappropriate, and done in a way to deliberately cause distress to the child.
101. Has refused to share prescribed medication with the other parent during access.
- 102. Alienator insists that the Target Parent's extended family is not the children's "real family" or that they are "no good".
- 103. Alienator tells the child(ren) that the Target Parent's new partner has replaced them.
104. Alienator tells the child(ren) that they have been replaced by children born to the Target Parent and any new partner – whether or not children have been born.
- 105. Alienator tells the child(ren) that they have been replaced by the Target Parent's new partner's child(ren) and that they are therefore not wanted or loved by the TP
106. Alienator denigrates all statements, answers, discipline and activities of the Target Parent when those statements, etc. are in regard to the child(ren)..
107. Alienator frequently suggests to the child(ren) that the Target Parent and/or new partner will do harm to the child(ren).
108. Alienator demands that the TP be subjected to and accept blame for any injury incurred by the child however minor and natural in the course of life.
109. Alienator forces the child to report minor injuries, bumps and bruises to a professional person and

Where Did I Go Wrong? How Did I Miss The Signs?

infers they were caused by the action or inaction of the Target Parent or their new partner.
110. Alienator shaves the child's hair off when the haircut has been provided by the Target Parent and claims that the haircut was bad and the child's hair was ruined.
111. Alienator will not allow the Target Parent to comfort the child when the child has been injured at play.
112. Alienator demands medical intervention for minor illnesses (i.e. demanding antibiotics for colds) and play injuries.
113. Alienator undertakes "doctor shopping" until a practitioner sympathetic to their cause is found.
114. Alienator does not comply with appropriate medical advice from practitioners who are not sympathetic to their cause.
115. Alienator actively damages (cutting, tearing or staining) clothing provided for the child by the Target Parent.
116. Alienator refuses reasonably required medical treatment when the Target Parent has sought review for a serious medical condition, which impairs the child or causes them to suffer.
117. Alienator allows the child to undertake activities after separation from the Target Parent, which were previously refused and blames the TP for denying the child such activities in the past.
118. Alienator refuses to allow the child(ren) time alone with other adults or children.
119. Alienator refuses to allow children to attend sleepovers with friends accusing friend's parents of abusive behavior
120. Alienator refuses to allow sleepovers stating that they 'do not want the children to see how others live."
121. Alienator frequently tells the child(ren) that the Target Parent will harm them or has mental health problems etc. that creates a fear of the TP.

122. Alienator informs the child(ren) that the Target Parent has a criminal record for harming children.
123. Alienator will not allow the child(ren) to undergo any medical or psychological assessment without being present.
124. Alienator informs the child(ren) that they were unwanted by the Target Parent and that the TP insisted that the pregnancy be terminated.
125. Alienator insists that Target Parent's family never accepted her or the children and insisted that the pregnancy(ies) be terminated.
126. Alienator blames Target Parent for poor food quality, housing quality and/or availability of funds where child support is paid and/or alienator contact is minimal.
127. Alienator blames Target Parent and new partner for stealing home, food and resources from the Alienator and child(ren).
128. Alienator ignores the child(ren) when they discuss activities with the Target Parent.
129. Alienator becomes angered when the child(ren) discusses activities with the Target Parent.
130. Alienator becomes angered when the child(ren) expresses a desire to see/phone the Target Parent.
131. Alienator becomes angered when child(ren) engage in mother's/father's day activities at school which are focused on the Target Parent.
132. Alienator becomes angered when child expresses desire for contact with the Target Parent to school teachers/mates/colleagues.
133. Alienator removes child from school and relocates child without cause if the child expressed a desire for contact with the Target Parent.
- 134. Alienator informs child(ren) that Target Parent is happier without them.
135. Alienator informs child(ren) that the Target Parent does not love them anymore, is never going to see them again and does not want them anymore.

136. Alienator accuses the child(ren) of causing rifts/separation in the marriage.
137. Alienator informs child(ren) that Target Parent is leaving THE CHILD(REN) rather than the marriage or the Alienator.
138. Alienator accuses the Target Parent of infidelity in earshot of the child(ren).
139. Alienator writes letters 'on behalf' of the child(ren) claiming that the child(ren) have had input into the content of the letters.
140. Alienator actively seeks to ensure that children believe that the Target Parent doesn't send letters, gifts or monies.
141. Alienator removes and destroys any items sent to the children through an outside facility (i.e. School, Grandparent.) This usually occurs after leaving the facility and after the AP appeared publicly to accept the items for the child.
142. Alienator actively destroys and discards any gifts or letters that the child(ren) was able to see.
143. Alienator insists that the child(ren) only refer to the Target Parent in derogatory terms (i.e. "The Bastard")
144. Alienator presents school teachers/principals with falsified documents/letters from practitioners of the AP.
145. Alienator pawns the Target Parent's personal and private belongings citing financial hardship to the child(ren).
146. Alienator pawns or returns to the retailer, gifts from the Target Parent citing financial hardship to the children.
147. Alienator takes every opportunity to belittle the Target Parent in the presence of the child(ren), when seeking assistance from welfare agencies and providers.
148. Refuses to provide the Target Parent with vital medical information thereby impeding the child(ren)s medical wellbeing.

149. Refusing to notify the Target Parent of identified allergies.
150. Refusing to notify the Target Parent of medical concerns or treatments for child(ren)
151. Accuses the Target Parent of stealing items the child has lost.
152. Attributing failure in school activities/studies to the Target Parent.
153. Accusing the Target Parent of neglecting the child(ren).
154. Denies essential medical care or treatment on the basis of financial hardship caused by the Target Parent.
155. Consumes drugs, cigarettes, or alcohol and blames the Target Parent for the addictions.
156. Purchases personal luxuries but won't buy essential items for the children and blames the Target Parent for their financial hardship.
157. Refuses to allow the child to show any affection toward the Target Parent, in front of the Alienator, when the child is saying goodbye to the TP after a visitation.
158. Makes derogatory noises/comments when the child or the Target Parent exhibits affection in the presence of the Alienator.
159. Accuses the Target Parent of displaying affection to child(ren) for an ulterior motive.
- 160. Accuses Target Parent of PAS behaviors.
161. Denigrates new partner or partner's children to PAS children.
162. Makes accusations of abuse against the Target Parent's new partner.
- 163. Makes accusations of abuse against the Target Parent's extended family.
164. Makes accusations of abuse against the Target Parent's consequent children or children of the new partner.

Where Did I Go Wrong? How Did I Miss The Signs?

165. Contacts Target Parent's extended family in presence of child(ren) to make false allegations of abuse/neglect/PAS.
166. Refuses to allow the child to give gifts, notes, paintings or letters to the Target Parent, new partner, children or extended family.
167. Alienating Parent is constantly rude, nasty, controlling and dictates when, where and what the Target Parent can do with the kids during their time together. This attitude is also permeated to the children who are rude, nasty, controlling and dictate when, where and how they will spend their time with the TP.

In addition to this list, the following chart was developed for use in determining the level of alienation that your child(ren) is exhibiting. Again, this is available in an excel format at www.KlothConsulting.com, click the hyperlink for Charts, Tests & Tools or go to www.PAS-Intervention.com, click on the link at the top of the page for Charts, Tests & Tools.

ALIENATOR INDICATOR FOR CHILDREN'S BEHAVIOR

If your child does or says any of the following, you might be experiencing Parental Alienation and Hostile Aggressive Parenting. Mark the empty box if it pertains to your situation.

1		Your child rejects anyone or anything having to do with you, but unconditionally accepts everything and anyone associated with the other parent.
2		Your child says explicitly or implicitly that you or anyone related to you is not part of their family; only members of the other parent's family is considered part of their family.
3		Your child refuses to visit with you claiming various excuses that are not true.
4		Your child claims that you do not love them, even after you have repeatedly told them how much you do.

215

5		Your child demands that you give them things to "prove" your love for them, or lists various things you have not given them or paid for them as proof that you do not love them.
6		Your child is violent and destructive when they come to your home.
7		Your child is violent and destructive when you take them places.
8		Your child displays latent hostility towards you, your family and/or your new spouse/partner when they do visit with you.
9		Your child refuses to bring their belongings from one home to the other claiming you will steal them.
10		Your child falsely claims you abused them, their siblings or the other parent, in any way, but yet has no concrete examples.
11		Your child claims to be afraid of you without any reason.
12		Your child claims to be afraid of you but yet still comes for visits.
13		Your child adamantly refuses to meet your new partner or spouse even though they willingly accept the other parent's new spouse.
14		Kids repeatedly say that they don't want to spend time with you or anyone in your family.
15		Child/ren use monetary threats such as if you really love them, you will buy or pay for various things for them.
16		Your child bursts out crying or becomes sullen/depressed all of a sudden, saying they miss the other parent, or other similar statements about the other parent.
17		Child/ren refuse Christmas presents from you or your family.
18		In public, the child/ren refuse to look at or acknowledge you or your family while in the company of the other parent or their family.
19		Are your phone conversations unusually short?
20		When you are on the phone with your child, do they all of a sudden shut down when the other parent comes into hearing range/ear shot?

Where Did I Go Wrong? How Did I Miss The Signs?

21		When you are on the phone with your child, do they become verbally abusive when the other parent is comes into hearing range/ear shot?
22		Does your child/ren only call to ask you for money or to buy them things and will not discuss or talk about anything else?
23		Do you leave messages for your children and they never return the calls?
24		Does your child no longer call you Mom/Dad, and only refer to you by your first name?
25		Does your child refer to the stepparent as their Mother/Father, while calling you by your first name only?
26		Your child tries to discuss the legal aspects of the divorce or custody with you, demonstrating that they have been shown documents or told about the case.
27		A child writes you mean-spirited letters designed to tell you why that child doesn't want to visit with you.
28		A child acts increasingly anxious when the time approaches to return to the other parent.
29		A child becomes reserved and quiet when the other parent is around, but is jovial when he's with you only.
30		Add your own behavior that concerns you.
		Total Score

Scoring:
1-3 = Could be the beginnings of PAS
4-6 = Mild PAS
7-9 = Moderate PAS
10 or more = Severe PAS

All of these worksheets are meant to be used as tools to help prove that Parental Alienation is being enacted upon your children and yourself. They help to establish a pattern of behavior, which gives the judge, the counselor and the agencies a visual picture of what is really going on. And in some cases, it will help to establish the level of support and intervention that will be needed.

Interviewing a Child to Determine if PAS Exists

As usually, I am driving and get one of those brain storms. Well, at any rate, the topic of therapists came up and it dawned on me that the first most important question that any therapist can ask a child of high conflict divorce is the following:

What would your mom/dad say if you asked to live with your other (targeted) parent? Yes, I know the child is going to say, but I hate them. And the therapist would say, what if you did not hate them. What if things were different and you wanted to try it out. Then what. I think the child's response as to what the other parent would say would be extremely telling of what is really going on. In other words, it has to start with the Counselor asking the right questions and then understanding the actual dynamics of PAS.

> *LIN NICHOLSON writes:*
> *Kids are usually coached by the parent that they are living with, as to what to say. Art work doesn't lie. Drawing pictures gets at the truth. Ask a child to draw a picture of each parent in their house --- then draw their picture in each house. Then ask the child to talk about the pictures.*
> *Peace,*
> *LIN NICHOLSON*

> *Author writes:*
> *Actually that does not work either all the time. Yes, under a situation where one parent is NOT coaching the children what to do and say, picture drawing can be very helpful. But I can also see your point that a child could be coached as to what to say. Though, typically, a parent does not coach a kid to say, I want you to go visit your other parent. They coach them to say that they hate the other parent. So in actuality, what a parent would say to that child if they wanted to go live at the other parents house would be more accurate a description. For example, I think a child would end up saying something like this: "If I wanted to go there, my*

Where Did I Go Wrong? How Did I Miss The Signs?

parent would say that I was stupid because you know that your father is no good and hurts people. That if I go there she will not love me because I am just like my...." In other words, the kid is not going to say, that my mother would say it is okay, because that is absolutely NOT what the other parent has coached them to say.

As for the picture drawing, unfortunately, I am a prime example of the drawing process not working. When I was about 8 or 9 years old, I had learned to draw the picture of Frankenstein's head really well. I was drawing it over and over so I could get really good at it. At about his point, one of my stupid ass teachers told my parents that they needed to send me to a therapist as they swore that I had mental problems because I could not read fast enough or something. (Do not even go there about how stupid this was and that this teacher ultimately destroyed many a child's life). At any rate, the therapist asked me to draw a picture of my sister. Well, being that the only thing I had been drawing for the past few days was that Frankenstein head, well, that is what I drew. So the therapist concluded that I hated my sister. In fact, it was probably the opposite. As her older sister, I was protective of her. I would loan her anything I had. I would even help to do things, such as schoolwork. I went as far as to even draw pictures for her for her to help explain how to do things. So the picture thing does not necessarily work. And probably could also be easily coached by a parent as that is a typical child psychology test.

The other picture test that I think is absurd is the Rorschach Test. That is the test with the ink blots and you supposed to say what they look like. I come from a medical background family along with the Lung Cancer van had just come to my school showing us pictures of diseased black lungs, hearts and things. So when they showed me these inkblots, and asked me what I thought they looked like, I did not say butterflies or whatever else you are supposed to say. I said they looked like black lungs and so on. Again, it was deemed that I had a mental problem by these counselors. I had to sit my parents down and the other extenuating circumstances related to this test that the counselors did NOT take into consideration. So my point, drawings can actually be a false reading if they have been influenced by an outside source or they can be very telltale if the circumstances have NOT been tampered with.

AN writes:

High conflict divorce does not automatically equate to PA. LIN NICHOLSON beat me to the basic punch as to the kids being programmed. When mine were young, and attended "art therapy," she "knew" to create volcanoes, dark clouds, generally disconcerting objects. (The therapist was onto the issues and realized the programming. So what, that was ten years ago. When he was called on it, he escalated the abuse and alienation.) As a teen, my kid regurgitated everything programmed into her for "therapy sessions" and was especially vile if I was present. Just to make sure any therapist didn't miss her points, my ex would call the therapist to make sure she understood precisely what the child meant!

Unless the child is allowed to feel safe with the therapist, they KNOW what the responses are that ought to be given. These kids don't consider their feelings as "hate," they are too ambivalent to hate (just saying "I hate him" doesn't SOUND like hate) -or, sadly, truly allow themselves to love.

I believe the therapist needs to build a relationship w/ the child and then find ways to elicit info that is truly his or hers. However, with the child "owning" so much, I found that when my daughter had break-through moments in counseling, she became angry shortly after the session. Guess who the safe target was for the anger?

Where Did I Go Wrong? How Did I Miss The Signs?

> *In some cases, the kids apparently keep the darkness and it becomes a key characteristic of their personalities. In my child's case, by middle school she was choosing dark subjects, writing and drawing in ways that any normal parent would at least question. I glimpsed her facebook page today......as a soph in college, apparently in response to something at a meeting, she wrote a lengthy "metaphorical" article that was deeply dark and bloody, very bloody. It is clear that this is a creative use of the darkness and a mechanism to get newer friends' attention. But, it is dark.*
>
> *I'd guess my daughter chose the wrong house. However, the next question becomes what do therapists do w/ the answers to the question you posed? Brave question! [?]*

Author writes:

> AN, all very good points. And yes, high conflict divorce does not automatically equate to PA, especially if there are no children involved. But the reality is that High Conflict Divorce is used to define a divorce that drags out everything into a conflict. And sadly, 99% of the time that includes the children and even can include pets. Your divorce was absolutely high conflict, when it came to the kids. He just beat you to the punch on it but you still fought back with court.
>
> As for the therapist question, actually, I kind of answered this in an earlier email because the reality is that the other parent will tell them to say they hate the targeted parent. So when asked what the other parent would say if they wanted to go live with the Targeted parent, the child is programmed to say, exactly what the Alienator wants them to say about change of custody. i.e. the child would say, "My ... would be very upset and tell me that I was in danger and ....." In other words, you will be getting exactly what they are programmed to say but from the Alienators perspective. Does this make sense?

I am not saying this is fool proof. In fact, I think there is no one-way to investigate PAS. It is a pattern of behaviors and statements that determine if PAS is going on.

Anonymous:
Maybe I'm missing the point on this. However, it would seem to me that a therapist/clinician could, with relative ease determine whether or not a child is being programmed. I was completely baffled and confused when my kids first started and continued to display such behavior. At the time I had never heard of PAS and had no idea it even existed. So, naturally I thought I actually was a horrible father and deserved what I got. But it never really made sense. The evidence of such a degree of abhorrent fathering just wasn't there. Then I happened upon Gardner's book and sure enough, every symptom of PAS was right there in black & white. And, in many instances the examples cited used almost the same exact language I had heard from ex and my kids over and over again. The point I'm making is that as a layperson I was actually able to make the diagnosis by reading a couple of books. Today there is a wealth of accumulated knowledgeon the topic so it should not be very difficult to spot PAS – assuming that is the clinician first has a fundamental belief in its existence as an identifiable pattern of behaviors and reactions. That said, once the existence of PAS is identified and confirmed, of course the therapist must work with the child to ameliorate the effects of the offending alienating parent. But, more importantly, intervention somehow has to be primarily geared toward stopping the alienator and working toward

cooperative co-parenting. I know it's much easier said than done but without that level of intervention, to stop the alienation, (and if I'm accurately interpreting AN's note), the child just becomes more of a pawn because he or she is now being played against the therapist as well, thus creating a triangulated rather than dual cycle of conflict. Not sure that I'm making any sense but seems that therapy accomplishes little as long as the alienator is allowed to continue to pull the marionette's strings.

Author writes:
  Yes, I agree that the situation is not going to get better if the alienator is allowed to continue behaving the way they do and if the child is not helped. The purpose of my question was because I wanted to know if anyone thought that asking this type question, might be another tool for a therapist to use to find out from the child's own mouth what they thought the alienator would say or what the alienator was actually saying to them if they decided to live with the other parent. In fact, I am not sure I have ever heard of a child telling a therapist that the alienator ever told them they could not live with the other parent directly. I think alienators suggest this by using other means. And so instead, it is how it is interpreted, by the child that they cannot go to live with the other parent. So what I am actually wondering, I guess, is if this question would illicit more of an interpretation of the child's understanding of what the alienator is truly saying to them about living with the other parent.

MH writes:
  Hmmm..... very interesting question. Thinking of N, he would say nothing. As usual, just flat out shut down. But, just for argument's sake, if he were to actually answer the question; some possibilities, "My Mom won't let me", "My Mom would take my Dad to court and make sure that never happens","I couldn't do that to my Mom",

Mom, mom, mom, mom, mom...... My guess is the first response- something along those lines. But, I would be really curious to hear what he would actually say to that question.

Author writes:
Exactly, this is what I was looking at myself. The child's initial answer would be another indicator of what is going on, because he is interpreting what he has learned from being alienated from the other parent as to what is expected of them or what the other parent would do or say.

BC writes:
What you should do is go in there and stand your ground. I think your mission should be telling and receiving the truth, i.e. "I want to know what I've done to you to warrant the hatred you have for me. In my life all I've done is love you. I've never -fill in the blank- to you so let's have it." And go from there. I think it would be a good idea to leave something for the therapist to educate her in PA. And then if things don't go well, suggest your own therapist.

Author writes:
Sadly, by this point, the damage is done. I have seen far too many cases where a parent has gone in and done this and in return, the uneducated therapist says that the Targeted parent is the problem. They look at you like you cannot even admit to what the child is saying or even just accept it and move on. They do not get that the child is so brainwashed that unless the programming is broken down, the therapists justifying of the child's reasoning and actions, versus the Targeted parents defending of them self, just increases the alienation. In fact, I think Dr. Gardner clearly warns parents to never go to counseling with a counselor who does NOT get PAS as it will destroy things even more.

Where Did I Go Wrong? How Did I Miss The Signs?

KG writes:

When my oldest children began accepting PAS, they were being subjected to my Ex and his soon to be wife degrading me in every facet of my life. They degraded my family, friends, integrity, decision making and falsely painted a picture of me as being an abuser and neglectful. Basically painting a picture of "Why in the world would you ever want to have that" in the minds of our children. From day to day they were told how wonderful and nurturing this soon to be step-mother was. Of course this is what they would want. It took only a few months for the bonds that my boys had with me to be broken. While all of this was transpiring, my phone calls would be left largely unanswered. If there was an answer, it was sometimes an immediate hang up or the boys would not be available. During one of our last conversations with my oldest, I could hear the resentment and lack of respect in his voice. He told me that his brother did not want to talk to me. I could hear the adults in the background, obviously within ear reach... they did nothing to intervene to try to foster my oldest sons relationship with me. While I do not think my ex ever said, no you can not go and live with your mother. I think my ex instilled a level of vile disgust, betrayal and resentment towards me to create his own sense and world of security.

Author writes:

Which is exactly my point in phrasing the question the way I did. I am not asking what the child thinks, but what his parent thinks. Thus, we are getting at what has been actually said to them.

SP writes:

M actually told her mom during an argument that she wanted live with us. She said her mom responded with: that will never happen.

Author writes:

> *So that kind of also proves my theory that this question could be used in an evaluation to determine if PAS exists. M actually told you what her mother had said, which is the same as what she knows to be what her mother would say, as in the question. This is just one key tool or question that could be used to evaluate for PAS in my opinion.*

CHAPTER 23

THE IMPORTANCE OF COUNSELING, DEPROGRAMMING CENTERS AND ALTERNATIVE PAS THERAPIES

Counseling is the key to success with any PAS case. Without specialized counseling with a therapist who understands PA as well as grief therapy, anger management and impulse control, no progress will ever be made and actually can go in the reverse. An improperly trained therapist or one who does not understand he dynamics of PAS will do more harm than good because they wrongly direct and allow the alienator to control the therapy. Below is a reprint from Dr. Lowenstein of a case study that clearly proves this point about how proper counseling can make all the difference in the world.

HOW CAN ONE OVERTURN THE PROGRAMMING OF A CHILD AGAINST A PARENT?

Ludwig.F. Lowenstein Ph.D
Southern England Psychological Services,
2005

Abstract

What will follow will in some cases make a considerable amount of sense. It will consist of viewing the specific approach to dealing with the problem with some concern since emotional factors come into play, which are not typically used in any therapeutic approaches otherwise. There are several ingredients necessary in order to reverse parental alienation, or what is often called Parental Alienation Syndrome (PAS). We will use one or the other of these terms interchangeably as there is still some uncertainty as to whether the syndrome, which has not yet been accepted by the American Psychological Association, is relevant. Certainly, parental alienation does occur and has been accepted.

How Can One Overturn the Programming of a Child Against the Parent?

The ingredients necessary for the therapist to have are: determination, resilience, frustration, resourcefulness and single mindedness. This is the only way that parental alienation can be reversed.

Few expert witnesses, be they psychiatrists or psychologists, take on cases such as parental alienation. This is because the methods which often need to be employed for overturning a child's animosity towards an alienated parent are strewn with dangers! It provides a minefield of visible and hidden dangers to the therapist to deal with such problems.

The chief dangers are the child and the alienator, who are opposed to the efforts of the therapist and will do almost anything and everything to sabotage the efforts of the therapist. They attend mediation sessions and assessment sessions merely because it has been ordered by the Court. They will go so far as to discredit the Expert and the manner in which he works in order to seek to change the thinking and behavior of the alienated child. Whatever happens, one side or the other will be critical of the therapist. Behind the main antagonists, and opposed to the efforts of the parental alienation therapist, are legions of family members on the alienators side, Solicitors, even Guardians ad Litem who are frequently very child-centered. The Court itself may also believe totally what the child has to say about the alienated parent.

The Court and the thinking of others are likely to be as follows: "Why would a child say such things about her father or mother if it were not true?" In this of course they are totally wrong in their thinking, unless such views can be confirmed by other, truly independent sources. The therapist is in the middle, attempting to discover three important aspects:

1. Are the allegations of abuse about a parent true, false or

Where Did I Go Wrong? How Did I Miss The Signs?

   exaggerated?
2. If untrue, and only if untrue, can the thinking and behavior of the alienated child be reversed? The alienator is unlikely to change in their views towards the programmed parent. Hence work with the alienator is not likely to bear much success as many have found.
3. If the allegations against the alienated parent are true such as when true sexual, emotional or physical abuse has occurred then the Expert witness therapist should not be involved further, except under very specific circumstances.

   Before commencing on how the present psychologist works and seeks to overturn the true effect of parental alienation we must consider the following:
   - Why does the 'programmer' carry out the process of alienation?
   - What are the psychological aspects involved in knowing that parental alienation has been carried out by the 'programmer' and what are its effects on the child?
   - What therapy can be used to overcome the effects of parental alienation?
   - To follow an illustration of rational emotive therapeutic approaches via a clinical case.

1. Why does the alienator program a child against the other parent?

   A parent who instigates accusations against another parent, for example, accusing the alienated parent as having abused a child sexually, physically or emotionally, are sometimes correct in this declaration. More often than not such accusations or allegations are wrong. Their allegations are frequently based on hostility towards a former partner. This can lead to one of two pathological reactions:
   - The accuser believes what he/she is assuming to be correct. That is he/she are deluded in their thinking or dangerously paranoid.
   - The accuser does not believe in the accusations

that he/she are making but makes them nevertheless out of conscious hostility and the seeking for vengeance against a former partner.

In both cases, acrimony and hostility are the basis for such false accusations. There is even a middle position between these two extremes. Let me illustrate this by an actual conversation I have had with an alienating mother who could be said to be 'stretching the truth' of 'insinuating the worst scenario':

Dr. L: "So you think your daughter does not want to be with her father because he once made her go to bed with him?"

Mother: "Yes, I don't think a father should ask a daughter to come into bed with him not at the age of 10."

Dr. L: "What do you think happened when the daughter got into bed with her father?"

Mother: "I really don't know, but I don't think….Do you think it is appropriate?"

Dr. L: "I'm asking you what you think about it. Never mind what I think about it. If you really do want to know, I don't think or see anything personally wrong with a child getting into bed with her father as indeed with her mother, providing they are having a cuddle and nothing more."

Mother: "Well I think it is totally wrong especially if the child does not want this."

Dr. L: "I do agree that if the child does not want to be in bed with her father he should not insist on it. You obviously believe the child did not want this and father did want her to get into bed with him."

Mother: "Yes, and I don't think it's right, and goodness knows what could have happened or perhaps did happen."

Dr. L: "You think perhaps she was sexually abused in some way by being touched?"

Mother: "I don't know but I wouldn't put it past him. Even if it didn't happen it could have happened."

Dr. L: "So you think your former partner might be a sexual abuser of his daughter?"

Mother: "I wouldn't go so far as that. I don't really think he would do that, but you never can tell."

As one may note no precise accusations have been made

Where Did I Go Wrong? How Did I Miss The Signs?

but "insinuations" are often sufficient for a claim of this kind to stick and the need for further investigations to be carried out in relation to it. It is often the accused who will need to prove innocence, instead of one needing to prove his guilt.

Paranoid ideations are infections. A deluded parent, or one filled consciously with hate for the former partner, can lead to an effort by that parent (the alienator) to control a child totally and to inculcate certain ideas that the former partner and parent is somehow dangerous to the child. This could lead to the next development which is that the alienated parent may eventually be considered repulsive and worthy of denigration and rejection. Children will often act this hatred out for a parent, especially when the 'programmer' (the alienator) is present. The child will seek to please that parent by taking on, or accepting the views of the alienating parent.

Paranoid ideation is illustrated when the child states that the father or mother have somehow, in general terms, done the wrong things, or been evil or lied etc. Here the child is "parroting" what the mother or father has said about the alienated parent. This is because the child has identified with the alienator and custodial parent, and the alienated parent eventually becomes the 'scapegoat' for all and any wrongs ever perpetrated against the alienator and 'ipso facto' those wrongs which the child has felt done to him/her. This is in contrast with the programming parent who is idealized by the child as being both 'all good' as well as 'all powerful'.

This occurs because a child feels, having lost one parent due to the acrimony of separation and brain-washing, there is a danger of losing the other parent as well. This fear is of a traumatic nature, leading to deep insecurity. The alienator senses this insecurity and works on the child making it clear that "I am all you have now.......Forget about your father/mother. They are no longer to be relied on."

2. How does the 'programmer' work and what effect does this have on the child?

There are a number of ways in which psychological aspects come into play in the alienation process. Among the methods which will be discussed are: reaction formation, identifying with the aggressor and the strong person i.e. the custodial parent, identifying with an assumed ideal or perfect parent, a way of releasing hostility, and the child identifying with the power of the alienator.

- The reaction formation When deep love formally felt for a parent is turned to hatred for purposes of disguising that love, this is not true rejection. True rejection is being indifferent to the parent, not hating that parent. Where there is hate there has been love and love can be rekindled. Alienated children do not so much love the alienator but fear losing the alienator by showing affection towards the alienated parent.

- Identifying with the aggressor Here the child backs the more powerful parent, the one who has custody of the child, and the one who is likely to be present more often than the alienated parent. The weak or alienated parent has been sidelined totally or partly. This is based on fear of a strong alienator.

- Identifying with an idealized or perfect parent Children who have been alienated cling desperately to the alienator. A common experience of a young child is "My mother/father is perfect.\ I don't need a father/mother.\ My mother/father is perfect in every way." This is especially when the alienating parent vilifies the alienated parent regularly, directly or more subtly, making that parent appear to be despicable to the child. Alienators cannot tolerate "ambivalence". One parent has to be always good and the other perfectly evil.

- Releasing hostility Most individuals have reasons for feeling hostile at different times. This is due to accumulated rage from other sources for which the alienated parent often becomes a ready target. The child therefore develops the same power as the alienator who can attack the alienated parent with impunity. The child will do this as well both verbally, physically and by rejecting.

- <u>The child identifies with the power of the alienator</u> Hence the child feels free to attack and humiliate a father/mother (depending on who the alienated person is). They will call them horrible names, spit at them, and even strike them, knowing they have the protection of the alienator or anyone who is present at this particular interview. The alienated parent is helpless to counteract this except by talking kindly and often with tears in their eyes.

3. What to do to do reverse alienation?

There are a number of ways of attempting to reverse the process of alienation.

- Firstly it is to appeal to the child's intelligence or rational thinking.
  This could be difficult for the reasons already quoted. Such children are often so brain-washed that their rational thinking is totally at odds with reality.
- Encouraging a child to confront the alienator
  This is difficult to achieve due to the likelihood of the child identifying with the 'programmer' (alienator) and therefore fearing what the 'programmer' will do if the child is friendly towards the alienated parent.
- Investigating specifics of pejorative remarks made by the alienated parent
  One must be cautious about the remarks made by the child about the alienated parent. Such remarks made as 'father is nasty, evil, stupid, abuses me etc. etc.'. This will be illustrated in the last section
- Making the child realize father loves him/her
  This can only be done eventually when father/mother and child are together. This is sometimes difficult to achieve especially when through the courts or some other source access to the child is barred to the Expert Witness and to seeing the child and the alienated parent together.
- To break down absurd or frivolous criticisms towards the alienated parent.
  It is vital to spend as much time as possible initially

listening to the child's complaints about the alienated parent before "hammering home" the absurdities, unfairness and cruelty the child is expressing. This includes phrases like, "Father is always bribing me to be with him". This is an example of a 'borrowed scenario' since mother could well have used this term to describe the alienated parent who gives the child presents or money. If that parent did not give the child presents or money the borrowed scenario from the mother could well be "He is such a mean man…..never gives me anything".

- It is important to explain to the child how frivolous, absurd statements, and borrowed scenarios come about and how it must be "hammered home" as originating not with the child, but with the alienator. This will not always be accepted by the child as the child thinks he is thinking "independently" of the alienator.
- The alienated child lacks ambivalence towards the alienating parent or the alienated parent. The alienating parent is 'all good' while the other is 'all evil'. There is not one good thing about the non-custodial parent and not one bad thing about the 'programming parent' in the child's mind.
- The term "independent thinking phenomenon" coined by Gardner is also of vital importance. Children must be shown how they have been alienated in thought and behavior against the targeted parent by the programmer. Such children then consider such thoughts and behaviors as originating in their own thinking rather than originating from the alienator. They fail to understand that because of the alienator such ideas are in their minds. Children who are directly or individually being programmed, cannot admit this. Firstly they do not want to blame the programmer to whom they appear to be "devoted". They will claim the alienating thinking and behavior is based on their own independent thinking rather than emanating from the alienated parent. This is a delusion and hence difficult to nullify strictly by rational methods. This is why in the following section emotional approaches will

4. How can rational emotive responses and methods be used to combat parental alienation (A case illustration)

   The present author has found it useful in a number of ases to combine vigorous and dramatic emotional responses with rational procedures. This has at least produced a breakthrough when the child who has had little or no contact with an alienated parent will, at least during the discourse within the therapeutic setting, re-enact a warmer relationship with the alienated parent. Unfortunately, very often the child will return to the custodial parent who will re-use any and all programming methods to reverse this tendency. It does however, indicate how even brief therapeutic approaches of 6-10 sessions can, for a time at least, change the child's thinking, until the child returns to the programming and custodial parent. The child should be seen in combination with the alienated parent whenever possible. It may be the very first time for a considerable period that both have been in the same room. The therapist at first sits between the two and later when some contact occurs, such as eye contact, the therapist will sit opposite the two. Still later, when some progress has been made via interaction verbally and otherwise between the child and the alienated parent, the psychologist briefly leaves the room and gradually extends the periods of absence. It will be noted that the psychologist becomes from time to time emotional to bring the child into reality thinking. The language tends to be 'down to earth', firm, rigorous and meaningful. The main objective is to make an impact on the brain-washed child, however difficult this may be.

5. Case illustration

   This will be a summary of a number of sessions carried out with a child and his/her father. When collected the child very frequently clutched the alienator tightly. The child eventually went with the psychologist. Initially, the child entered the room hesitantly, fearing to leave the alienator. The father was waiting in the room while the child was being brought in by the psychologist to be with the father for the first time. The child on the whole tended to avert her eyes so that no contact could be established. The father in the meantime looked at the child somewhat despondently but greeted the child in a friendly and caring manner. Frequently the father would remind the child of happy times together. This was reinforced by pictures or videos which had been brought along by the alienated parent to demonstrate how actually the alienated child behaved in the past when she was with her father. The dialogue went as follows:

Psychologist: "This is the first time that you and your father have been together for some time hasn't it?"

Child: Does not answer

Psychologist: "I would like you to speak to me even if you don't at the moment speak to your father. This is the first time you have been in the same room with your father for some considerable time isn't it?"

Child: "It's not because I want to. I'm being made to do it."

Psychologist: (speaking to the father) "Can you remind (child's name) of some of the happier times you were together by showing her some pictures of the past, or maybe some of the letters that she wrote to you before all this occurred."

Father then showed the child some pictures, and videos. The child averted her eyes in order not to look at these reminders of the past and happy times. Psychologist: "I would like you to look at those pictures even if you don't look at your father so that you can see how things were in the past and why things have gone wrong in the meantime and this we will discuss later."

The child then turned her eyes to look at the pictures without looking at the father.

Child: "I can't remember these pictures being taken. I was probably only pretending to be happy when I was with my father. I have never really been happy with him at all."

Psychologist: "Well these pictures don't indicate this at all. You seem to be smiling and cuddling your dad and generally showing signs of happiness. Can all this be pretense?"

Child: "Yes. I was only pretending. The only person I want to be with and love is my mother. She only needs me and I only need her. I don't need a father." Psychologist: "Don't you think your father loves you and deserves for you to be nice to him when he always tries to be nice to you. I believe be tries to telephone you regularly but you don't want to speak to him and hang up on him. Is that right?"

Child: "Yes. I don't want to speak to him. I don't want anything to do with him any more."

Psychologist: "Why is that? What are the reasons you have? I want specific answers why you don't want any contact with your father. I don't want general remarks like 'I don't like him' or 'He is horrible to me'. I want to know exactly what he does wrong in your eyes to make you wish to reject a loving father who cares for you."

Child: "I can't think of anything now but he always tries to make me go to places I don't want to go to and he sometimes asks me to come into the bed with him. I don't like that."

Psychologist: "And what else?"

Child: "He shows me off to other people and tells them how clever I am and I hate that. Also he always tells me what to do and makes me eat things I don't want to eat. He makes me go on holiday with him and do things I don't like doing. He makes me sleep on a dirty bed which he has in his house."

Psychologist: "Is there anything else?"

Child: "There are many other things I don't like. I don't even like being in the same room and talking to him."

Psychologist: "Again I want you to be civil and nice to your father. OK? He is one of the few people in this world who will give anything to help you in any way he can, and I don't think it's fair that you should treat him in this way. Do you?"

Child: Silent, says nothing at first. Then says: "You don't have to be with him like I have to be with him. You don't know what he is really like."

Psychologist: "No I don't really know. I am not always with him as you were in the past. There must be something good about your father that you enjoyed doing with him."

Child: Thinking, then says, "Nothing".
Psychologist: "There must be something that you remember that was good about him."
Child: Thinking, then says, "He used to make some nice meals for me when I was with him. Nothing else. Anyway he could probably hit me from time to time if I was with him."
Psychologist: "Has he ever hit you?"
Child: Answers, "No".
Psychologist: "Has he ever hit you?"
Child: Answers, "No".
Psychologist: "What makes you think he is going to hit you then ?"
Child: "He could hit me. He's the sort of person who would do that sort of thing."
Psychologist: "What makes you say that?"
Child: "Look at him, he is big and strong and he could hurt me."
Psychologist: "But has he ever done so?"
Child: Reluctantly says "No".
Psychologist: "If all these things you dislike about him and how he is with you were changed would you want to be with your dad after that?"
Child: "They could never be changed, and anyway even if they were changed I wouldn't want to be with him."
Psychologist: "So there is no sense in changing anything is there?"
Child: "That's right. I just don't want to be with him."
It is clear from this interchange that there has been no breakthrough of any kind while the father has been in the room demonstrating pictures and videos from time to time to show how the past had been and how happy the child had been in the father's company. It is now felt that a more emotional and direct approach is required. This approach could well be criticized by those who believe in pure therapeutic approaches of an orthodox nature. The current psychologist however, has found that these methods are totally ineffective with an alienated child who is obdurate about wishing any contact with a former affectionate, caring and loving parent. The psychologist

Where Did I Go Wrong? How Did I Miss The Signs?

from time to time therefore uses fairly emotional and direct expressions, and also the tone of his voice is louder to be emphatic to the child. Essentially it is, a way of "shocking" the child to reality.

Psychologist: "Now I am going to say something that has been on my mind for some time having read everything you've said about your father, and having talked to your father for a long period of time to find out how he feels about you. I think you have treated him abominably. I think you have been a horrible little girl. You have been too powerful for your own good. What right have you got to reject a father who loves you and cares for you and wants to do everything for you? You should be ashamed of yourself. Don't you feel guilty at all about the way you have treated him all this time by not even looking at him, by not talking to him, by hanging up on him on the telephone? What has he really done that is so terrible for you to behave in this way. I think you have virtually thrown your father into the rubbish pile. If that is what you want to do then so be it. I think your father is very, very caring or he would not persist in wanting to be with you and wanting to have contact with you, and wanting to show his love for you. I'll tell you one thing, many fathers would have given up and not bothered any more, and not bothered even contacting you or wishing you a happy birthday or a good Christmas, or providing for you financially. Many fathers would have given up and just said to themselves that this was the end and I am not having any more to do with this child."

At this point very frequently the child will develop thinking. The emotional tone of the therapist or psychologist will in may cases have 'hit home.' Sometimes one has to go on in this vein using very emotional expressions and very 'down to earth' expressions defending the father and drawing attention to the good times that the child has had with the father which has been substantiated by the pictures and other information provided by the father. The important thing is not to accept what the child says and how the child behaves since it is based on considerable programming or brainwashing. It is vital to continue to try to break through that barrier and very frequently one does break through.

Eventually in the case quoted above the child did look at the father having seen the pictures and seen what an impact this had on the father. It was then the chance of the father to talk to the child in a caring, loving manner and remind the child of the good times they had together in the past.

It is at this point that the psychologist would best leave the room for a short period to provide an opportunity for interaction between the two parties. It is surprising, very often, when the psychologist returns after the first or second time being away from the two how much closer the chairs are between the two parties and how their eye contact has improved and how they are now speaking to one another. Sometimes the child will even hold the parent's hand and even at a later stage give that alienated parent a cuddle (often for the first time in years) or a sign of physical warmth. Sometimes it takes a number of sessions of this kind before this can be achieved. Powerful emotional language is vital in order to break through the barrier that has occurred due to the alienation process. The child then begins to think again for him/herself rather than repeating the phrases and thoughts of the alienator.

It must also be said that the child feels safe interacting with the alienated parent as mother is not present. Were mother in the same room the child could be very reluctant to allow a breakthrough of this kind. The child would be worrying about the views of the alienator. The child would be concerned with the disapproval of the alienating party if the child is too friendly to the alienated party. It will take a considerable effort to redeem the damage that has been done to the child over a period of months or years in which the programmer (alienator) has 'hammered home' their own prejudices and the child has identified with these prejudices. Once the psychologist has completed the process of mediation there is a need for a report to go to the Court. The Court will either accept or fail to accept the views of the Expert Witness. In the extreme it will ignore all the views by psychologist and retain the situation as it was before with the

Where Did I Go Wrong? How Did I Miss The Signs?

child living with the custodial, programming parent. It is hoped more and more courts in future will in extreme and prolonged cases of programming consider the possibility of a change of custody, at least for a period of time, so that the alienated parent can have the opportunity of healing the wounds of the past. Only time will tell what occurs in the future.

Dr. Lowenstein's contact information is as follows:
Dr. L. F. Lowenstein, M.A.,DIP.PSYCH.,Ph.D.
Southern England Psychological Services (SEPS)
Allington Manor
Allington Lane
Fair Oak, Eastleigh
Hants, SO50 7DE
Tel/Fax: 023 80692621
http://www.parental-alienation.info

DEPROGRAMMING CENTERS AND INTERVENTIONS

If the situation has gone beyond the ability to make use of counseling, there are some other options. For those who are not giving up yet, and have the finances and energy to continue this fight, but whose children are completely programmed and brainwashed, there are several centers and workshops that might be useful. The key is to get the judge to agree to this type of treatment including removal of the children from the offending parent, with only supervised visitation, until that parent gets help for their mental health issues. This list will be updated online whenever new information becomes available.

Family Bridges and Welcome Back Pluto DVD
www.warshak.com
Dr. Richard Warshak's is a counter-parental alienation program With a 3 to 4 day workshops that kick starts the process to deprogram the child/children. Please contact Dr. Warshak directly about this program.

Clinical Psychology Associates,
16970 Dallas Parkway, Suite 202,
Dallas, Texas 75248,

Dr. Craig Childress – www.drcachildress.org
The Strategic-Behavioral-Systems Intervention "is a treatment intervention designed to alter the meaning of the Delta child's rejection of the Delta parent." It is a positive reward program to encourage a positive relationship with the ousted parent using a points system.

Craig Childress, Psy.D.
547 S. Marengo Ave., Ste 105
Pasadena, CA 91101
(909) 821-5398

The Rachel Foundation - http://www.rachelfoundation.org/
The Rachel Foundation for Family Reintegration has identified and developed a flexible, four-step program for the reintegration of returned abducted children and children who have been severely alienated from a parent.

It has applied this program with remarkable success, even in cases estimated to be close to hopeless: for instance where children are severely alienated from a parent and in cases where children have had no contact with a parent for many years.

Each case is different and the program can be adapted to meet the needs of the individual family unit, either residential or non-residential, short term (3 days to one week) or longer term (up to several months.) The Rachel Foundation for Family Reintegration delivers practical, affordable, structured reintegration programs on several levels:

> Bridges ™ - intensive residential program for returning abducted or alienated children and their left behind parents. This program also facilitates Clauses 13(b) and 21 of the Hague Convention, by working with Federal Courts.
>
> Footsteps ™ - short-term supportive residential access program to strengthen damaged or at-risk parent-child bonds. For non-custodial parents and parents whose bonds with their children have been damaged through divorce or other reasons.
>
> Rachel Community Reintegration Program – outpatient, in the family's community.

Where Did I Go Wrong? How Did I Miss The Signs?

Rachel Outreach – Consulting and counseling services, multidisciplinary networking with appropriate social and legal agencies and Courts. This includes a developing network of trained reintegration facilitators.

ALTERNATIVE THERAPIES, STUDIES AND RESEARCH FOR TREATING PAS

1. **The Personality and Emotion Research and Treatment (PERT)** Laboratory within the Department of Psychiatry and Human Behavior at UMMC is a translational research laboratory combining basic experimental research on the mechanisms underlying personality pathology, posttraumatic stress disorder, and additional….
http://pertlab.umc.edu/people/klgratz.html
Personality and Emotion Research and Treatment Laboratory -University of Mississippi Medical Center, www.pertlab.umc.edu

2. **Horse Therapy Grants**, www.ehow.com Horse Therapy Grants. Children and animals seem to have a special bond, and sometimes animals can even get kids to open up in a way that adults can't. Horses are often especially good at making that…

3. **Psychology Today:** Find an Emotional Disturbance Therapist in Grants Pass, Josephine County, Oregon (OR), Therapists specializing in Emotional Disturbance, http://therapists.psychologytoday.com/rms/prof_results.php?city=Grants+Pass&county=Josephine&state=OR&spec=198
Grants Pass Emotional Disturbance Therapist - Emotional Disturbance Therapist Grants Pass, Josephine, www.therapists.psychologytoday.com

4. **Horse Therapy Grants | DailyPuppy.com**, www.dailypuppy.com
Children and animals seem to have a special bond, and

sometimes animals can even get kids to open up in a way that adults can't. Horses are often especially good at making that emotional connection, especially with both kids and adults who have physical...

5. **Equine Therapy for PTSD - Disaboom**
   www.disaboom.comInformation about equine therapy for veterans with PTSD, or, post traumatic stress disorder. Military veterans are healed through therapeutic horseback riding.

6. **Emotional Therapy from the UK**
   http://emotionaltherapy.co.uk
   Write to: emotionaltherapy.co.uk

7. **Special Kids Therapy**
   http://www.specialkidstherapy.org/pdf/Grant_Application.pdf
   SKT is pleased to offer through the gifts of generous donors, grants to individuals orgroups to:♥ Obtain books, journals videotapes, software and other learning tools;♥ Make equipment purchases♥ Provide complimentary/alternative therapy or other needs for CSHCN
   http://www.specialkidstherapy.org/pdf/Grant_Application.pdf
   www.specialkidstherapy.org

CHAPTER 24

DIVORCE RULES
By
Susan Boyan and Ann Marie Termini
co-founders of the Cooperative Parenting Institute (CPI)

Directions : Post these rules on your refrigerator as a reminder of your commitment to care. Ask your child to let you know if you forget one of the rules. Never reprimand your child when they give you this feedback.

Dear Mom and Dad, I'm just a kid, so please…
1. Do not talk badly about my other parent. (This makes me feel torn apart! It also makes me feel bad about myself.)

2. Do not talk about my other parent's friends or relatives. (Let me care for someone even if you don't.)

3. Do not talk about the divorce or other grown-up stuff. (This makes me feel sick. Please leave me out of it.)

4. Do not talk about money or child support. (This makes me feel guilty or like I'm a possession instead of your kid.)

5. Do not make me feel bad when I enjoy my time with my other parent. (This makes me afraid to tell you things.)

6. Do not block my visits or prevent me from speaking to my other parent on the phone. (This makes me very upset.)

7. Do not interrupt my time with my other parent by calling too much or by planning my activities during our time together.

8. Do not argue in front of me or on the phone when I can hear you! (This just turns my stomach inside out.)

9. Do not ask me to spy for you when I am at my other parent's home. (This makes me feel disloyal and dishonest.)

10. Do not ask me to keep secrets from my other parent. (Secrets make me feel anxious.)

11. Do not ask me questions about my other parent's life or about our time together. (This makes me uncomfortable, so just let me tell you.)

12. Do not give me verbal messages to deliver to my other parent. (I end up feeling anxious about their reaction. So please just call them, leave them a message at work, or put a note in the mail.)

13. Do not send written messages with me or place them in my bag. (This also makes me uncomfortable.)

14. Do not blame my other parent for the divorce or for things that go wrong in your life. (This really feels terrible. I end up wanting to defend them from your attack. Sometimes it makes me feel sorry for you and that makes me want to protect you. I just want to be a kid, so please, please…stop putting me into the middle!)

15. Do not treat me like an adult. It causes way too much stress for me. (Please find a friend or therapist to talk with.)

16. Do not ignore my other parent or sit on opposite sides of the room during my school or sports activities. (This makes me very sad and embarrassed. Please act like parents and be friendly, even if it is just for me.)

Where Did I Go Wrong? How Did I Miss The Signs?

17. Do let me take items to my other home as long as I can carry them back and forth. (Otherwise, it feels like you are treating me like a possession.)

18. Do not use guilt to pressure me to love you more and do not ask me where I want to live.

19. Do realize that I have two homes, not just one. (It doesn't matter how much time I spend there.)

20. Do let me love both of you and see each of you as much as possible. Be flexible even when it is not part of our regular schedule.

Thanks, your loving child.

Reprinted with permission from Boyan & Termini (1999). Cooperative Parenting and Divorce.. Copyright, 2007; Stephanie K. Glassman, Psy.D. All rights reserved. http://www.glassmanpsyd.com/divorce-rules

Collaborative Law Center
3128 Clairmont Road, N.E.
Atlanta, Georgia 30329
susanboyan@gmail.com
404-315-7474 Ext 1
Fax: 404-982-0006

WHAT IF?
What If one parent is breaking these divorce rule? Here are some things that the other parent can say to give the children the ability to permit themselves to stand up and not be put in the middle. To just not have to choose and be able to love both parents without being stressed about insulting the other parent.

EMPOWERING THE CHILDREN WITH WORDS
By Kathy Turetzky

Tell the children:
- You have every right to have both parents in your life.
- You have every right to enjoy being with both parents.
- You have every right to love both your parents.
- You have every right to spend time with both parents.
- You have every right to enjoy these gifts I give you.
- You have every right to stand up to wanting the life all other kids have and that is both parents in your life.
- You have every right to tell your parents to not put you in the middle.
- You have every right when a parent says hateful things about the other parent that "You don't want to hear it."
- You have every right to tell your parent to stop badmouthing the other parent.

AND THEN THERE IS GASLIGHTING

The term comes from a play of the same name about a husband who attempts to make his wife think she is crazy. The actual definition is a form of intimidation or psychological abuse in which false information is presented to the victim, making them doubt their own memory and perception. (http://en.wikipedia.org/wiki/Gaslighting) In other words, the victim is made to believe that someone or something is not what they think it is. In the case of parent-child relationships, this could involve one parent deliberately destroying the once positive memories of their other parent with the express purpose of severing all ties to the targeted parent.

To follow is a list of feelings and thoughts that one might have who is being gaslight into not having a relationship with one parent. Your own personal experience may not involve all of these experiences or feelings, but if you recognize yourself in any of them, you may be a victim of psychological abuse and parental alienation from one of your parents.

Where Did I Go Wrong? How Did I Miss The Signs?

1. You are constantly second-guessing yourself.
2. You ask yourself, "Am I too sensitive?" a dozen times a day.
3. You often feel confused and even crazy at school, work, home, or around friends.
4. You're always apologizing to your mother/father
5. You wonder frequently if you are a "good enough" son/daughter.
6. You can't understand why, with so many apparently good things in your life, you aren't happier.
7. You buy clothes for yourself, furnishings for your apartment, or other personal purchases with your parent in mind, thinking about what he would like instead of what would make you feel great.
8. You frequently make excuses for your parent's behavior to friends and family.
9. You find yourself withholding information from friends and family so you don't have to explain or make excuses.
10. You know something is terribly wrong, but you can never quite express what it is, even to yourself.
11. You start lying to avoid the put-downs and reality twists.
12. You have trouble making simple decisions.
13. You think twice before bringing up certain seemingly innocent topics of conversation.
14. Before your parent comes home, you run through a checklist in your head to anticipate anything you might have done wrong that day.
15. You have the sense that you used to be a very different person - more confident, more fun loving, more relaxed.
16. You start speaking to your parent through another person so you don't have to tell him things you're afraid might upset him.
17. You feel as though you can't do anything right.
18. Your parent begins trying to protect you from your other parent based on things that don't make sense or you do not remember or that you know are lies.
19. You find yourself furious with people you've always gotten along with before.

20. You feel hopeless and joyless.

CHAPTER 25

THE HEALING POWER OF LAUGHTER

One of the biggest things that helped my family through this high conflict divorce crisis was laughter. When things got tough, though we might yell or cry or vent or scream, at some point we would also turn it around and make a joke of it. The more we could make light of the little things in our lives as well as the big ones, the easier it was for us to get through the hard times.

Laughter is good for the soul. When we laugh it also helps us to heal from the inside out. It helps us to believe that maybe this is not all that bad and we can survive it. It gives us hope. And it gives us a mental break from the real world. And when we are able to look and laugh, we are able to have a clearer perspective of our lives. We are able to enjoy our lives - something the ex-spouse does not want us to do. We are able to move forward and see that there is still so much fun and laughter left, even when the relationship with the children is being severed and impeded.

They say, laughter is the best medicine, and I couldn't agree more. Laughter actually releases all sorts of good hormones and chemicals that calm, soothe and make us feel better. It helps to ease stress and calm nerves. It almost seems to stop the roller coaster ride of emotions that plague victims of PAS.

The benefits of laughter are incredible. Just a quick Internet search came back with the following partial list on the following page.

Physical Health Benefits:
- Boosts immunity
- Lowers stress hormones
- Decreases pain
- Relaxes your muscles
- Prevents heart disease

Mental Health Benefits:
- Adds joy and zest to life
- Eases anxiety and fear
- Relieves stress
- Improves mood
- Enhances resilience

Social Benefits:
- Strengthens relationships
- Attracts others to us
- Enhances teamwork
- Helps defuse conflict
- Promotes group bond

From the website:

http://www.helpguide.org/life/humor_laughter_health.htm

SO LAUGH. LAUGH HARD. LAUGH TILL YOU CRY. LAUGH TILL YOU CANNOT LAUGH ANYMORE.

CHAPTER 26

MOVING FORWARD AND LETTING GO SO THE FESTERING WOUND HEALS

None of this is ever easy and none of it ever will be. Below is an excerpt from a support group member whose family put every dime of money they had into trying to save their relationship with the alienated child and in the process, they caused their own financial demise and it was beginning to harm the other members of their family. They felt like they had done everything in their power but did not know what more to do. It describes the guilt they were feeling and what others had to say about it. Remember, there is no right or wrong answer as to when enough is enough. After her post, there were responses from many of the members as well.

> *MH writes:*
> *I haven't posted in a while. Not much to report on. I think we just keep making wrong decisions, but no matter what we do, it always seems to be wrong. =(*
>
> *I think we're almost to the point where your husband ended up. N is only coming every other Saturday... if he doesn't manage to make other plans ahead of time.*
>
> *S is done fighting the losing battle. He is letting N go with love at this point. When it gets to where N states he no longer wants to be here, S will let him know that the door is always open.*

The Author writes:

First, I know exactly where you are, because that is exactly where one of my family members were at, broke, emotionally, financially and physically. And they still had their eldest son from a first marriage in their lives that needed and loved them as well as their own daughter. And no, you are not doing anything wrong. Biological Mother (BM) is.

Don't worry about not posting for a while, sometimes, it just is overwhelming and you are at a loss for words. And lastly, do not ever worry about long emails. Sometimes that is just the way it is. Keep in touch more often so we can help you through these tough times.

MH writes:

I hear what you're saying. But, I think at this point, S is done. Just done. He has not been able to do or say anything at all without it being turned around on him to look like the bad guy and he feels at this point, he just wants to try and live his life with his other children. As I'm typing this, I feel as if you're right- he should do this or he should do that- but how much more can we take? I worry about my 11 yo's safety and my safety because of his outbursts and worry that pushing him will send him over the edge. And ex will support him in anything that he does. She has trained him to do her dirty work for her. Maybe we are letting him down by letting go, but to keep pushing only seems to make it worse. He is being told constantly that his father is a loser and treats him like a child. When, in fact, ex is the devil and treats him like he's the other adult in that house- which is NOT good.

There is going to come a day, probably in the very near future, when N will get himself in a lot of trouble because of his lack of respect for authority and his sense of entitlement. And ex will be pointing fingers at his father telling everyone it's his fault etc. Well, how can it be his fault if he hasn't been able to see him or have any say in his upbringing?

Where Did I Go Wrong? How Did I Miss The Signs?

We have given up... is that horrible? Sometimes I think it is, other times, I think it's a blessing.

AB writes:
No, it's not horrible. We gave up, we're trying again, and somewhat cuz he's out of his mother's house now. But the troubles followed him. He's very self-centered and manipulative. But, life for our kids and us was a lot better after we let his stepfather adopt him. Our ex wasn't happy with us just backing away, not calling, and not asking for visitations. She'd keep taking us to court for more child support, complain how we didn't care about our son, and then complain because we'd call. But, in the end all she wanted was an adoption to make it "like you never existed". The way we feel/felt was that my stepson was old enough that if he had some strength of character he would have been able to say no or to make an effort to know his dad. Comes a time when a person has to decide, "Do I let my upbringing dictate my life or do I make my own choices"? Ya know? And, you're really not giving up so much as being pushed away. There is a difference.

The Author writes:
You are at the point that my family member was. S can give it one last try, and if that does not work, then he tells N to meet him at the therapists office, so he can tell him a bunch of very important things. Doing the following at the therapists office makes it a matter of record and that there is a third party involved. And this is an idea of what S can say to his son.

N, I have always loved you. Always will love you. I have always tried to respect you and treat you like the young man you have grown to be. But I am no longer going to ask you to comply with the court orders to visit with me or spend time with me. There is no point anymore as you refuse to spend the time with me anyway and when you do you are rude. I will no longer tolerate you abusing my family or me. I know your mother is *going to bad mouth me for this, and tell you how I do not care and that she told you so. But the truth is that if I had not cared, I would not have spent every dime we had trying to make this work. This was the money that should have gone into my own home and family, but instead, I invested into trying to get your mother to allow you to have a relationship with me. And for the record, when you do finally get in trouble for your disrespectful and arrogant attitude, you mother can try to blame it on me all she wants. But the truth is that since I was no allowed into your life to raise you, then how could I be the influence of your problems. There is only one person who influenced your behavior and upbringing and it was not I as I was not even allowed to be part of it.*

It does not have to be exactly like this, but it needs to be said, loud and clear and with a third professional witness. N may not get it right then and there, but down the road it will hit home. And in fact, you can ask the therapist to give him a copy of that days session so that when he is older, he can look back and see what really happened and not what he was brainwashed to believe.

MH writes:

Its a struggle not to feel like we're horrible- shoulda, coulda woulda.... and who knows, maybe we will try again when he's older...or if by some miracle, N shows some sort of sign that he wants to know the truth, or even just "start over".

A writes:

Ya, I know. I think a lot about the story of King Solomon.... you know the one with the baby being split in two. That mother probably felt terrible, too. This 'fight' is not physically tearing the kid apart, but it is emotionally. We will never know if we did the right thing. We hoped that his mother would stop bad mouthing his dad. But I now think it didn't. But what did stop was him seeing his parents fighting. I don't know if that sent the message of "we don't care about you". I do know that's how he

Where Did I Go Wrong? How Did I Miss The Signs?

choices to see it. Even with all our affirmations to the contrary. But, we can't control that any more than we could control him believing the stuff his mother said when we were trying. It was a lose/lose situation. But our 'giving up', turned it into a win for our kids, if nothing else, and, in some ways, a win for us. We were able to concentrate on us, our family and we didn't get more 'surprise you're going back to court' sessions. We also lost the stress of trying to deal with my stepson... do we call? do we stay away? It was a daily struggle. There was no question of it after. Before, EVERYONE was losing, except maybe the ex. But, it's different for everyone. I don't want you to think I'm trying to talk you into this. Just giving you other options of how to look at it, if you do take that road.

The Author writes:
You hit the nail on the head here. It is sad that we cannot have a relationship with these kids, but it is not fair to the rest of our families to keep fighting this losing battle. It would be like pining away for a person who has already been dead and gone to us for many years. It does no one any good and least of all, us any good.

The above excerpt is an example of what I like to call, The Festering Wounds and it goes like this.

THE FESTERING WOUND
By Joan T. Kloth-Zanard

At first it starts as a red rash that itches, so you scratch it. But it just itches more and more. So you scratch it more and more. You scratch it so much that it starts to get raw. Soon you are scratching it so much that it starts to bleed. Now, it is not just bleeding but infected and oozing. In fact, it is a festering open wound. And the only way for it to heal is to cover it with a bandage and ointment and just leave it alone for a while, so that eventually, you can reach out and touch again. That is to say, we must move forward and come back to this when the time is right and the healing has begun or been done.

But what is moving forward? Moving forward is not the same thing as moving on. Moving on means to leave things behind and conjures up the idea of not turning back. Whereas moving forward, says you are going on but in a positive way to continue your life and grow. It is not about leaving anyone behind, but instead about trying to get to the next stage or cycle in your life.

Part of moving forward is accepting that we cannot force people to change. But on the other hand, we can change ourselves. And in changing ourselves, we can hope that it assists or provides a positive example for others to change and move forward with their lives too. This is not something to feel guilty about because you are putting your foot down and not allowing the children or your ex to abuse you any more. You are moving forward with your life and there is no reason for you to take this abuse with you.

I want to further back this up with some information from the book, Stop *Walking on Egg Shells* by Mason and Kreger, pages 127-128. Set limits for your self because it is important for your mental health and for your children's mental health. Without limits and boundaries, there are no borders and without borders there is no line as to where to stop and when to keep going. If you continue to permit the children to violate your personal boundaries or space, you are allowing them to get worse, because it does not fix the problem by letting them continue. They are not learning that this is inappropriate or even how to set their own boundaries or limits. They are learning that this is okay to do and thus they continue to act irresponsibly and poorly.

It is also important for you to NOT continue to accept responsibility for your children's feelings and behavior or they will never know how to do if for themselves as they never see it being done. All people need to know how to accept responsibility for their own actions. The children cannot get better if we continue to allow them to never take responsibility for their own behavior and in reality, this lack of responsibility

Where Did I Go Wrong? How Did I Miss The Signs?

will actually get worse when they get into the real world as an adult.

When your children are enacting this much pain and suffering toward others, it is not healthy for you or for them. If we continue to allow them to do this, what lesson are we teaching them? That it is okay to abuse others and treat them with disrespect? Is this the lesson you want them to learn that it is okay to do this? Sometimes being a parent is about teaching some very hard lessons and having to put our foot down firmly.

By setting limits, you are presenting a good role model as well. Maybe they will learn to create their own person limits and will have learned a valuable lesson about what is okay to tolerate and what is not. In the end, it might help them to battle the constant barrage of negativism from the other parent about you. So DO NOT feel guilty about putting your foot down to preserve yours and their mental and physical health, along with teaching some very valuable lessons about life. You are not just doing it selfishly for your own mental and physical wellbeing, but for their safety and security too.

CHAPTER 27

STRESS MANAGEMENT

What is stress management? It is anything that helps someone to control or have power over their situations that cause them anxiety or depression. It can be anything to anyone, so long as it helps to lower your heart rate and pulse, calm you down or provide you with positive thoughts and energy. Why do we need to manage our stress? Because if we do not, it will take over and start to make our own health, both mental and physical, deteriorate. And if our health deteriorates, the chances of us being around for our kids when they "finally get it", will be lessened. The healthier we are, the better chance that we will be there for them when they do "come around". Below are just some examples of activities that can help with managing your stress.

CREATING VISUAL IMAGES TO KEEP YOU GOING
I know none of this is easy and is just a lot of words, but let it sink in. Start imagining your ex-spouse as this decrepit old person, pushing an apple cart with one bad wheel. The cart, which is completely out of whack, is listing to one side. Imagine them constantly trying to stand it up so it doesn't look crooked. Imagine that a passerby sees the old person and wonders why he doesn't fix the wheel. All it would take is a hammer and a nail, (i.e. correcting what they have said and done to the children) Then imagine yourself as a kindly lady who passes him on the street and out of pity buys one of his apples so that he can at least make a little money for the day. You are the better person by trying to make a difference, while they are still pushing their rotten agenda and falling deeper and deeper into disrepair.

PHYSICAL EXERCISE AND WHY IT WORKS

I am a big believer in exercise to relieve tension and clear our heads. I have done some research and study on this but for the purposes of this book, I will make it short and simple. Stress, anxiety and depression cause chemical changes and build up chemical imbalances in our bodies. These chemical changes need to be addressed and one-way is through exercise.

When we exercise, even if it is just a 20-minute walk around the block, it has many cathartic or cleansing properties. First of all, within the first 10 minutes of exercise, our brains start amping up and moving the files around in our head, like a filing cabinet. Our brain pushes things around until the most important stuff comes to the forefront. All the non-important stuff is moved to the back. This is a form of meditation and it helps to clear our brains. We can see important issues more clearly and get a new perspective on them. We get fresh, clean thoughts about our problems and what to do about them.

In addition, when we exercise, it increases the flow of oxygen and pumping of our blood through our circulatory system. As well as it assists our lymphatic or cleansing system to do a better job. That is they help to pump fresh clean oxygenated blood and antibodies through our systems while flushing out toxins and wastes. When we increase the system flow, we are helping our bodies to rid themselves of excess toxins, hormones, and poisons that have built up from stress, anxiety, depression, We also increase the oxygen supply to our organs and this helps us to function more efficiently.

Not only is this cleansing process helping to clean our hearts and souls, but it providing fresh oxygenated blood to our brains, so that we can think more clearly, which brings us back to the meditative state that exercise creates if we do it for a long enough period, (i.e. clearing up those dusty files in our heads.)

In the end, all of this adds up to using exercise to eliminate the stress and keep us healthy, both mentally and physically. Hopefully, this will extend into other successes in our lives.

BECOME A SUPERHERO

Superhero's are people who have been wronged, harmed or hurt in some way. But instead of becoming depressed, letting themselves go, turning to substance abuse or some other vise, they stand up and fight for what they believe in. The stand up to help the little people so that this harm never happens again. They turn their anger and frustration into positive energy and move forward to help others in need. They become Superhero's for a cause and this gives them reason to live and move forward in a positive way in their lives. It allows them to be there when for their children or others, when they are need them. It is gives them a purpose in life. This is NOT about being a vigilante but about standing up and protecting others from the destruction and pain of PAS, such as by educating others, standing on court house steps at rally's, speaking up about the abuse, making signs, protesting, writing letters, handing out flyers and so on. It is about taking on the Superhero mentality that you are NOT going to let this destroy you but instead, you will destroy it and not let it hurt another sole.

HAPPY MEDIUM - MANTRA VIEW

Sometimes, despite everything we do, we still come back to the pain and suffering that the ex is inflicting upon us through the children. Maybe the happy medium is to just accept that our children cannot say anything positive or nice right now, because there is nothing positive or nice in their lives. Also, this is really not about you, but about the other parent. Though this is hard to remember when you are upset, maybe there is a mantra you can repeat in your head when you hear crap from the kids. Like, "My Ex Sucks" or "Words Cannot Hurt" or "Her Pain is Her Pain" or "Let the Pain Go" or "Breathe and Let Her Vent". And don't forget to think good Karma thoughts for yourself.

Where Did I Go Wrong? How Did I Miss The Signs?

CHAPTER 28

PARENTAL CHARACTER ANALYSIS AND INDICATOR – A SCALED QUESTIONNAIRE

With the help from many support group victims who wanted to a way to help counselors and courts to recognize PAS, the following questionnaire was created. Unfortunately, if the other parent is narcissistic, they will be able to pass almost any psychological evaluation they are given. Therefore, a behavioral analysis or other testing will need to be added for all psych evaluations. For the purposes of this questionnaire, ex-spouse will refer to an ex-spouse, ex-partner or soon to be ex-spouse or partner. This questionnaire is used to indicate the level of PAS being used by an ex-spouse.

DIRECTIONS:

For each statement in the following chart, please mark the answer that reflects your true feelings about the statement. Answers range on a scale of strongly agree; to agree; to neutral; to disagree; to strongly disagree. A professional with the appropriate answer key and score ratings must score this questionnaire, which can be obtained from the developer, Joan T. Kloth-Zanard.. They also should have a strong training and education in grief, anger management and impulse control so they can properly gage the responses to the questionnaire and the essay questions that follow it. Please go to www.KlothConsulting.com or www.PAS-Intervention.com, then click on the words Charts, Tests & Tools for the excel version.

	Strongly Agree	Agree	Neutral	Dis-agree	Strongly Dis-agree
1) Your ex-spouse is late picking the kids up. You should not make a big deal in front of them and let them go on their visit.					
2) You're mad at your ex-spouse for not paying child support. You should never discuss this with the children.					
3) Your ex-spouse and you disagree about visitation and child support issues It is appropriate to discuss and involve the children in this argument.					
4) The children reside primarily with you, but you feel they should spend time with the other parent as					

Where Did I Go Wrong? How Did I Miss The Signs?

equally as is possible.					
5) You hate your ex-spouse and feel the children would be better off with you.					
6) Your ex has finally met a new partner. Encouraging a relationship with the new spouse/partner is important.					
7) Even though the children reside primarily with you, the other parent is entitled to medical information and should help with decisions, which relate to the children.					
8) You are fed up with your ex-spouse. You feel like they abandoned you. If you refuse visitations between the children and					

your ex-spouse it sends a clear message about how you feel and this will not hurt the children.					
9) Since the children reside primarily with you, they no longer belong to your ex-spouse.					
10) You want to take the children away on vacation during your ex-spouse's visitation weekend. Your ex-spouse has already made special plans for that same weekend. You should change your plans.					
11) Even though the children reside primarily with you, the other parent is still entitled to the children's school information, schedules and appointments.					

Where Did I Go Wrong? How Did I Miss The Signs?

12) The children are refusing to go visit the other parent for no real reason or are refusing to return home from the visit. It's best if you make them go on the visit or conversely, make them come home from the visit even though they don't want to.						
13) The children's after school schedules and events are not important to the other parent because the children reside primarily with you.						
14) The courts have ordered everyone into counseling, but you don't think you or the children need to go. It's okay to skip counseling.						
15) The judge has						

267

given your ex-spouse more visitation time with the children but it conflicts with the routine you've already established. You should change your schedule to accommodate the new orders.					
16) Since the children reside with you, you should have more rights and control over the children's lives and schedules, including visitations with the other parent.					
17) Child support, which is contingent on both your incomes, should also take into consideration the pain you are suffering because of your ex-spouse.					
18) Telling your children the other					

Where Did I Go Wrong? How Did I Miss The Signs?

parent hates them and doesn't love them will not affect them.					
19) There is no need for my children to communicate with my ex-spouse.					
20) Your ex-spouse admits that he/she no longer loves you, and wants a divorce. If you deprive the ex-spouse and the children from having a relationship, the ex will be forced to know what rejection feels like. This will not hurt the children.					
21) Children need both parents.					
22) The children need to hear the "truth" about the other parent even if it hurts them.					
23) It is perfectly					

legal to ignore the courts, judges and attorney's advice if it's not what you requested in court.					
24) Your child has been recommended for counseling because of the divorce, but the child is refusing to go. Sending your child is the right thing to do.					
25) Divorce laws were made for others not me.					
26) Sometimes I feel useless.					
27) Sometimes I am full of energy.					
28) Taking my anger out on my ex-spouse by refusing visitation makes me feel better.					
29) A court order has been made for visitation every					

Where Did I Go Wrong? How Did I Miss The Signs?

Wednesday and every other weekend. But you usually spend the time with your kids on the weekends and Wednesday nights doing something special. It is okay for the children to drop the new visitation schedule because it is not what they have been doing in the past, and interferes with my schedule.					
30) Your ex does not deserve to see or speak to your children.					
31) Do you feel like a victim and have no control?					
32) Your ex refused you visitation this weekend, therefore you do not have to pay child support.					

ESSAY QUESTIONS:

33) Essay Question: This is called the Miracle Question. And it goes like this. You go to sleep tonight and in the morning, a miracle has happened. What would be different? How would you know? In other words, if everything in your divorce/separation went smoothly, how do you envision your life?

34) Essay Question: Why would it be in the best interests of "X" for custody to be awarded to you?

35) Essay Question: If I were to award custody of "X" to you, what visitation would you want for the other parent?

In addition to this questionnaire for parents, on the following pages is an evaluation created for children with the help of my support group members. It is just a guide and idea of things that one might notice or hear from the children.

EVALUATION QUESTIONS FOR CHILDREN
Contributors:
Joan T. Kloth-Zanard
Lin Nicholson
Karen Godfrey
Kat Lai
January 2010

When evaluating children for the presence of Parental Alienation, it is not just a single response that will acknowledge this abuse, but a pattern of responses. The list of questions in this document is only suggested questions that could be used with children of varying ages. Not all questions need to be asked, nor do they need to be asked in this format. Not all questions will be useable in all circumstances. For example, if a child has been alienated from the other parent since a very young age, they will not have any recollection of the targeted parent at all. This must be taken into account, as all answers related to memories will solely come back with only the Alienating parent having been there for them. These are only suggestions for types of questions that will illicit answers to help evaluate the existence, or non-existence as well as the extent/level of existence of PAS.

For most kids.
1. Do you think you look like your Mom or your Dad?

2. Are your eyes the same color as your Mom or your Dad?

3. What do you like to do to make your Mom smile?

4. What do you like to do to make your Dad smile?

5. What is your favorite food? Is that your Dad's or your Mother's favorite food?

6. If you were hurt in school, would you want your Mom or your Dad to pick you up?

7. If you had a booboo/cut or injury -- what would your Dad say -- what would your Mom say?

8. Do you think it is OK to say bad things about your Mom or Dad?

9. How do you feel if you say bad things about Mom or Dad?

10. What is the best and worst thing about a divorce?

11. Who do you think loves you?

12. Who do you love?

13. Do you think it is OK to hate anyone?

14. Are you happy or sad?

15. When anyone says bad things about someone, how do you feel about that?

16. When is it OK to say something bad about someone?

17. What is your best memory of your mom? Your dad?

Once the evaluator has the child's confidence and trust, this next question is very important as it tells us what the child believes the other parent would say and often indicates exact wordage from that parent.

1) What would your mom/dad say if you asked to live with your other (targeted) Parent?

For Younger children but might work with older as well:
2) What are some of your first memories that you can remember?

Where Did I Go Wrong? How Did I Miss The Signs?

    3) Who is it that you can remember first kissing your cut or bruise?

    4) Do you remember Mommy and Daddy tucking you in at night?

    5) Do you ever remember having a bad dream? Who was it that you went to?

    6) Tell me how you learned to ride a bike.

    7) Who helped you learn your alphabet?

    8) Do you remember going to the park, who did you go with?

    9) What is your favorite game, who plays that with you?

    10) When you were sick and went to the Dr, who would rock you...

    11) Do you like hugging your mom? Your dad?

For an older child:

    12) In a perfect world, what would your world be like?

    13) What do you do when you're happy?

    14) What do you do when you're sad?

    15) What do you do when you're angry?

    16) What do you do when you hate?

    17) Does anyone at school make you laugh? Why?

    18) Does anyone at school make you sad? Why?

19) Does anyone at school make you angry? Why?

20) Do you hate anyone at school? Why?

21) Is it all right to hate? Why?

22) Who else do you hate? Why?

Evaluating the level of independence vs. control a child is allowed...

23) Does your Mom or your Dad let you go over to your friends house?

24) Do you spend the night with friends?

25) Are there any friends, your parents do NOT let you spend time with and why?

26) With the friends, that you can spend time with, when you spend the night, do they spend the night at your house or do you spend the night at your friend's house?

27) Do you walk or ride over to your friend's house?

28) When was the last time you saw your other parent?

29) So what do you and your _____(parent that child is NOT alienated from/the aggressive parent) do for fun? When was that? Is there anywhere else that you go?

Though many of these questions are to elicit specific facts such as if the abundance of outings are to amusement parks or other vacation type outings as well as the timing of these outings in relation to the targeted parent, the majority of these questions are just suggestions and ideas of ways to determine the depth of the alienation. But they might even be helpful in helping a child to critically think and maybe put 2+2 together.

CHAPTER 29

SOLVING FOR HAP/PAS USING A PREVENTION AND INTERVENTION PROGRAM

JUSTIFYING A PREVENTION AND INTERVENTION PROGRAM FOR HAP & PAS

Please Note: The following chapter is more technical than all the other chapters. You may need to read it several times to absorb it all, so do not worry if you do not get it all at once.

Back during my Graduate workdays, I was asked to read a book by Mark Hubble, the Heart and Soul of Change. It brought many issues to the surface that are important to me. For example, from letting the client be more involved in the theoretical and practical process; to the theory of hope and encouragement; to the importance of a strong therapeutic bond; to understanding that everyone is different and no one method works for everyone and that change is possible. Critiquing this text gave me food for thought but I would like to hone in on just one small Hubble aspect that of the Proactive Therapeutic interventions in Chapter 8 on page 250-251, especially in relation to divorce and the family courts.

A proactive intervention according to Hubble involves the therapist actively bringing the program to the client rather than being beholden to the "wait-till-they-come" attitude. (Hubble. P.250) By this he is implying that if we can extend the olive branch out that has the olives already on it, offering them the food for thought and change, that people will grab hold of this fruit and devour it for salvation. If we can bring an offer of hope in a special program designed for them, that this is equal to or better than waiting around for the client to finally realize they need help. Thus we are actively seeking out clients who we can help to make positive changes in their lives. Hubble uses the example of addictive behaviors to show the cause and effect of an intervention program that is proactive on page 250. But what if we could use this process to prevent psychological abuse of children in high conflict divorce situations?

It is becoming a more commonplace problem in a divorce or separation situation, to see one parent alienate and denigrate the other parent in front of the children, to the point that children refuse to have a relationship with the targeted parent. Behavior such as this causes severe psychological trauma to the innocent children and even the targeted parent. This phenomenon has many names but is most often referred to as Parental Alienation Syndrome (PAS), Hostile Aggressive Parenting (HAP) or just simply Alienation. But what if we could be proactive and develop tools that could predict those parents who were at a higher risk of committing HAP and PAS, so that a preventative program could be offered or court ordered to change this high-risk behavior?

It is my belief that with the test/questionnaire and/or list of 167 Red Flag behaviors I have created, that this could be administered to divorcing/separating parents, and thus predetermine the likelihood of a parent committing PAS. And with these tools, there is a pretty good chance that we could stop this epidemic. This type of proactive approach brings the program to the people, instead of waiting for the abuse to occur and then trying to back track the psychological traumas. These tools could track parents with a higher propensity or score who would be characterized as having a potential to alienate and destroy the children's relationship with the other parent. With this knowledge, Hubble's idea of proactive interventions would enable the courts and counselors to help place these high risk parents in a cognitive/behavioral preventative program to change their thought patterns and behavior.

The Hubble text backs up this contention on page 250, when the authors make an interesting comparison between

Where Did I Go Wrong? How Did I Miss The Signs?

proactive and reactive therapy. The theory, which is partially backed up by studies, revealed that when a program is brought to the people, rather than waiting for them to come to the therapist, the positive results were equal to if not higher in it's success rate for improvement. That is to say, that going to the people and intervening before the issue got to a harder to manage state, worked as well if not better than just sitting around and waiting for the bomb to drop.

From this perspective, one can take the position that by predetermining those parents who are more likely to alienate their children from the other spouse, a preventative program can be developed to meet the families immediate needs to change distorted thoughts and behavior patterns before it is too late for the children and other victims. A simple scaled test/questionnaire or list of behaviors would be the best first line of inquisition to preliminarily determine which parents might be at risk. Using a liken-scaled test of 30 questions with responses ranging from strongly agree to strongly disagree, and with highest potential for risky behavior scoring a 5 and lowest risky behavior scoring a 1, we could easily calculate a parents risk factor and degree from questions that illicit red flags. In other words, questions would be phrased so that responding more often with answers valued at a 5 would produce a higher risk level score. Thus a score of 30-39 is a very low risk, while a score of between 40-60 means a mild risk, a score of 60-90 is a moderate risk, a score of 90-120 is high risk and over 120 is definitely a parent who will do anything and everything to interfere with the children and other parents relationship and rights. Once administered, any parents with a moderate to high risk potential could then be administered a more thought probing questionnaire which would further help the courts and therapists to determine the appropriate type of therapy for change, as well, the secondary questionnaire could illicit why they responded the way they did.

Another tool is a list of red flag behaviors in an excel format worksheet that allows a targeted/alienated parent to mark off the number of times that a particular event has occurred. A score of more than 10 would indicate a propensity for alienating behaviors that would put the children at risk of psychological abuse.

The severity of Alienation and Hostile Aggressive Parenting issues warrants serious consideration of this proactive intervention. Alienation of the children from the other parent can have tragic life-long psychological and physical consequences for the children, which are passed on from generation to generation. Since children are like sponges, absorbing every piece of information out there for them to learn about negotiating life, whether appropriate or not, if all they hear are derogatory comments about the other parent, then this is how they learn about intimate relationships and their fear of abandonment is exasperated if they do not agree with the alienating parent's point of view. If we can avoid the psychological abuse from happening by preventing the parents from perpetrating it, then we are stopping generations of children from growing up in severe emotional pain and confusion. As well, with proactive therapeutic intervention, we have a chance to stop a tragic chain of events from robbing our children of love, happiness and a relationship with both parents but most of all the positive memories of childhood with both parents.

For this reason, Hubble's theory of proactive intervention merits serious consideration especially by family courts, counselors and judges so as to further prevent the agony of divorce. Preventative medicine is the best medicine I know of. And preventing the psychological abuse of children with the simple administration of a test could be the answer to many divorcing family's problems and the overburdened caseload of the Family Courts.

On the following pages is my Prevention Intervention Program Initiative developed as Proactive approach to solving for Hostile Aggressive Parenting (HAP) and Parental Alienation Syndrome (PAS). You may notice various elements that have already been discussed previously but they are all part of this program. This work is in constant change and growth, so ideas and comments are always welcome to the development of this project.

Where Did I Go Wrong? How Did I Miss The Signs?

PREVENTION INTERVENTION PROGRAM INITIATIVE (PIPI)

For Divorcing Families and High Conflict Divorce (HCD) a preventative intervention approach program for Divorce Initiated psychological abuse to help families, courts, counselors and attorney's to work in a positive democratic manner for the benefit of all involved.

Purpose: To provide a low cost and where applicable free counseling for families of divorce, while equipping the courts, counselors, agencies, attorneys and families with a more suitable program of dealing with high conflict divorces that involve custody, visitation and child support.

Today's courts are torn with knowing how to protect the children of divorce and protecting the parents' rights. Everyone wants to do the right thing, but no one is willing to do it by working together. They all seem to be on a different page. While child support enforcement is doing one thing, family court is doing something else, and in the meanwhile, family court services is completely left out of the loop and the parents and their attorney's are on completely different wave lengths. We need to pull everyone in together so that we are all working on the issues as a team. This should be a democratic team effort so that more can be accomplished for the good of all, monetarily, emotionally and in a timely fashion.

Unless we break this chain of events caused by HCD, it will waste enormous amounts of resources such as time and money because of the emotional roller coaster that these children will have to ride to finally get to the realization of the lies and the genuineness of the other parents love for them. Probably hardest of all will be the AP's unwillingness to be treated, which then spreads to the children. If the AP refuses treatment it can completely devastate any chance of recovery for the children. Though in most cases, counseling is court ordered for the children, the Alienated Parent and the TP, the AP will refuse to go or will do everything in their power to prevent the children from attending. At this point, it is important for the abusive parent to find specialized counseling or they will continue their tirade of hatred through the children. If the courts would just comply with their own court orders, fines and consequences for any violations, it would be a deterrent for the offending parent. A combative and resistant AP, who constantly refuses to be treated or cooperate should send up red flags for everyone involved to question whether the children are in the right parental home where a healthy relationship between both parents can be nurtured.

PREVENTION AND INTERVENTION PROGRAM INITIATIVE (PIPI)

The Prevention and Intervention Program Initiative (PIPI) was developed to deal with the growing problem of parents destroying their children's relationship with the other parent during a separation and divorce. With a growing body of evidence supporting the destruction of these relationships it was felt that more needed to be done to help prevent and intervene before the "alienation" and Cross-generational Coalition destroyed the children lives and the lives of the targeted parent. I personally began my research into this area of psychological maltreatment 12 years ago, but it has been a problem for well over 20 years as evidenced by Dr. Gardner who coined the name Parental Alienation Syndrome to describe the behavior patterns of children who are forced to detach from the targeted parent by the alienating parent. With over 200 peer review articles on the subject, the passing of the Frye Test in Court and recent recognition in more and more courts, it is time to find a solution that will prevent and intervene to keep the trauma of divorce to a minimum.

Positive and Negative Approaches

Negativity seems to abound when the word divorce, custody, visitation and courts are mentioned. With 50% of marriages ending in divorce, we need to stop seeing it as a negative enactment. Instead we need to find the positive implications of these words. We need to implement programs and practices that breed positive attitudes. If we attempt to look at things in an Appreciative Inquiry (AI) way, we increase the support and probability of success for the families and the system.

Where Did I Go Wrong? How Did I Miss The Signs?

AI is four-stage program, which begins with the Discovery stage, and progresses to the Dream and Design stage and culminates in Destiny. Basically it breaks down as bringing the whole team together to discover the positives, dreaming clear thought out solutions, designing and planning solutions and then creating a positive destination that produces strength and power to believe the job can be accomplished. It is a way of putting a positive light on situations, which normally would be viewed as terminal. It is a way of pulling all the pieces and parts together to work as a fully functioning unit with specific positive goals in mind. And it finishes with a resounding chorus of rejoicing as everyone works together toward a common held belief in the positive initiatives they have developed together.

To look at Divorce positively, one must first understand that a failed marriage is not about failing in life but about life changes and growing apart. It is about a new stage in their life, much like going from being an infant to a toddler, from a toddler to a pre-juvenile, from a pre-juvenile to juvenile, from juvenile to adolescent, from adolescent to young adult, from young adult to adult and adult to elder. Through out this entire process we are growing, learning and going through emotional, physical and personal changes.

In addition, it is important to realize that when marriage was instituted people did not live much past the age of 35. Today people live into their 70's, 80's and 90's and even 100's. And that means marriages must last for nearly 50 years or more, not 15 years. This puts a lot of pressure on the two adults to continue to love, honor, cherish and continue to grow together. If we do not grow and learn together in the marriage, then we grow apart. But this is not necessarily bad.

If we look at divorce as just being another step or stage in our life cycle, then we can view it as just another process in our aging. It should be a time for growth, letting go and moving on. It can be a time for us to explore things we dared not do while married. It can be a time to find new partnerships and relationships, which are more compatible with whom we have matured into. And for our children it is a chance to gain new relatives and extended family members. It is a chance to increase our networking potential and have more family and friends to communicate, count on and even get the other necessary ingredients that make up their our hierarchy of needs.

With divorce being so prevalent and the ravages so detrimental, it just stands to reason that we need to find another way of understanding and accepting this new change in our lives, without making it into a horrific event. If we can change our attitude to see Divorce as a stepping-stone to the next level or stage in our life, it will open up endless doors of opportunity for all involved.

Presently, one of the biggest issues we are seeing in the courts is the negative attitude that develops when one parent interferes with the relationship between the children and the other parent. This bitterly destructive behavior is also called Hostile Aggressive Parenting (HAP), which is the precursor to a mental disorder that develops in children who are victims of this abuse. (http://familyconflict.freeyellow.com/General1/Recommendation sHostile-AggressiveParenting.pdf)

As this behavior takes hold and wreaks havoc on the children and the targeted parent, it produces Parental Alienation Syndrome or Cross-generational Coalitions. This negative perspective overtakes the whole divorce proceeding process as it wastes tremendous amounts of money, time and resources while ignoring the best interests of the children. The problem is compounded when the courts refuse to penalize the parents who are isolating the children from the other parent or when child support enforcement thinks that throwing more money from one parent to the other will resolve the problem. The situation breeds nothing but negatives and animosity for all involved. This is where Appreciative Inquiry may be useful. If we can refocus the view of the divorce in a positive light, working to make everyone feel and respond positively and responsibly then we are on the first step toward preventing the alienation from occurring. Part of the process of doing this is to understand clearly what PAS is, the signs, the symptoms and how to prevent it.

PAS or Parental Alienation Syndrome Defined

Dr. Richard Gardner, of Cresskill, NJ, a child psychologist, was one of the leading authorities on children of dysfunctional families. What he found in his research is that no

Where Did I Go Wrong? How Did I Miss The Signs?

matter the financial or cultural background, alienation of one parent from the other could occur. (www.rgardner.com, now owned by Dr. Richard Warshak)

According to Dr. Gardner, PAS is described as "a disturbance in which children are obsessively preoccupied with depreciation and/or criticism of a parent, in other words, denigration that is unjustified and or exaggerated." (www.familycourts.com/pas.htm). PAS is the erosion of the relationship between the children and a once loved parent using a very slow and insidious behavior that at first just seems minor but ultimately eats away at the relationship, bit by bit, until the damage is permanent. (Threlfall, Penny) In effect, these children are taught to hate the other parent to the point of wanting to eliminate them from their lives. This type of parental behavior is called Hostile Aggressive Parenting or HAP. Dr. Gardner considers this psychological abuse and it is the only form of psychological abuse that has clear-cut unmistakable signs, symptoms and behaviors by the alienating spouse, therefore the only psychological abuse that can be easily diagnosed. (Chapter 22. Kloth-Zanard, List of Behaviors Exhibited by Alienating/Hostilely Aggressive parents) PAS or Parental Alienation Syndrome can also be classified as Domestic Violence in the Form of Psychological Maltreatment. (Chapter 3: Kloth-Zanard)

PAS can be further described as a form of psychological kidnapping (www.familycourts.com/pas.htm) where the child's mind has been forced to prejudicially believe and discriminate against the other parent. This is perpetrated by creating fear, not of the outsider parent, but of the parent whom the child must reside with, or as Gardner calls it, the "hostage taker" parent. (www.familycourts.com/pas.htm) It has also been compared to the Stockholm Syndrome and best exampled with the Patti Hearst kidnapping. (http://www.yahoodi.com/peace/stockholm.html) And all of this leads to a fear of abandonment.

PAS's behaviors, signs and symptoms are so classic and straightforward, that there is little discrepancy in a properly trained professionals mind when PAS is in existence. The following is a more comprehensive list of sign, symptoms and behaviors exhibited by children that I have compiled (from websites and information by Richard Gardner, Deirdre Conway-Rand and the Divorce Source) of the most basic signs and symptoms of PAS. (www.R.Gardener.com, Covey-Rand, www.robin.no/~dadwatch.pasdir/rand01.html & Dishon, A., http://divorcesource.com/info/questions/visitation.shtml)

1. A campaign of denigration against the Target Parent (TP) with no real substance. Also seen as relentless hatred for/towards the TP.
2. Weak, absurd, or frivolous rationalizations for the deprecation of the TP to the point of delusional and irrational.
3. Animosity toward the TP lacks the ambivalence, which is normal to human behavior.
4. The "independent thinker" phenomenon where in the child asserts that the decision to reject the TP is his or her own.
5. The child reasons for not wanting to visit or spend any time with the TP are obscure and not even of a threatening nature.
6. Impulsive support of the AP (Alienating Parent) who is impeding the relationships in the parental conflict. In fact, they are totally enmeshed with the AP.
7. Absence of guilt over cruelty to and/or exploitation of the Alienated Parent.
8. The presence of borrowed scenarios such as the child's statements reflects themes and terminology of the AP. In fact, they have difficulty making any differentiation between their experiences and the APs.
9. Spread of the animosity to the friends and/or extended family of the Alienated Parent.
10. They can appear like normal healthy, even studious children until asked about the TP, which triggers their hatred.

The Alienating parent, on the other hand, will exhibit quite different behaviors, signs and symptoms. Their behavior is described as hostile and aggressive toward the other parent or anyone who is friends, family or agrees with the other parent. The following examples of Alienators behavior are called Red

Where Did I Go Wrong? How Did I Miss The Signs?

Flags. The more of these a parent exhibits or enacts, the higher the probability PAS will or is occurring. (This is only a partial list. See Chapter 22 for a more complete list.)

1. Impeding with visitation, despite orders
2. Denigrating the other parent in front of anyone who will listen, including the children, as well as calling the TP or stepparent derogatory names in front of the child.
3. Filing allegations of abuse while constantly dragging the ex into court for child support or alimony. (Note: A truly abused individual wants to have nothing to do with the abuser, making face-to-face confrontation out of the question. See stats in Chapter 12)
4. Stopping any contact with the children and the ex's extended family or friends who disagree with them
5. Believing that they are above the law, and that all orders/laws were made for everyone else but them.
6. Impeding Communication with the children, including blocking access to school records and meetings and events.
7. Grilling the children about their visit, asking the children to spy or collect evidence.
8. Refusing visitation because the ex spouse has been unable to afford the child support or not made a payment.
9. Statements of constant hatred and vengeance about the ex-spouse
10. Refusal to disclose their home address
11. Refusal to supply or keep the other parent in the loop on medical issues, educational issues, events pertaining to the child/ren and so on.
12. Continually referring to the child as their own children and not the spouses.
13. Continually not enforcing the visitation with the other parent by claiming the children do not want to go (Barring no true abuse is truly going on) and using the excuse that they are not going to force the children to go see their other parent if they do not want to.

14. Impeding any court orders, including Counseling orders.
15. Moving the children away from a parent they once had a loving relationship with, and thus making visitation and a relationship next to impossible.
16. During visitation times, constantly calling the house, to speak with the child/ren or leaving nasty disruptive messages.
17. On days that TP is in a public place the parent shows up to push, swear at or just intimidate them or the stepparent in front of the child.
18. Making the child feel emotional responsible for the parent's happiness so that the child is as protective as an adult might be towards a young child.
19. Lying or even involving the child in the divorce proceedings and custody or child support issues.
20. Making the child feel uneasy about talking to their therapist or other official person.
21. Having the child call his non-custodial parent by their first name; instead of Daddy or Mommy
22. Preventing the children from contacting their father by pulling the phone out of the wall, changing their phone number, refusing to allow them to accept calls, refusing to allow them to make phone calls or lying and claiming the children are not home or are asleep.
23. Discussing and involving the children in court, child support and other legal matters, which they should not be involved in.

Further Red Flags have been compiled in a list of over 167 typical tactics used by one parent to alienate the children from the other parent. These have been taken from countless cases and documentaries of parents whose relationship with their children has been impeded by the other parent. For the complete list, see Chapter 22.)

In addition, the psychological affects upon the children range from Attachment disorder; to fear of abandonment; to Dissociative Personality; to Emotional Neglect by the Alienator. The last in this list, emotional neglect, which can only be

Where Did I Go Wrong? How Did I Miss The Signs?

considered as one thing, abuse, forces these kids to endure the most horrific of abuses as it is inside of them and they cannot put a finger on. They cannot put a Band-Aid on. They cannot even control it because it is being controlled by one of their parents. This leads to attachment disorder (DSM Diagnosis 313.89) along with Acute Distress Disorder (DSM 308.3), where in the children never form proper relationships or attachments with their primary caregivers, which leads to inability to appropriately behave socially. They never quite get what the normal procedure or process for responding and reacting to significant others is supposed to be and thus impedes their ability to communicate appropriately with others in the real world.

Tack on their fear of abandonment. This fear is not just the fear of the alienating parent hurting them or abandoning them, but the fear that if they get to close to the Targeted parent, that they will leave them too like they left the alienator in the marriage when it broke up.

But probably the worst of these is that 10% of these kids develop Dissociative Personalities. The children actually detach themselves from the real world, creating alter personalities and lives for themselves. It is the only way they have to escape from the trauma of being caught between their two parents and wanting to be part of both parents lives but are too afraid to say anything. And this brings us back full circle to their fear. These psychological damages to the children are devastating and in some cases irreparable. We need to stop this before more children are permanently harmed.

Impact and Effects of PAS and Hostile Aggressive Parenting on the Children

Recently the Massachusetts General Hospital (MGH) conducted a research project on the effects of High Conflict divorce on the children. What they discovered was an overwhelming and profound impact on the children's emotional well-being. It did not matter the age of the child, the anxiety of divorce is overwhelming. In their minds, no matter the age, the children think, if Mommy and Daddy no longer love each other, then will they stop loving me too? This fear ultimately leads to anxiety, which invariably can cause an emotional meltdown at various levels. MGH also discovered that the more the parents fought or where at odds with each other, the more intense or disturbed the children became mentally and emotionally. And the more disturbed and upset the children became, the more their emotional wellbeing was affected. The following are the statistical results from MGH's project on the Impact of High Conflict Divorce on Children:

- 65% had anxiety severe enough to require therapy
- 56% Developed Attachment disorder;
- 48% had abnormal fears and phobias;
- 44% of both boys and girls became physically aggressive;
- 31% had sleep disorders
- 29% withdrew from activities including ones that they loved to do
- 24% developed opposition defiant behavior, including temper tantrums and uncontrolled outbursts
- 21% prematurely became involved in sexual activity
- 13% began bed wetting
- 10% developed dissociative personality disorders (once known as multiple personality disorders)

Amy J. Baker backs this up with her research in her article, The Cult of Parenthood: A Qualitative Study of Parental Alienation, Cultic Studies Review and her book, Adult Children of Parental Alienation Syndrome – Breaking the Ties that Bind (2007). Ms. Baker's research and interviews of 38 adults who were victims of PAS as children revealed seven (7) precedents about the effects of PAS. Furthermore as Baker points out, these abused interviewees suffered lifelong pain as a result of being alienated from a once loved parent (36). Ms. Baker's results from her interviews are as follows:

- High rates of low self-esteem to a point of self-hatred
- 70% of the adults suffered with serious depression episodes in their adult life.
- 30% had substance abuse problems with drugs and alcohol

Where Did I Go Wrong? How Did I Miss The Signs?

- 42% had trust issues with themselves and/or others
- 50% were alienated from their own children, thus proving that PAS is multigenerational
- 66% had been divorced and of those 25% was divorced more than once
- And the last pattern was Identity issues

Dr. F. L. Lowenstein of Southern England Psychology Services describes the problems that children of PAS suffer. His list includes:
- Anger
- Loss or lack of impulse control in conduct
- Loss of self confidence and self esteem
- Clinging in separation anxiety
- Developing fears and phobias
- Depression and suicidal ideation
- Sleep disorders
- Eating disorders
- Educational problems
- Enuresis
- Encopresis
- Drug abuse
- Self destructive behavior
- Obsessive compulsive behavior
- Anxiety and panic attacks
- Damaged sexual identity problems
- Poor peer relationships
- Excessive feelings of quilt.

What this means is that these children are loosing the battle to have a normal life. Because of the anxiety disorder, which leads to attachment disorders, they never learn how to have a normal emotional relationship with others. If the fighting continues, the child has no choice but to spiral out of control becoming more and more anti-social in their behavior and responses. Ultimately, if the war is not ended, these children can and will end up with personal and mental problems for the rest of their lives. This is why it is so important for parents to put aside their differences, anger and need for retaliation/revenge. This is why PIPI, Prevention and Intervention Program Initiative is so important. If we can get to these parents before this happens, then we can stop the ravages of high conflict divorce on the children.

The Courts, Court Orders and PAS

Proper education of the court, judges, counselors, agencies and attorney's of the signs, symptoms and proper process for dealing with a non-compliant parent is very important at this point. So for example, though in most cases, counseling is court ordered for the children and TP, it is often only recommended for the AP and even when court ordered, the AP will refuse to go or will do everything in their power to prevent the children from attending. PAS would not be so difficult to solve if everyone was willing to cooperate. The AP's unwillingness to be treated is probably the hardest part of solving for PAS because they spread this negativity to the children. If the AP refuses treatment it can completely devastate any chance of recovery for the children. It is also important at this point for the abusive parent to be court ordered into specialized counseling or they will continue their tirade of hatred through the children, even if it means having the court mandate it with strict penalties for non-compliance.

In addition, the present trend in the courts is to not penalize and force the offending alienating parent to comply with the court's orders. If the courts would comply with their own orders utilizing the legal remedies afforded by the law, it would be a deterrent for the offending parent to violate the orders. Too many alienating parents know that the courts will do nothing about their anti-social behavior and so continue to assault the children mentally. And unfortunately, these cases remain in family court were there seems to be no penalties for violations of court orders. (See Chapter 18, Kloth-Zanard, Penalties to Include...)

It is also important for the courts to recognize the signs of parents who are at a higher risk of impeding the children's relationship with the other parent. For example, a combative and resistant AP, who constantly refuses to be counseled or cooperate with court orders, should send up red flags for everyone involved

Where Did I Go Wrong? How Did I Miss The Signs?

to question whether the children are in the right parental home where a healthy relationship between both parents can be nurtured. And when this same alienating parent claims that they are actually encouraging the relationship and have moved on, yet, refuse to be in the same room with the other parent and children to apologize for their behavior, quite clearly, this parent is using lip service and has not moved on. Unless we break this chain of events, it utilizes all the resources of time and money because of the emotional roller coaster that these children will have to ride. With the courts present position of not penalizing the offending parent, the courts are inadvertently helping to manifest PAS in the children.

The courts, children's attorneys and Guardian Ad Litems involvement should establish authority over the offending parent. In this way, it is recognized as officially the prevailing or final word and thus supersedes the offending parents influence. And it warns this parent that their actions are being monitored. This authoritarian influence of public officials also tells the children that it is the courts making the orders and that these orders must be followed, no matter what the other parent says. It also solves a very important issue for the children, that of allegiance to one parent over the other. This gives the children permission to love the other parent unconditionally.

Preventative Measures Lead to Specialized Programs

Since 1997, I have been working on a program, which incorporates short test/questionnaires to help determine the parents who are at a higher risk of using Parental Alienation (PA), Hostile Aggressive Parenting (HAP) and Cross-Generational Coalitions. This type behavior ultimately leads to a broken relationship between the children and another parent known as PAS (Parental Alienation Syndrome). These are simple tests that could be administered by trained professionals in either the courts, counseling settings or through other qualified agencies at the commencement of separation and divorce proceedings. And even if a parent answers the liken-scaled questions appropriately, it is their essay answers that shows if there are discrepancies, such as the parent knowing the right answer but choosing to do otherwise by sighting false excuses.

The first test developed by Alison Benitz, is a short 12-question test about parenting practices. (See Chapter 2) It starts the process of determining appropriate and inappropriate parental behavior patterns. This test is the 1st key indicator of Red Flags (See Chapter 22), if answered honestly. The next or 2nd Test/Questionnaire is a bit more in depth with essay questions to help determine the validity of the liken-scaled questions. (See Chapter 28) When a parent answers a question one way but makes excuses for not doing it that way in the essay with no proof, basis or compromising solution, this is a red flag, and means that parent knows their behavior is wrong but makes excuses, often blaming it on everyone else.

This 2nd Test Questionnaire consists of 30 Questions plus 3 essay questions, which allow the parent a range of 5 possible answers from Strongly agree, Agree, Neutral, Disagree and Strongly Disagree. Depending on the question, each answer would have a score from 1 to 5, along with several essay style questions that further determine the validity of their answers. A parent scoring from 60 to 70 would indicate a slight risk for perpetrating HAP or PAS or creating difficulties during the divorce. While a parent scoring 71 to 90 would indicate a higher risk for impeding the relationships. And where as a parent scoring 90 and above is at a progressively higher risk of interfering and committing PAS. An added idea is for each parent to also score the other parent on each of these questions.

Once a score is determined for each parent, including new spouses, in the family, those with higher scores would then be referred to a special counseling program designed specifically for parents who are at a risk of committing PAS or HAP. This special counseling program would have a first main goal of helping to put a positive light on the divorce/separation while assisting the alienating/abusive parent/s to deal with their own demons and feelings of low self-esteem and low self-worth and loss of their spousal relationship. The test question responses would help the counselor to explore with the parent the reasoning for their answers. This helps the patient gain insight into the dysfunctional or distorted thought patterns and processes. It is thus a way to change perception to a more healthy way of thinking and responding.

Where Did I Go Wrong? How Did I Miss The Signs?

In the same way, it would then help the TP, Targeted Parent, to learn how to deal with the abusive parent. Instead of antagonizing them, they would learn to understand why the Alienating Parent responds the way they do and to give the TP the tools to assist the children as well. (See Amy Baker's, Beyond the High Road, www.amyjlbaker.com) The program would further help the children to gain the knowledge and tools necessary to negotiate the anger and hostility of the parent or parents in the divorce as well as help the innocent extended families that have been dragged into this custody mess by stopping the projection upon them. And most important to all, it would help everyone get on with living happy healthy lives as individuals, families and extended families.

In addition to these tools, in Chapter 28, there is an additional evaluation questionnaire created with the help of my support groups members to determine if a child is alienated or being affected by the alienation attempts.

A Venn of a Democratic View and the Preferred Model

Taking this one step further, we can apply Doherty's model of a Democratic View to explain how the whole process could work. Using a Venn diagram, (see figure 1), it can be visualized as three circles with three sub-circles in each. The Left hand circle would be entitled "The Family" and would include three inner circles entitled the Mom(and her extended Family), Dad (and his extended family) and the Children. The Right hand Circle would be entitled "The Professionals" and would include three circles labeled the Attorneys, Counselors/Therapists and Agencies. The third or lower circle would be entitled "The Courts" with three sub-circles called Family Relations, Child Support Enforcement and Criminal/Civil courts. This brings the family's entire divorcing world together under one "Doherty" Democratic roof. (See figure. 1 on following page) This model helps to keep everyone on the same page of the process, and thus a united front. Furthermore, I have honed my direction for this program using the Preferred Model with the use of Cognitive Behavior Theories. (See figure. 2 on following page)

Figure 1

[Diagram showing overlapping circles: Family (containing Mother & Family, Father & Family, Children), Professionals (containing Counselors and Therapists, Attorneys, Agencies), and Courts (containing Family Relations, Child Support Enforcement, Civil and Criminal Court).]

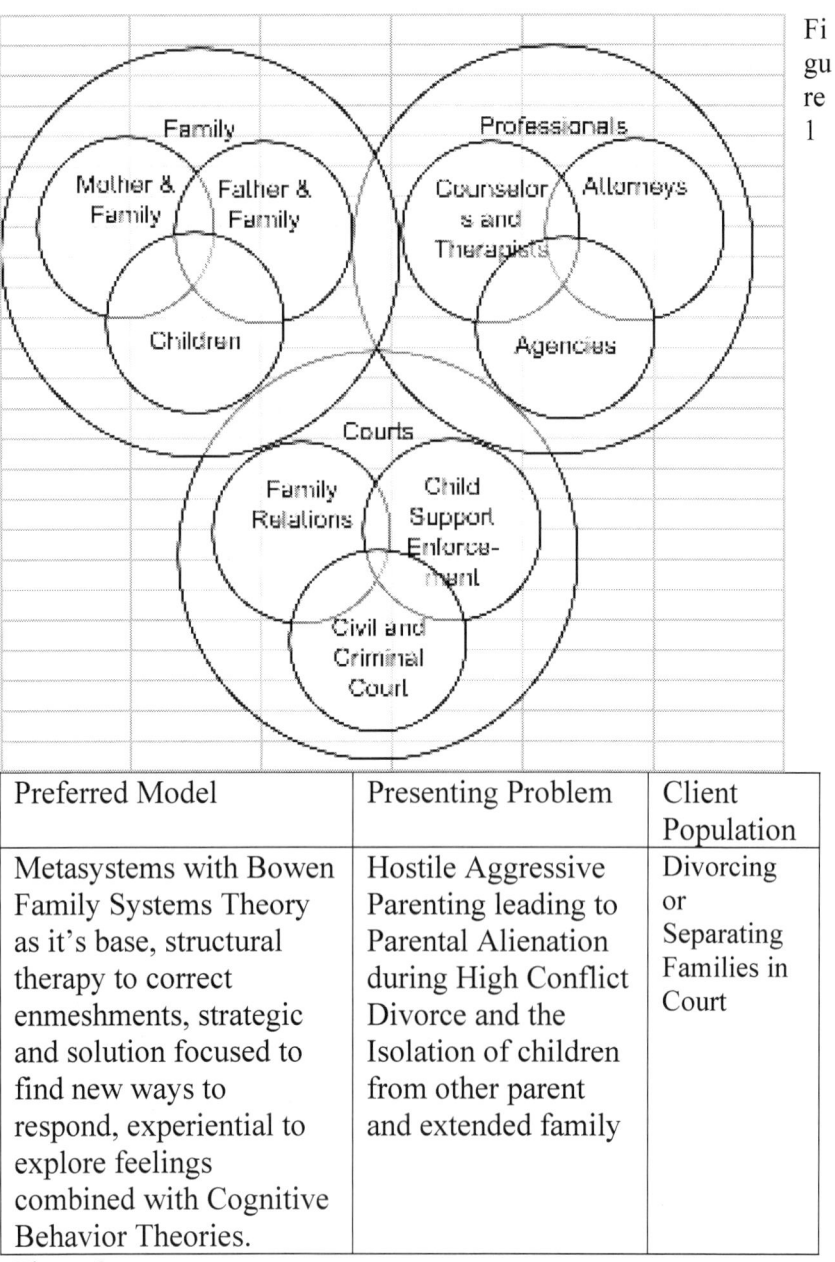

Preferred Model	Presenting Problem	Client Population
Metasystems with Bowen Family Systems Theory as it's base, structural therapy to correct enmeshments, strategic and solution focused to find new ways to respond, experiential to explore feelings combined with Cognitive Behavior Theories.	Hostile Aggressive Parenting leading to Parental Alienation during High Conflict Divorce and the Isolation of children from other parent and extended family	Divorcing or Separating Families in Court

Figure 2

Where Did I Go Wrong? How Did I Miss The Signs?

A Metasystems Approach

Though much of the emphasis for creating a working counseling program for victims of PAS is based on Bowen Family Systems Therapy (BFST), it was realized that BFST, though an asset, does not work for every situation, especially since it brings up some pretty deep and heavy things in our lives. Through my studies it became apparent that a multitude of techniques combined with BFST seems to be the best answer. Bowen Family Systems Therapy was initially used as a basis especially for the parents because it helps them to differentiate themselves from the very enmeshed relationships that may have developed between them, their parents and the children. It is also believed that BFST when used with the parents helps them to put their own lives in perspective and start to differentiate themselves from the issues at hand and their own parental relationship problems. However, the children might benefit more from structural therapy to understand the enmeshed relations and crossed boundaries while learning new ways of reacting and dealing with the stresses.

In the same token, in order to accomplish this, it was felt that many of the techniques of the other theorists compliment the Bowenian process, such as the strategic, solution-focused and structural strategies, including Gestalt chair, Play Acting, Miracle Questions, Sculpting, Anger Management, Mapping or Genogramming and so on. Since every family unit is unique and thus it's members are unique, we need to consider their traits, assets and behavior patterns when choosing the appropriate method to work with them. For example, some people are more auditory thus responding better when they can hear everything rather than the visual person, who needs to see everything. Others need more behavior modifications than cognitive awakenings. By knowing our clients better, we can better detail a program that will fit them.

Types of Treatments

It is very important to note that the aggressive parent or alienator is usually expressing some kind of anger and fear directed at the targeted parent based on control. They realize that their ex-spouse no longer loves them unconditionally, while expressing unconditional love for their children. As well, there may be some perceived transgression, whether real or imagined, the aggressive parent feels has been done to them.

In an article by Lisa Pisha published in Family Therapy Magazine (Pisha, January/February 2009), she discusses how children emulate the fear that their parents model for them. Parents control how children "handle or mishandle" fear as well as the manifestation of those fears. In other words, an alienating parent fears the loss of their ex spouse and thus fears loss of their children. These parents instill that same fear into the children, that they will loose the other parent's love because the alienator has lost the other parent's love. In addition, how the alienator handles that fear is passed down to the children as to how they handle the fear.

If we can get the courts to hear that the fears of loss is very real, but it is the parent's ability to handle and properly deal with it that is directly proportional to the children. The alienator needs to get counseling to overcome these fears and to learn how to appropriately manage them, so that they are not instilling the same fears into their children. With court intervention, we can better direct the type of counseling and treated so that it is specialized to deal with the low self-esteem and unrealistic fear of loosing their children because they lost their spouse.

The anger that afflicts these parents and stimulated by this fear is defined by Howard Kassinove at Hofstra University is:

"A negative, phenomenological (or internal) feeling state associated with specific cognitive and perceptual distortions and deficiencies (e.g. misappraisals, errors, and attributions of blame, injustice, preventability, and/or intentionality), subjective labeling, physiological changes, and action tendencies to engaged in socially constructed and reinforced organized behavior scripts." (Kassinove, 7) Furthermore there is *"a variance in the frequency, intensity, duration, pervasiveness and chronicity. "* (Kassinove, 47) *This behavior associated with anger is learned, reinforced and "refined" as to how we display it.* (Kassinove, 26)

Though Anger is not listed as a diagnosis in the DSM, several possible options are presently being used to describe and

Where Did I Go Wrong? How Did I Miss The Signs?

diagnose people with anger problems. Some of these are as follows: DSM 309.4 Adjustment Disorders with Mixed Disturbance of Emotions and Conduct, (APA, 679-683), DSM 301.7 Antisocial Personality Disorder (APA, 701-706), DSM 301.81 Narcissistic Personality Disorder, (APA, 714-717) Acute Distress Disorder (308.3), Attachment Disorder (313.89) and 301.9 (Personality Disorder NOS such as Passive Aggressive Personality Disorder, (APA, 729, 789-791).

Kassinove and his colleagues' research discovered that anger is not properly represented in the DSM but by expanding the definition of Adjustment Disorders to include Angry Mood disorders, a more accurate diagnosis could be made for persons experiencing this dysfunction. The categories they have come up with are Adjustment Disorder with Angry Mood, Situational Anger Disorder without Aggression, Situational Anger Disorder with Aggression, General Anger Disorder without Aggression and General Anger Disorder with Aggression. Kassinove and his colleagues have tried to separate anger from aggression by stating that aggression is indicated by a behavioral response or action. Bandura goes further in his definition to include verbal assaults or behaviors that though not physically assaulting are antisocial.

These are the stuff that many PAS cases are made of. Though no physical harm has occurred, the anger aggression from misinterpreted and perceived violations of a person leads to verbal and non-physical acts of disrespect and disregard for others and in turn harms those it is directed at and through. This aggressive action is clearly psychological and helps to further establish PAS as a form of Domestic Violence and abuse. (Kloth-Zanard, PAS or Parental Alienation Syndrome Defined in Domestic Violence Terms. Chapter 3)

Furthermore it is possible to classify PAS as DSM V62.89 or a Phase of Life Problem. The DSM IV TR describes this as the following:

> This category can be used when the focus of clinical attention is a problem associated with a particular developmental phase or some other life circumstance that is not due to a mental disorder or, if it is due to a mental disorder, is sufficiently severe to warrant independent clinical attention.

Examples include problems associated with entering school, leaving parental control, starting a new career, and changes involved in marriage, divorce, and retirement. (DSM IV TR, 742)

The complexity of this issue may require various techniques to resolve it with some models and styles of treatment available to combat psychological trauma having more merit in an abusive situation such as PAS. In addition, PAS seems to be triggered by low self-esteem especially for the abuser who also needs total control but does not deal well with the anger, anxiety and fears of loss, aloneness, not being loved, loss of control and so on, that accompany divorce. In fact, it seems that much of PAS is triggered by anger that cannot be controlled. It may not necessarily come out physically, but subtle aggressive techniques that can be classified as Hostile Aggressive Parenting.

In a recent article by Dr. Worth, a series of questions were developed to help determine where a parent's anger was coming from and how much they "desired" to deal with it. (Worth. 40-41) In addition, there are now several new tests available to determine the various types of anger. Some of them are as follows: State-Trait Anger Expression Inventory (STAXI) (Spielberger), Anger Response Scale (ARS) (Eckhardt, et.al), and Five Factor Model of Personality (FFM) such as NEO-Personality Inventory-Revised (NEO PI-R) (Costa & McCrae).

As noted previously, anger is not listed as a true disorder in the DSM. This leads to a major issue of classification of Anger, for the purposes of treatment and reimbursement of counseling services. Though this can be termed a "mood disorder not otherwise specified" (Worth. 40), it is rarely as simple as just one issue causing the problem and can stem from FOO or the Family of Origin learned behaviors.

The DSM IV does list "Intermittent Explosive Disorder" as a possible diagnosis but this does not cover for the psychological abusive person who subtly induces their anger toward the other parent through the children. Eckhardt and Deffenbacher do offer another criteria for organizing "pathological anger". (Worth, 41)

Where Did I Go Wrong? How Did I Miss The Signs?

Using a breakdown into five categories, it seems that it is easier to classify the type of anger a person exhibits. The categories, Adjustment Disorder with Angry Mood, Situational Anger Disorder without Aggression, Situational Anger Disorder with Aggression, General Anger Disorder without Aggression and General Anger Disorder with Aggression, are differentiated by the degrees and behaviors that can be exhibited by a person with these diagnosis's. A therapist can use these categories to help work with a client and tailoring where to direct their treatment.

Using this in relation to PAS, we see many parents angry with their ex, the divorce, their life and other issues that are now affecting them. Their natural response system they learned while growing up is not appropriate, thus causing them and the people around them severe pain and discomfort. Using both the PIPI Questionnaire, Alicen Benitz Test, along with the 10 questions posed by Dr. Worth, a therapist would be able to help the family and it's members break through the anger and get on with their lives in a healthy format by diagnosing the type of anger and their responses they presently use and exhibit to deal with this anger. With these tools, the ravages of High Conflict Divorce can be dealt with before they reach epidemic proportions.

In addition to these tools, the Relationship Belief Inventory (RBI), developed by Epstein and Eidelson as a test to determine a couple's different worldviews about relationships, would be of assistance with Pre-Divorce and Divorcing situations. (1981; Eidelson & Epstein, 1982) Furthermore, the Inventory of Specific Relationship Standards (ISRS) developed by Baucom, Epstein and their contemporaries to evaluate 12 standards (household tasks, leisure time use, sexual interactions, parenting, positive/negative communication) that individuals can be rated on in their relationship along with subscales related to boundaries, investment and power/control in the relationship could assist in diagnosis and treatment techniques. These tests would help a counselor and others to get a better picture of the relationship and how each person fits into their own version as well as their partner's version.

In addition to this medium, Ethnography, or the therapeutic idea of showing ethnic or cultural experiences, can be accomplished using stories, pictures, theatrical performances, tests, demonstrations or even poetry. These techniques have a very positive approach to teaching parents better ways of parenting and handling the difficulties of marriage and divorce. (Piercy and Kristen, 2005, 111-113) An idea might be to do a performance play depicting the cumulative distress of death, when a child is still alive but alienated from their parents and thus both sides can not grieve openly for fear of being ridiculed. (Piercy and Kristen, 2005, 113) In fact, Mad Elf Productions does a dramatic presentation about a family going through divorce. The show depicts a set of parent's inappropriate behaviors and how it affects the children, who in turn express their issues in their own way. A video or DVD documentary or live performance like this could be used to help a family explore and visualize better what is happening to them or could happen to them. Just as watching a movie has a dramatic affect on people, so might a presentation of this magnitude such as Dr. Warshak's DVD, Welcome Back Pluto. (www.warshak.com)

Another ethnographic medium would be the use of note cards with various statements made by parents and children in high conflict such as PAS. These comment cards are then passed around for all the family members to read and respond to with no explanation as to who made the statements. The members would have the chance to read the cards and absorb what was being stated un-adulterated by a person emotions but giving them a chance to see how and what the other sides feel. They would be asked to respond to how the statements made them feel and so on. These comments might not necessarily be ones made by a family member but by someone outside the family who is also experiencing the same emotions and situation. (Piercy and Kristen, 2005, 111-113)

Ethnographic discoveries can also include experiences expressed metaphorically or in poems of how each side of the parent's situation is viewed. This helps each family member to understand. And again, outsiders who are going through the same trauma might write these. In the test arena of ethnology, a performance test might be a respondent statement pertaining to the loss of a parent and how one would respond, then taking it

Where Did I Go Wrong? How Did I Miss The Signs?

one step further to the PAS level. (Piercy and Kristen, 2005, 111-113)

Also as stated previously, self-esteem has a serious impact on many parents and thus triggers anger when they can no longer control their situation. In Carl Roger's research on Personality Psychology and Self-concept, he discovered that therapists could raise low self-esteem using "client-centered" or "non-directive' therapy. (Baron & Byrne, P. 174-175) This is accomplished by having the therapist behave as a non-judgmental, open-minded parent/person who does not pass any judgments or values onto the client but instead allows the client to do their own soul searching and growing. In effect, the client is allowed to relive their infancy and childhood, experiencing all the emotions they should have had in the first place. Via this method, it was proved that a client would be able to change their self-image and concept to a more positive one. (Baron and Byrne, P. 174-175)

The children also need to change their perspective of themselves and image of the relationship with the TP. A terrific approach to resolve this conflict is centered around the Contact Hypothesis (Baron, P.234). This Hypothesis states that the more contact the children have with an individual, the more chances they have to enjoy that person's company, love and support.

Unfortunately, the AP's refusal to allow the children "repeated expose" via visitation with TP reduces contact and positive lifetime experiences with the TP. This action lessens the children's interest and positive attitude toward the TP. (Baron, P. 258-259). They begin to miss out on all the positive experiences and life processes necessary for a normal family and parent relationship. Once the pattern of dislike has been established, repeated exposure tends to create even more hatred for the TP because the children now fear repercussions from the AP for having a good time. This in turn enhances the AP's views and claims that the children hate the TP. This type exposure is an example of how negative Contact Hypothesis can further drive the children away from the TP. (Baron and Byrne, P. 234). In affect what the contact hypothesis says is that loss of contact breeds a loss of relationship and remembrance of the other parent. This pattern of interference between the children's relationship with the other parent must be broken.

To combat the negativity, under this hypothesis, if we instead increase the contact in a positive nature, such as working together as a whole family unit, the AP no longer divides them. The AP looses any control of the situation and a re-categorizing or new association with the in-group is established. (Baron and Byrne, P. 237). In fact, this change in prejudice has a two-fold affect, by actually diminishing the AP's overall control; it puts them on the aggressive and defensive side. In a sense, it would be pushing the AP's buttons thus showing their emotional defects and true devious nature. With this evidence, a counselor can more easily hone in on what is needed.

This by itself is not enough, though. One must also change behavior patterns and erroneous thought processes as well. Such treatment for this type of case may require using many different techniques to illicit the necessary changes. Some of the different techniques that could be utilized include Models of Psychoanalytic, Client/Person-Centered, Behavioral, Cognitive, Affective, Structural Family Theory of Cross-Generational Coalitions as well as Family Therapy. The type of treatment will very much depend on the client's personality.

Using Psychoanalytic Theories, Freud may have some basis with his idea that our behavior is controlled by our desires. Freud's belief that our desires to seek pleasure and to avoid pain, may very well explain why the abuser behaves in such a destructive manner toward the children and ex-partner. They maybe looking to avoid the pain of feeling abandoned and seek the feeling of pleasure from revenge by hurting the other spouse any way possible. As for the children, their avoidance of pain would include always siding or agreeing with AP's views of the TP. The children will do anything not to loose the AP's love, or feel their wrath or even becoming ignored by the AP. (Vacc & Loesch P.76) In these ways, Freud's theories would make sense. The Psychoanalytic process may continue deeper and co-involve the Adlerian, Experiential and Analytical Theories.

From an Adlerian point of view, it seems that these behaviors are directly correlated with interaction to others, our life experiences, socially learned behavior (Vacc and Loesch, P.

Where Did I Go Wrong? How Did I Miss The Signs?

37) and our self-selected goals. In theory, people should have control of their own destinies and to make the necessary changes; if their respective environments permit them too. (Vacc and Loesch, P.77) In the case of the abuser, they refuse to be civil toward anyone who does not agree with them, whether they are their equal, older or an innocent child. They have minimal respect for ex-spouses or their own parent of the same gender. All of this may have been learned from the family life experiences, which are now passed on to the children. For the children, they are experiencing and learning to process this information as being the way to behave. They are rewarded for following the AP's lead and complying with their anger toward the TP. Their family environment rewards them for showing hatred toward the other parent.

In this respect, this is an example of Pavlov's 1927 theory of Classical Conditioning. That is the re-enforcement of a response to a stimuli, i.e. anger toward the TP, elicits rewards from the AP. (Vacc and Loesch, P. 42-43) For example, a mother might use "withdrawal of love" (Vacc and Loesch, P. 44). She might show them love and affection when they behave as she wants in relationship to their father. But if they show any signs of support, happiness or love for their father, she withholds her love. She gives them a warped perception of life and then re-enforces it with conditional love. The more they turn against their father, the more she seems to reward them. Their environment is solely responsible for their reactions and actions toward their father. (Vacc & Loesch P.77)

With the Adlerian Theory, we can strongly see why these children are behaving disrespectfully toward the TP. After all these years of tormented feelings, it would probably stand to reason they have suppressed feelings as well. Thus in order to reverse this situation using the Adlerian theory, one would need to establish a set of norms for dealing with family members that would allow the children to relieve themselves of these burdens and try to relearn proper family etiquette. This is assuming that the children can be convinced to want to heal and regain a relationship with the ousted parent.

With classical conditioning, Thorndike and Skinner discovered that cessation of a behavior could be accomplished by removal of the positive negative re-enforcement. (Vacc and Loesch, P. 43) In other words, if the AP was kept out of the equation or forbidden to interfere with the children's attempts at a relationship with TP, no negative responses would be elicited when the children show affection toward the TP. They would not be scared away from loving the TP and finally having a possible relationship. As well, the AP would no longer be permitted to reward rejection, thus removing control from the AP. This would have to be constant to make it consistent and produce a change so the children could regain a positive view of the TP without outside influences opposing it.

From an Experiential Therapy point of view, alienators are experiencing the anxiety, which comes along with change from divorce. It is a defense mechanism to protect them from the unknown or foreign feelings. They are avoiding the challenges of going on with life as their anxiety grows about losing their spouse and false fear of loosing their children. They may even feel like nothing is left without their spouse, thus there is no meaning to life. In order to prevent this loss from happening, they fight it and try hard to keep some kind of contact with the ex-spouse, even if it is negative. (Corey, P.246-247) Hence why we see many ex's accusing their spouses of abuse while harassing them for child support. A truly abused individual wants nothing to do with the abuser, especially if it means seeing them at all. The abused would much prefer not to have anything to do with their abuser, including receiving child support as it means having to face their attacker in court. This is something called a red flag. It is a strong indicator that allegations of abuse are probably false, but that this is the only way the alienator has to keep engaging with the TP.

But if we can "peel away" at the layers of the anxiety, like peeling the skin of an onion, then we may be able to help the Alienator deal more appropriately in being "receptive to accepting and dealing with the insecurity and anxiety" brought about by the divorce and failed marriage. (Corey, P. 247) We are shedding the resistance to change and grow while the alienator begins to come into their own, creating a new self-image. (Kloth-Zanard, Divorce Does Not Have to Be a Dirty

Where Did I Go Wrong? How Did I Miss The Signs?

Word & Divorce is the Most Negative Word in Any Language. www.KlothConsulting.com)

Life is not easy, but people need to face the challenges that make life not so dull and boring. Because alienators are afraid of change and loss, anxiety develops. But this anxiety and insecurity is part of the growing process. It is the beginning of a new stage in their lives. And if we can help them to see this, then we help them to let go of their anger, hatred, fears and warped system rules, to get on with the business of living life with a meaning and purpose that is healthy. By doing this, we get them to see a positive in the process of divorce.

Gestalt therapy, another method, emphasizes the here and now. It looks at resistances and boundary disturbances to communication as being both healthy and unhealthy depending on the circumstances. While alienators often use projection to express their resistance to change, their children use confluence to express their resistance to same life situations. Gestalt techniques, such as using the empty chair and bringing the past into the present, might just help them to get through the roadblocks in their lives.

In addition, we can look at the existentialist belief in the theory of Death and Nonbeing. For alienators, they cannot move on to the next level. They are stuck as nonbeings, fearing the death of their relationship and translate this as the death of their whole existence. They lash out to stop this from happening. If we can get them to move on, then a process of change related to the divorce can occur, which leaves room for growth. This growth occurs because "as part of us dies, it makes room" for us to expand our life experiences. (Corey, P. 249) If an alienator does not move on, they get stuck in an angry, hate-filled life of lies and dead experiences. We want to move them out of this perspective and into a healthy self-image that allows them to handle what life is going to throw them. We want to give them the tools to deal with anxiety appropriately so they can apply it to other life experiences. We want them to find a new meaning for their life so that going on is not a negative but a positive.

Another useful therapy developed by Marsha Linehan (1993) is Dialectical Behavior Therapy (DBT). Through her work with Borderline Personality Disorders (BPD), she was able to create a program that helped a person control their internal responses to worry and anxiety instead to tolerance and emotional regulation. The following list of skills is the main characteristics of the tools she used to teach her BPD patients.

    For Distress/worry/anxiety, the skills are:
1) Learning how to divert ones focus to other thoughts
2) Learning how to comfort ones self.
3) Find ways to improve the present situation using tension relieving exercises such as meditation, or other relaxing skills
4) Considering the "pros and cons" of behavior (p. 148).

    For Emotional control:
5) identify and label affect
6) identify obstacles to changing emotions,
7) reduce vulnerability to hyper-emotionality through decreased stress,
8) increase the frequency of positive emotional events, and
9) develop the ability to experience emotions without judging or rejecting them (p. 147-148)

    Linehan's work has actually been taken by John Briere, Ph.D. and applied to the treatment of Adult Victims of child abuse with great success. And thus this provides another avenue for treatment of all the victims involved, i.e. alienating parent, targeted parent and child(ren). Linehan offers training programs for professionals in this line of treatment.

    As for the Targeted parent, Amy J. L. Baker has done extensive work to help them to understand what their children are feeling and how to handle them. In her book, Adult Children of Parental Alienation Syndrome: Breaking The Ties that Bind, Baker conducted a study of over 40 adults who as children were victims of PAS and HAP. She found that many of these adults wished the targeted parents had pushed to be more involved but

Where Did I Go Wrong? How Did I Miss The Signs?

understood the gravity of the abuse the targeted parent was taking.

It was further determined that taking the "high road" or not confronting the issue at hand was far worse of a way to handle PAS. But many targeted parents were and are so beat up by the system and their ex's, that they are afraid of making things worse for their kids, and instead mistakenly back off, or take the "high road".

Further, from the original 40 interviews of the adult children of PAS, Baker was able to come up with 17 strategies targeted parents could use to help thwart off the tactics used by the other parent to impede the relationship between the children and the targeted parent.

In her subsequent eBook written by Baker, Beyond the High Road: Responding to 17 Parental Alienation Strategies without Compromising Your Morals or Harming Your Child, she provides targeted parents with healthy tools to respond with. These tools make the targeted parent better prepared to appropriately respond to the impediments and comments stated by the Aggressive parent and children. These tools also help the children to not feel they must side with one parent or the other, thus struggling to protect one parent or side from the other.

By giving independent thinking back to the children to rationally look at both sides, the children are allowed to mature and learn to stand on their own two feet and not be dependent on one parent or the other. And by doing this, control is removed from the Alienator, which as previously touched upon, alienation is about control or loss of control, especially when it comes to the children.

This type behavior is not in the best interest of the children and defeats all attempts at a reconcilable divorce. But by moving an aggressive parent into a passive more cooperative parent, we create a healthier outcome for all. And if we can do this with the proper and appropriate responses and tools for the targeted parent and children, as Baker suggests, we may just thwart the Hostile and Aggressive actions of an Alienating Parent and prevent a tough situation from escalating out of control.

Healthy Conclusion to an Unhealthy Situation

In conclusion, PAS appears to be a form of Domestic Violence in the form of psychological abuse. From the isolation of the children and targeted parent, to the denigration and verbal attacks toward the targeted parent in front of the children, to the using of the children as pawns to inflict pain and suffering upon the Targeted parent, the Alienator is a true perpetrator of abuse. But there could be a happy solution if properly planned program of prevention and intervention were instituted at the beginning of the divorce and separation process. If the courts and agencies could work hand in hand along side the families, a community-based support system would be developed that could help to monitor and prevent this type of abuse long before it wreaks irreparable damages on the families.

Where Did I Go Wrong? How Did I Miss The Signs?

CHAPTER 30

BOOKS, MOVIES AND WEBSITES ON PAS AND THE SYNDROMES ASSOCIATED WITH IT

Adams, Kim. Book: The Parentectomy: A Memoir. A Perspective on Rising above Parental Alienation. 2009, Xlibris Corporation.
Baker, Amy J. EBook: Beyond the High Road, Offers advice for Targeted parents.
Baker, Amy J. Book: Adult Children of Parental Alienation Syndrome: Breaking the Ties that Bind. What happens to children who are manipulated by one parent to turn against the other? Do these children ever figure it out and reconcile with their "lost" parent? Adult Children of Parent Alienation Syndrome presents answers based on research interviews with 40 adults who were alienated from a parent as a child.
Baker, Amy J. Book: I Don't Want to Choose! How Middle School Kids Can Avoid Choosing One Parent Over the Other Dr. Baker is pleased to announce her latest book, co-authored with psychologist Dr. Katherine Andre written to provide middle school children with the tools and language they need to resist the pressure to reject one parent to please the other. This book is for kids, their parents and other caring adults in the lives of divorcing families. View the table of contents.
Baker, Amy J. Book: I Don't Want to Choose! How Middle School Kids Can Avoid Choosing One Parent Over the Other.
Baker, Amy J. Books: http://www.amyjlbaker.com
Behary, Wendy T. Book: Disarming the Narcissist. This book has signs of recognizing a Narcissist as well as other

information about how to deal with Narcissists.
Birke, David. Movie: A Kidnapping in the Family. Made: 1996. Genre: Crime Drama. Stars: Kate Jackson, Tracey Gold Pairing "Charlie's Angels" star Kate Jackson with "Growing Pains" darling Tracy Gold — do you really need to know anything else about this movie to want to watch it? Just in case, here's the scandalous storyline: An over-the-edge mom doesn't think twice about making false accusations or kidnapping (or even worse) to get her grandson from her own daughter!
Borderline Personality Disorder (BPD) Family Forum Site. Link to a great forum about BPD. http://www.bpdfamily.com/discussions/message-board.htm
Bryan, Mark. Book: The Prodigal Father. Trade Press. 2008.
Burns, Dr. David Book: Cognitive Behavior Therapy. It provides some very good self-help information to help deal with our partners who are struggling with BPD and maybe it could help them too.
Carnes, Patrick. Book: The Betrayal Bond: Breaking Free of Exploitive Relationships Carnes describes PTSD in relation to Stockholm Syndrome, PAS, as Trauma bonding
Clawar, Dr. and Dr. Rivilin. Book: Children Held Hostage: Dealing with Programmed and Brainwashed Children
Eddy, William. Book: High Conflict People in Legal Disputes. Summary: This book discusses the impact of High Conflict People (HCP) in legal disputes from the perspective of professionals working within the court system; however, those involved in litigation (petitioner or respondent) will also find it extremely helpful as it discusses strategies for discovery of evidence and presentation, as well as challenging distortions and lies introduced during court.
Eddy, William. Book: The Explosive Child. Excellent read on how to Collaboratively Problem Solve with a child or even an adult who has difficulty with transitioning and changes.
Egizii, J., 2009, Book: The Look Of Love, Seven Locks Press, Santa Anna, CA.
Engel, Beverly. Book: The Emotionally Abusive Relationship - How to stop being abused and how to stop abusing.
Evans, Patricia. Book: The Verbally Abusive Relationship.

Where Did I Go Wrong? How Did I Miss The Signs?

Gives helpful information on how to change your behavior patterns in response to the verbal abuse so that you gain strength and confidence, which in the end, this change in our reactions changes, the tone of the abuse.
Forward, Susan. Book: Emotional Blackmail: When the People in Your Life Use Fear, Obligation, and Guilt to Manipulate You.
Hotchkiss, Sandy. Book: Why Is It Always About You? Saving Yourself from the Narcissists in Your Life.
Jeffries, Michael and Dr. Joel Davies Book: A Family's Heartbreak A Parent's Introduction to Parental Alienation. This is a quick fast easy to read and entertaining book. http://www.afamilysheartbreak.com/
Mason, Paul T., M.S. and Randi Kreger. Book: Stop Walking on Egg Shells: Taking your life back when someone you care about has Borderline Personality Disorder. This book actually is good for both the person with BPD and the people without BPD to read.
Miller, JP. Movie: The People Next Door. Made: 1996. Stars: Fay Dunaway, Nicolette Sheridan, Tracy Ellis and Michael O'Keefe. In this one, the couple living next door to a single mother demonstrates alienation tactics and end up kidnapping two children. I found it to be a good depiction of how children are easily influenced and threatened into rejecting their own mother by their captors.
Minas, Alan. Movie Short: A Morte Inventada. This little film is on the internet and though originally done in Portuguese, it is translated in English as well. Translated it means Fading Away. http://www.amorteinventada.com.br
Psychology Today. Article: Narcissistic Personality Disorder, http://www.psychologytoday.com//conditions/narcissistic-personality-disorder
Reaves, John and James B. Austin. Book: How to find help for a troubled kid: A parent's guide to program and services for adolescents A resource book of treatment programs for children/adolescents.
Richardson, Pamela. Book: A Kidnapped Mind. http://www.akidnappedmind.com/

Roth, Kimberlee and Freda B. Friedman, PHD, LCSD, Book: Surviving A Borderline Parent - How to heal your childhood wounds and build trust, boundaries and self-esteem.
Santoro, Joseph and Ronald Cohen. Book: The Angry Heart: Overcoming Borderline and Addictive Disorders; An Interactive Self-Help Guide It is a book and workbook all together that Helps you heal and find yourself. Dealing with psychotraumatic stress, borderline behavior patterns, psychotraumatic experiences, Borderline Zone, Recovery Exercise, Recovery Zone (more...)
Simon, George K. In Sheeps Clothing. A Book that might help understand the Alienator.
Stout, Martha, Ph.D, The Sociopath Next Door. A Book that might help understand the Alienator.
Tinman, Ozzie. Book: One Way Ticket to Kansas. Here is a link for the book itself and the author, Great book for BPD highly recommended. http://www.onewaytickettokansas.com/
Warshak, Dr. Richard. Book: Divorce Poison. www.divorcepoison.com
Williams, Mary Beth, Ph.D., LCSW, CTS and Soili Poijula, Ph.D.Book: The New Harbinger Self-Help Workbook; The PTSD Workbook. A very intense workbook and very descriptive of PTSD. A lengthy process that should be done at a person's individual pace.

Where Did I Go Wrong? How Did I Miss The Signs?

CHAPTER 31
PARENTECTOMY REDEFINED AND NEW INSIGHTS TO FAMILY DYNAMICS

A BI-MONTHLY NEWSLETTER OF ARTICLES

Every two months, as part of PAS Intervention work to promote awareness and help victims to deal with the stress of PAS, a newsletter with articles is produced and sent out to donors and subscribers. PAS Intervention is a501(c)(3) non-profit dedicated to the prevention, intervention of PAS and providing support to the victims of PAS for free. All revenue from the sale of this book is donated to PAS Intervention. To follow are some examples of the articles in the newsletters produced by PAS Intervention.

PARENTECTOMY*
The unauthorized removal of a parent from their child's life via Hostile Aggressive Parenting (HAP) & Parental Alienation (PA)!**

*Peshkin, Dr. M.M. 1940's, original author of Parentectomy based on the concept of removing the parents to heal asthmas.
http://www.medterms.com/script/main/art.asp?articlekey=40066
**New revised definition based on Hostile Aggressive Parenting and Parental Alienation*

Family Disharmony Hurts Kids

Reprinted from July 2011 issue
Joani T. Kloth-Zanard, RSS, ABI, LC
Internationally Available
PASIntervention@aol.com
www.PAS-Intervention.com

Are You Helping Fuel the Anger and Rage of someone else? Are you unwittingly helping another parent destroy the relationship between the other parent and their children?

Sometimes when a relationship ends, the grief of this loss can be overwhelming for either partner. Grief is a very real emotion that has several basic stages, such as denial, anger, bargaining, and acceptance. Though this is not necessarily the order that one goes through it, many times a person gets stuck in the anger phase of this process. They often cannot move forward and become filled with rage and hatred. This rage and hatred though directed at the ex-spouse/partner can often manifest itself in the children of this relationship as well as the extended family on either side. This angry parent will do anything and everything to make sure that no one likes the targeted parent (TP). They rage and spew anything that will make sure that the TP has no friends, family but most importantly, that the children are removed as painfully as possible from their lives. When this happens, the targeted parent becomes a victim of bullying to satisfy the grief, anger, hurt and rage of the other parent.

Remember not all people show grief the same way. Some are masters of disguise do to their sociopathic tendencies while others are more on the manic depressive end. Either way, these grief stricken ex-partners will do anything to make the TP suffer and hurt as much as they do. Including creating false stories and lies to get the children and other extended family members and friends to hate the TP. When this happens, the damage to the children, the target, the aggressor/angry parent (AP) and even the innocent bystanders who have been pulled in, is terrifying.

Where Did I Go Wrong? How Did I Miss The Signs?

When a person is filled with this much anger grief that they are stuck, it becomes a tragedy for all involved. Their mental state is in jeopardy. Their sense of reality becomes skewed. They actually become so fanatical about the hatred and rage that the stories they tell become their reality, a false reality that makes it impossible for them to ever heal. They may appear sane, normal, a pillar of their community, but in reality it is just a façade. They are so damaged by their inability to move forward and get past the grief of the failed relationship that they literally will start to deteriorate. No one is exactly the same, but sometimes they cannot hold down a job or keep true friends. In other cases, they are so sociopathic that they come across as the perfect parent and person, who could never do any wrong. But in the end, the truth is that they rely on terrorizing the children to follow them until the children are finally brainwashed to fear or hate the other parent. And they often rely on others to help them perpetrate their anger and hatred.

Examples of Alienating Behavior:
From Dr. Warshak's DVD, Welcome Back Pluto
- Restricting Contact by impeding visitation and communication
- Discouraging Good Feelings & Memories of the other parent
- Badmouthing/Bashing of the other parent
- Selective Attention by only looking for the negatives and mistakes, and never seeing any positives in the other parent
- Referring to the other parent by their first name and not as Mom or Dad

What happens to the Victims of this deceit?
For the children, they are consumed with fear that the angry parent will also be angry with them if they do NOT hate the other parent. These children become riddled with guilt and sadness, until they can take no more, and become either just as filled with hatred and anger, or become self-destructive. These children want to love both parents but know they cannot without risking the love of the angry parent. The children are caught between

the Favored vs. Rejected Parent (Dr. Richard Warshak, 2010, Welcome Back Pluto DVD).

For the extended family and friends, they are duped into believing these stories about the TP because they cannot believe that someone could really go to this length to make something up this horrendous. In the back of their minds, they think, well it has to be true because they are no longer together or because of some past vague memory that the AP has warped and used as evidence and besides the children are saying it. These people are so convinced that the TP is bad, that they do not even question it nor ask for the TP's side of the story

For the TP, they are forced to hurt silently for fear of breaking in two. They know that no matter what they do, the AP will find a way to twist it to look bad, leaving them no way to rectify the damages. The TP knows that as long as the AP has followers in their cult of hatred, they will always be made to suffer. Often their only choice after years fighting for their kids is to just move on themselves, so that the kids are spared any more emotional pain.

The children and extended family/friends become pawns of the AP's anger and rage. They actually become unwitting warriors in the battle to continue the AP's rage and hatred campaign against the TP. The saddest part of all is when these people finally do find out the truth, they are mortified, and the guilt they have is incredible. Those that are strong enough will apologize and hope for forgiveness, but those that are weakest, such as the children, the damages are lifelong, resulting in relationship issues, trust issues, substance abuse issues and even suicide.

For the AP having others to corroborate their hatred and anger just helps to fuel it. In fact, it causes the AP to continue in this very unhealthy lifestyle and mental state. The AP's can never truly be happy, because their happiness is based on hatred and revenge. They are never able to move on with their lives because they still live in this world consumed with anger, hatred, rage and revenge. Imagine living with nothing but anger, hatred and rage, year in and year out. One's mental state does not get better but actually worsens. Especially having all of these victims to feed the ego. In reality, these children and extended family/friends are

Where Did I Go Wrong? How Did I Miss The Signs?

unwittingly helping to further desecrate the AP's mental health by following along.

What can be done to help the AP?

So what can be done to help the AP's to move on and not continue to hurt themselves and the people around them? It starts with the victims learning about this type of mental illness. It is a form of depression related to grief and the inability to move on. It also involves extreme low self-esteem, where by the AP believes that if they are not perfect, that they are not lovable and if they are not lovable that they will be abandoned, which leads to the terrifying fear of being alone. This is Parental Alienation.

Once someone can understand it from this point of view, then one can instead of following the AP's anger, revert it by helping the AP to see that being a perfect parent is impossible and not even necessary. That there are no perfect parents because parenting is not an exact science as no two families are ever completely alike. Also, by helping the AP to grieve in a healthy way and stop them when they fire off assaults and attacks against the other parent, helps to stop fueling their agenda of revenge. When the AP has no one following their "orders" or believing their tales, then they have no choice but to learn how to move onward and upward. They have no choice but to look for a different way of life and future.

It is very important for the children and extended family/friends to not be pulled in to the AP's rage and anger campaign against the TP. To do this means that they must learn to think critically for themselves and question whether the stories being told are true or being said out of hurt, anger and rage. Being able to differentiate between the truth and things said out of anger is key to not getting dragged into this vicious circle. It also helps the AP because if no one is listening and following what they are saying, then they no longer have control. The control we are talking about is control of their out of sync emotions of grief that have festered into anger, rage and hatred. AP's believe that if they do not have total control, then they will be disrespected and left behind. They believe control of everyone and everything will prevent them from being abandoned and alone. They are actually obsessed with being in control. If we can take this away and help them to see that control leaves no room for growth, and progress, then maybe we can get them to let go of the anger and need to have revenge too.

Instead, the AP needs to be helped to move forward in the grief cycle. They need to be helped to move on and finally get to an acceptance stage that the relationship may be over, but their life is not. The AP needs to be helped to see that being perfect does not mean they will not be loved or will be left behind. Not being perfect is part of being a person and it is part of how we learn in this life. The AP needs to find a positive in this experience instead of seeing it as all negative.

To see it as a positive, the AP has to realize that the relationship falling apart now gives them some freedoms and the chance to make changes or do things they could not do while in the relationship. Such things as maybe going back to school, traveling, meeting new people, starting a hobby, getting out more often, reading more books and so on.

Life goes on and can be very productive and happy, if we can get the AP to leave their grief behind. And once the AP leaves their grief, then their need to control can be released. And as they do this, they start to gain respect for themselves and with that respect comes a newfound level of positive self-esteem. And just maybe their pain, anger, rage and hatred can be left to the wind as they grow into a new mentally healthy and sound person to be around.

Where Did I Go Wrong? How Did I Miss The Signs?

Parental Alienation is a Multi Diagnosis for the Family

Reprinted from September 2011 Issue
Joani T. Kloth-Zanard, RSS, ABI, LC
Internationally Available
PASIntervention@aol.com
www.PAS-Intervention.com

Do you feel like you are dealing with more than one mental illness at one time when it comes to your family and divorce? Do you know what it means to have a co-morbidity or dual diagnosis?

First, let's start with some technical jargon. When a doctor or counselor uses the term co-morbidity, it literally means that there are two or more occurring issues at one time or a dual diagnosis. What this means is that there is not one problem going on that needs to be addressed but more than one and they often interplay on each other. It was not too long ago, that the mental medical community believed that you could only have one mental illness diagnosis at a time. In fact, because of this misbelief, many clients were never able to get well because the doctors would be treating only one of their problems and not the route cause.

Let me give you an example. My daughter's biological father definitely had a substance abuse problem. He was placed in and out of rehabs as well as the jail. Through some 30 years of his life or more, the doctors and counselors were constantly treating his substance abuse but not the real heart of the problem. Her father was extremely jealous type person. He constantly found himself in fights or battering women. He had extreme low self-esteem and probably depression. More than likely he was bi-polar/manic depressive and using substance abuse to control this problem. Because no one ever bothered to look into his other issues but only address his substance abuse, he never got well and continued to have problems his whole life. Eventually at age 42, after having been in jail 3 times for Assault and Battery, and in the rehabilitation centers no less than 4 times, he was found dead of an accident overdose of drugs and alcohol. As no one addressed his true medical condition, bi-polar manic depression, coupled with substance abuse, and only addressed the substance abuse, there was no possible way for him to ever get well.

Why is this important to Parental Alienation? In the context of high conflict divorce families, there is a co-morbidity of issues that are going on. It is not just about the children having a relationship problem with one parent. It is not just about a parent who is unable to control their anger and grief to the point of using the children as pawns. And it is not just about the targeted parent whose whole world is turned upside down and devastated by the loss of their relationship with their kids. It is about a combination of all of these issues rolled up into one Relational Problem. Just like the above case scenario where the undiagnosed manic depression/bi-polar issue was led to substance abuse, so is the case in Parental Alienation, where one parent, the aggressor, is unable to properly move forward in their lives, despite any outward image, and their actions (the bi-polar/manic depression) in turn cause additional problems (the substance abuse) for the children and targeted parent. When we can look at Parental Alienation as a combination of diagnoses, we have a better chance of solving it and for that matter classifying it in the DSM or Diagnostic and Statistical Manual.

Furthermore, when the professionals misdiagnosis or do not attend to the initial cause of the problem, the alienator or aggressive parent can actually slide even further backwards into a more antisocial diagnosis. These individuals will actually begin to hover on the borderline of narcissistic and sociopathic behaviors. If not addressed immediately, the aggressor can eventually become a full -blown narcissist and sociopath.

This does not bode well for the children or targeted parent. Sociopaths and narcissists are extremely convincing people who know how to control their surroundings and the people in them. They can be extremely successful or complete failures, but the key for them is total control by convincing everyone else around them that they are the perfect person and parent and therefore anything they say about the other parent must and has to be true.

For the children from a scientific community view, the children have a Folie a Deux complex or shared delusional belief

Where Did I Go Wrong? How Did I Miss The Signs?

system with the aggressive/alienating parent(AP). The children actually parrot the AP's words and feelings, taking them on as their own. If not eradicated early on, the children become to believe this is their own thoughts and feelings. Like a child taught to hate and discriminate by a family that follows the KKK (KluKluxKlan), they believe this is the only truth there is. But in the case of Parental Alienation, these kids are also grieving the loss of the Targeted Parent (TP) and are filled with anger, hatred, rage and mistrust even after the TP is replaced with a surrogate parent. These children are brainwashed, programmed and trained to hate the other parent because they are no sharing the same warped anger, hatred and rage that the AP is dealing with.

For these reasons, it is imperative that preventive measures be implemented from the start by the courts, counselors/therapists and others involved. There need to be consequences for violated court orders and impediments. If this is not done, then the aggressive parent gets too much control of everyone from the children; to the targeted parent; to the courts, therapists and agencies. Once they have this undying control and power over everyone, they are pretty hard to stop. It would be like trying to stop a train with no brakes. The only way to stop that train is to literally put something in its way. That something has to be removal of all custodial rights and unsupervised visitation. A situation, I am quite sure no one, not even the courts, agencies or persons involved ever wants to be put into the displeasure of having to do, let alone enforce.

So what can be done? The courts need to start ordering specialized counseling for grief and low self-esteem issues for everyone. The courts need to start penalizing for court violations and contempt of court orders with loss of custody or time with the kids for any parent that does not comply. Counselors need to keep the courts up to date on all progress with all family members so that if one of the parents or children is NOT cooperating, it can be dealt with immediately and not after the damage is done. For those situations, where the aggressive parent is now sociopathic or narcissistic in nature, it may be necessary to remove the child(ren) from this parents care until proper counseling with progress has occurred. Or threaten them with loss of custody and jail if they do not stop their antics. Or worse case scenario, if the child(ren) become a danger to themselves or others, them in mental hospitals or juvenile detention centers. The point is to stop the process of NOT allowing the children to spend the time with the other parent without interference and unadulterated by the aggressive parent. Judges need to put their feet firmly on the group when it comes to the parents who are impeding or they will loose total control and the children will suffer along with the targeted parent for the rest of their lives.

Parental Alienation is not just one diagnosis but should be viewed as a Co-morbidity that affects the entire family. It starts with an alienator who can look perfectly normal on the outside, but who's grief, anger and need for total control mars the family dynamic, thus causing psychological problems for the children and the targeted parent. There is a co-morbidity of issues that are going on that need to be addressed all at the same time.

At the end of the day, we need to stop treating just the symptom, the children and targeted parent, instead treat the cause, the alienating, aggressive parent. Even if the alienator never completely heals or stop, it may just make it easier for everyone else involved.

Where Did I Go Wrong? How Did I Miss The Signs?

Stages and Concepts for Grief:
Is one way or belief better than another?

Reprinted from November 7, 2011 Issue
Joani T. Kloth-Zanard, RSS, ABI, LC
Internationally Available
PASIntervention@aol.com
www.PAS-Intervention.com

There is no one-way to grieve. It is an eclectic process that could follow any one of several venues and/or all of them. There is no right or wrong way, only the way that works in a positive move forward for you. In this article, we will try to apply the issue of bereavement and grief to Parental Alienation and the loss of once healthy relationships for everyone involved.

One of the many theories about the grieving process is based upon the Kübler-Ross Model. This models uses 5 stages or phases that a person might go through when experiencing a loss or tragic event. The Kübler-Ross model or the Five Stages, is often referred to as DABDA, which stands for Denial, Anger, Bargaining, Depression and Acceptance. Though this model was originally designed for explaining the grieving process involved in death, as victims of Parental Alienation we actually experience a living death of our children. They are physically and emotionally dead to us, but yet still living in this world. For the targeted parent and even the child, we are stuck grieving a loss that is only partial. This same model can be applied to the alienators, who are stuck in the grieving process over the loss of their marriage and relationship.

To follow are the stages of the Kübler-Ross model based on someone with terminal cancer. Where the word death is, try substituting the word divorce in and see if it feels and sounds like what you, your ex and children are going through. Try to figure out what stage of this model you fit into, as well as your children and ex. Also, be aware that the order of these stages is NOT definitive and can happen in almost any sequence.
Kübler-Ross Model.

1. Denial — "I feel fine."; "This can't be happening, not to me." Denial is usually only a temporary defense for the individual. This feeling is generally replaced with heightened awareness of possessions and individuals that will be left behind after death (divorce, loss of my children/other parent).
2. Anger — "Why me? It's not fair!"; "How can this happen to me?"; "Who is to blame?" Once in the second stage, the individual recognizes that denial cannot continue. Because of anger, the person is very difficult to care for due to misplaced feelings of rage and envy. Or in divorce the rage, hatred and anger over loosing control of the relationship.
3. Bargaining — "I'll do anything for a few more years."; "I will give my life savings if..." The third stage involves the hope that the individual can somehow postpone or delay death (divorce, loss of my children/other parent). Usually, the negotiation for an extended life (relationship) is made with a higher power in exchange for a reformed lifestyle. Psychologically, the individual is saying, "I understand I will die (be divorced, may loose my relationship with my kids/other parent), but if I could just do something to buy more time..."
4. Depression — "I'm so sad, why bother with anything?"; "I'm going to die (be divorced, loose my relationship with my children/other parent)... What's the point?"; "I miss my loved one, why go on?" During the fourth stage, the dying (aggrieved) person begins to understand the certainty of death (divorce/loss). Because of this, the individual may become silent, refuse visitors and spend much of the time crying and grieving. This process allows the dying (divorced/targeted parent/targeted child) person to disconnect from things of love and affection. It is not recommended to attempt to cheer up an individual who is in this stage. It is an important time for grieving that must be processed.
5. Acceptance — "It's going to be okay."; "I can't fight it, I may as well prepare for it." In this last stage, the individual begins to come to terms with her/his mortality or that of a loved one (or lost relationship).

Where Did I Go Wrong? How Did I Miss The Signs?

Kübler-Ross, E. (2005) On Grief and Grieving: Finding the Meaning of Grief Through the Five Stages of Loss, Simon & Schuster Ltd, ISBN 0743263448

After this version about grief was published by Elizabeth Kübler-Ross, George Bonanno did further research that did NOT agree with Kübler-Ross. Bonanno, a bereavement and trauma expert, believes in patterns of grief. One of those patterns is persistent resilience. Or much what I talk about when I say moving forward in a positive way. He also expressed a strong faith that laughter was more important to healing than crying. We can all agree that when we are laughing, we are letting go and feel good. So again, in my eclectic approach to grief, I think that laughter could very well be incorporated in the healing process.

Though most of Bonanno's experience shows people grieving using resilience, he also saw two other patterns of importance. One he termed "prolonged grief" and was based on the inability by people to move forward. He says people who experience prolonged grief, "struggle for years, yearning and pining for the lost loved one. They never seem to get any better. For them, grief is one long horrible experience and it only seems to get worse over time." Without a doubt, we can see how this is true with most, if not all alienators.

The other pattern he recognized, he named "recovery" pattern. These individuals grieved for much shorter times but at most only a year. Then they would start to restore themselves to their original personas, and from all outward appearances seemed to be back on track. But underneath, they still felt pain and tremendous loss and thus never completely get to the resilience level of the bereavement process.
(Bonanno, George. 2009, http://www.psychologytoday.com/blog/thriving-in-the-face-trauma/200910/grief-does-not-come-in-stages-and-its-not-the-same-everyone)

Next in this eclectic view comes the finding of the Grief Recovery Institute started by James W. James after the death of his own 3-year old son. James, in coordination with Russell P. Friedman, grew the Grief Recovery Institute into a huge non-

profit with over 2500 centers. He felt the terminology and concepts of Kubler-Ross were not accurate and thus reinterpreted the 5 stages as the following:
1. Denial
    a. Disbelief, Shock, Numbness was a more appropriate feeling than denial.
2. Anger
    a. He felt this was not a universal feeling as not all deaths are the same, such as someone finally dying after suffering from a long disease or someone who was killed by a drunk driver. Yes, there is anger at the disease or the drunk driver but he did not believe this was a stage.
3. Bargaining
    a. Yearning for their loved one instead.
4. Depression
    a. He believed that though the following list were symptoms of grievers as well as symptoms for clinical depression and that this did not mean a person was depressed.
        i. Inability to concentrate
        ii. Disturbance of sleeping patterns
        iii. Upheaval of eating patterns
        iv. Roller coaster of emotions
        v. Lack of energy
5. Acceptance
    a. Was relative to the person and event and required someone to admit that it was over and the person gone.

Friedman, Russell and James, John. The Myth Of the Stages of Dying, Death and Grief, Grief Recovery Institute http://www.grief-recovery.com/Articles/Myth%20of%20Stages.pdf

We can all see how these ideas above can work both ways for all of us. And it seems that there is no one right or wrong answer about how one handles it. It is more about what we go

Where Did I Go Wrong? How Did I Miss The Signs?

through and if that process is a positive one for us or a negative one that needs to be attended to.

When it came to the children's grief, VNA or Visiting Nurses Association wanted to focus on how educators could assist children with their grief. They based their finding on age appropriateness of responses. The Grief Institute compiled this information and came up with a booklet on the subject of grief related to death and the affects on children. Again, change the words death to Divorce and I think we can see how this applies in our children's cases.

Child Development and Possible Reactions to Death (Divorce)
Age Range (3-5 years old)
Concepts of Death(Divorce)
- It is temporary and reversible
- Death/divorce is mixed up with sleep and trips
- May wonder what the deceased/missing are doing
- They will never die
- Sees death(divorce) as special, but not why
- Death (Divorce) occurs when something bad is done

Feelings
- Cranky (feelings are acted out in play)
- Confused about changes
- Angry and scared
- Withdrawn

Actions
- May be interested in dead (divorced) things
- Cry
- Fight
- Act as if death (divorce) never occurred

Age Range (6-9 years old)
Concepts of Death (Divorce)
- Views death (divorce) as real, though real is distant
- Begins to understand that death (divorce) is irreversible
- Realizes everyone, including self, will die (Divorce/have family problems) someday
- A spirit gets you when you die (divorce) because you are

too slow to get away
- Who will care for them if a parent dies (divorces)?
- Asks questions about the biological processes of death (divorce)
- Magical thinking can still overcome death (divorce)

Feelings
- Anxiety
- Sad
- Confused about changes
- Withdrawn
- Angry
- Scared
- Moody

Actions
- Able to articulate their feelings and thoughts more clearly
- Older children may revert to younger behaviors
- May seek honest, simple answers about situation
- Act as if nothing happened
- Behave aggressively
- Become withdrawn
- Experience nightmares
- Lack concentration
- Decline in grades
- Try to control body as they cannot control external environment (may make self vomit to get the "bad" out of belly)

Age Range (9-12 years old)
Concepts of death (divorce)
- Their words or actions caused death (divorce)
- Death (divorce) may happen again
- Who will take care of him/her if parents die (divorce).
- Sees death (divorce) as irreversible
- Can tell difference between living and non-living , ((divorce and married)
- More adult in thoughts, but still has child-like beliefs

Where Did I Go Wrong? How Did I Miss The Signs?

Feelings
- May internalize anger or sadness
- Depression
- May have preoccupation with the deceased (divorced)
- Guilty
- Scared
- Confused
- Vulnerable

Actions
- May revert to younger aged behaviors •
- Become protective of remaining parent
- Interest in rituals at death (divorce) (funerals, wakes, etc...)
- May play act these rituals
- Act as if it never happened
- Behave aggressively
- Lack concentration
- Decline in grades

Age Range (13 years and Older)
Concepts
- Can joke about death (divorce)
- Their actions and words caused death (divorce)
- Weakness if they show their feelings
- More typical of adult conception of death (divorce)
- Able to look toward the future without parent
- Able to comprehend permanence of death (divorce)
- Guilt in their own growth and development when faced

Feelings
- Adolescent vulnerability is magnified
- Isolated
- Worried
- Abandoned
- Scared
- Anxious
- Lonely
- Confusion around need for growth vs. regression

Actions
- Delay grief until they feel it is a safe time
- Desire to participate in rituals
- Engage in risk taking behaviors
- Display dramatic emotional responses
- Expresses grief more with peers than adults
- Has common adult reactions, (fatigue, depression, somatic complaints)
- May seek relief through substance abuse

VNA Hospice Care, When Children Grieve: How Educators Can Help. http://www.hospicecarema.org/atf/cf/%7B503349D3-99A9-40CD-A8AE-CAAAD384BCAD%7D/Griefbooklet.pdf

All of this information is just another step in the process for us to all understand the different stages or phases that we go through when processing a loss, such as death or alienation. Processing things in a way that is positive for us and produces happy, healthy and successful end results for us, is what is important. How we got there is not as important as it is different for everyone.

So how can we apply all of this to Parental Alienation and understanding why and what is going on? Most alienators are stuck in the stage of grief called anger. They are so filled with hatred, anger and rage at the other parent for not staying in the marriage that they literally are stuck and cannot move forward. Instead of compartmentalizing and realizing that their anger is their issue, they reach across the boundaries and borders of parent child relationships and perpetrate their hurt and grief onto the children and through the children to the other parent . This is NOT a positive move forward for them or the children. But it might also explain the responses that we see in both the children and the ex-spouses.

If we can see the initial problem or trigger for the Alienator, i.e. loss and inability to complete the grieving process, or just not having control anymore, then maybe we can better protect the children and targeted spouse with proper correction/direction for the alienating spouse. In other words, we

Where Did I Go Wrong? How Did I Miss The Signs?

find a proper method of helping the Alienator to move forward in their lives by recognizing their part and inability to let go and move on. This in turn trickles down to their treatment of the children and the targeted parent, which in turn, then stops Parental Alienation.

ABBREVIATION INDEX

AP	Alienating Parent
BF	Biological Father
BD	Biological Daughter
BM	Biological Mother
BS	Biological Son
CPS	Child Protective Services
DH	Darling (Dear) Husband
DSM	Diagnostic and Statistical Manual of Mental Health
FIL	Father-in-law
HAP	Hostile Aggressive Parenting
MIL	Mother-in-law
PA	Parental Alienation
PAS	Parental Alienation Syndrome
SD	Step-Daughter
SF	Step-Father
SM	Step-Mother
SS	Step-Son
TP	Target Parent

REFERENCES

Abandonment.net. August 2009. www.Abandonment.net/therapist.html
Alliance for Children and Families, http://www.alliance1.org/
Amato, P. R. Nonresident Fathers and Children's Well-being. Department of Sociology, University of Nebraska-Lincoln, Lincoln, Nebraska. http://law.gov.au/aghome/commaff/lafs/frsp/mensforum/people/amato.htm.
American Academy of Child and Adolescent Psychiatry (AACAP). Children and Divorce. www.aacap.org/publications/factsfam/divorce.htm.
American Society of Clinical Hypnosis, http://www.hypnosis-research.org/hypnosis/
Arndt, B. Paying the high price of divorce. The Age. April 13, 2002. www.theage.com.au/articles/2002/04/12/1018333416832.html
Ayob, C., Deutch, R. Andronicki, M. (1999) Emotional Distress in Children of High Conflict Divorce; Impact of Marital Conflict and Violence. Family & Conciliation Courts Review, Vol. 37, No. 3. P. 297-315
Azar, S.T., Nix, R.L. & Makin-Byrd, K.N. (2005) Parenting Schemas and the Process of Change. Journal of Marital and Family Therapy: January 2005, Vol.31, No. 1, p.45-58.
Baker, A. Accessed March 2005)The Cult of Parenthood: A Qualitative Study of Parental Alienation, Cultic Studies Review, Vol. 4, No. 1 http://f4.grp.yahoofs.com/v1/kGNgQpS2btksTX7hfl_BAGMbqPtYtOeMa4RdGXV1vXRdH4R58xD3bmeG0R6ObDPj_bvMvSaYayJczdsEcTxu/CultofParenthood%20final%20version.doc
Baker, Amy J. L. (2007) Adult Children of Parental

Alienation Syndrome – Breaking the Ties that Bind. NY, NY. W.W. Norton & Company.

Baucom, D. H., Epstein, N., Daiuto, A. D., Carels, R.A., Rankin, L.A., & Burnett, C.K. (1996). Cognitions in marriage: The relationship between standards and attributions. Journal of Family Psychology, 10, 209-222.

Baucom, D. H., Epstein, N., Rankin, L.A., & Burnett, C.K. (1996). Assessing relationship standards: The Inventory of Specific Relationship Standards. Journal of Family Psychology, 10, 72-88.

Baskerville, S. The Myth of Deadbeat Dads. Liberty, Expose. Received June 2002. P. 27-32. baskers@msn.com

Baskerville, S. The Real Responsibility of Man. Human Events, Retrieved April 8, 2002, vol. 58, no. 13, p.14. baskers@email.msn.com or baskers@msn.com.

Baskerville, S. The Truth About Child Abuse. Human Events, vol. 58, no. 16, Received April 29, 2002, p.14. baskers@msn.com or baskers@msn.com.

Bauserman, R. (2002) Child Adjustment in Joint-Custody Versus Sole-Custody Arrangements: A Meta-Analytic Review. Journal of Family Psychology:Vol.16, No. 1, P.91-102.

Beck, M. & Friedlander, M.L. (2006, July) Three Perspectives on Clients' Experiences of the Therapeutic Alliance: A Discovery-Oriented Investigation. Journal of Marital and Family Therapy, Vol. 32, Number 3, 355-368.

Bennett, S. Parental Alienation Syndrome. www.prairielaw.com/articles/article.asp?channelId=18&articleId=1558.

Bieniewicz, D. J. (2002) Advise to Judges-Just Say "No". Received 2002.

Briere, J. (2002) Treating adult survivors of severe childhood abuse and neglect: Further development of an integrative model. The APSAC handbook on child

Where Did I Go Wrong? How Did I Miss The Signs?

maltreatment, 2nd Edition. Newbury Park, CA: Sage Publications.. http://www.johnbriere.com/STM.pdf

Brown, T., Sheehan, R., & Frederico, M., Hewitt, L. (2002) Resolving Family Violence to Children. Monash University. Family Violence and Family Court Research Program, Monash University.

Caring Dad. Collaboration of Articles. www.custodyreform.com.

Case Western University Reserve, http://connection.cwru.edu/ai/ , http://connection.cwru.edu/ai/intro/default.cfm, http://connection.cwru.edu/ai/uploads/whatisai.pdf

Castagno, J. T., My Testimony in Waterbury, CT. Retrieved April 10, 2002. Castagnojean@aol.com

Center for Disease Control Prevention. http://www.cdc.gov/health/violence.htm

Child Access Center of Maryland, The. Guidelines for parents when the other parent is angry, hostile and uncooperative. Email.chldxsctr@aol.com

Cincinnati Family Service Agency, http://www.beechacres.org/

Clawar, S. S., Ph.D., C.C.S. & Rivlin, B. V., M.S.S. Children Held Hostage: Dealing with Programmed and Brainwashed Children. American Bar Association. 1991.

Cloer, S. (2002, Aug. 14). Don's Story, My Success Story…I'm the custodial parent and a Father!. Message Posted from sacs1@mindspring.com.

Cloer, S. My Domestic Abuse Story. Norcross, GA. Sacs@mindspring.com

Cloer, S. Specific Case Law for NCP Rights. Sacs@mindspring.com.

Coachville, Venn diagrams. http://www.venndiagrams.com

Controlling Styles. The Eight Styles of Controlling Parents. www.controllingpartnes.com/stylesof.htm.

Conway-Rand, D. (1997) American Journal of Forensic Psychology, Volume 15, Number 3, 4 & 5,

23, Parental Alienation Syndrome, The Spectrum of Parental Alienation Syndrome, Parts 1–3. Balboa Island, CA: Forensic Psychology. Also available at Dad (Pappa) Watch, <http://www.robin.no/~dadwatch/pasdir and http://www.robin.no/~dadwatch/pasdir/rand01.html and http://www.robin.no/~dadwatch/pasdir/rand02.html and http://www.robin.no/~dadwatch/pasdir/rand03.html and http://www.robin.no/~dadwatch/pasdir/rand04.html and http://www.robin.no/~dadwatch/pasdir/rand05.html and http://www.robin.no/~dadwatch/pasdir/rand06.html

Cooper, M. (2002, June 10) "Going to the Chapel". Time: , 31.

Cooperride, D. and Srivastva, S (1987) Case Western Reserve University. http://appreciativeinquiry.case.edu

Corey, G. Theory & Practice of Group Counseling. (6th Ed.). (2004). Belmont, CA: Thomson Brook/Cole Publishing.

Corry, Charles E. (2002). Chaos and the borderline personality. Colorado Springs Gazetter, Aug 29-31, Denver Post August 29-31, September 1-5, Associated Press reports.

Council on Accreditation for Children and Family Services (COA), http://www.coanet.org/front-end/index.cfm.

Darnall, D. Parental Alienation: Not in the Best Interest Of The Children, North Dakota Law Review, Volume 75, 1999, p 323-364

Dishon, A. (2000, 2 Nov.) Divorce, Source: Parental Alienation, http://cadivorce.com/php/aritcles/parental_alienation.php.

Dishon, A. Divorce Source, Featured Question: Can I

Deny My Ex-spouse Visitation? http://divorcesource.com/info/questions/visitation.shtml.

Dishon, A. Divorce Source, "Parental Alienation: Recognizing a Severely Alienated Child", http://divorcesource.com/info/alienation/child.shtml.

Dishon, A. Divorce Source. Parental Alienation: What Can the Courts Do? http://divorcesource.com/info/alienation/courts.shtml>.

Dishon, A. Divorce Source, Reestablishing and Increasing Visitation. http://divorcesource.com/CA/ARTICLES/dishon8.html

Dobson, J. Father has key role in daughter's life., Focus on the Family. (2002, Feb. 17). The Washington Times. [Electronic Version]. www.uexpress.com/focusonthefamily.

Doherty, W. University of Minnesota, http://fsos.che.umn.edu/doherty/

Doherty, W. http://fsos.che.umn.edu/doherty/

Domestic Violence Against Men. The Face of Battering. www.dvmen.org/dv-94.htm.

Donald, M. Access-Denied. (2001, May 10). Dallas Observer. New Times, Inc. Retrieved 2002. www.dallasobserver.com/issues/2001-05-10/feature.html

Downing, J. Re: Visitation Enforcement Laws. (2001, Oct. 10). E-mail from author. http://www.acf.dhhs.gov/programs/cse.

Dricoll, M. New Deal for Divorced Fathers. (2002, March 17). The Sunday Times. www.Sunday-times.co.uk/article/0,,179-238134,00.html.

Dunne, J. & Hedrick, M. (1994) The Parental Alienation Syndrome: An Analysis of Sixteen Selected Cases. Journal of Divorce and Remarriage, Vol. 21, 21-38.

Eden, B. Fathers Rights Association of NJ & Mid-Atlantic Region. How to Handle Corrupt

Uncooperating Custodial Parents. Email Dialogue. Nikky@icdus.com and family@stone.net.

Eidelson, R. J., & Epstein, N. (1982) Cognition and relationship maladjustment: Development of a measure of dysfunctional relationship beliefs. Journal of Consulting and Clinical Psychology, 120, 599-605.

Ellis, E. Divorce Wars, Interventions with Families in Conflict. (2000). APA Books. What We Have Learned From 30 Years of Research on Families in Divorce Conflict.

Eckhardt, C., & Deffenbacher, J. (1995) Diagnosis of Anger. In Kassinove, H. (Ed.) (1995) Anger disorders. (pp.27-47). Washington, DC: Taylor & Francis.

Epstein, N. (1982) Cognitive therapy with couples. American Journal of Family Therapy, 10(1), 5-16.

Epstein, N., Chen, F., & Beyder-Kamjou, I. 92005) Relationship Standards and Marital Satisfaction in Chinese and American Couples. Journal of Marital and Family Therapy, 31(1), 59-74.

Family Conflict Resolution. http://familyconflict.freeyellow.com/General1/RecommendationsHostile-AggressiveParenting.pdf

Farell, W. Why Dads Matter. (2002, May 12)..Men's New Daily. www.mensnewsdaily.com/stories/harrell051202.htm

Feibert, M. S. References Examining Assaults By Women on Their Spouses or Male Partners: An Annotated Bibliography. http://www.csulb.edu/~mfiebert/assault.htm

Foundation Center, The. http://fdncenter.org/

Gardner, R. A. Denial of the Parental Alienation Syndrome Also Harms Women. www.rgardner.com/refs/ar13.html.

Gardner, R. A. Family Therapy of the Moderate Type of Parental Alienation Syndrome. www.Fact.on.ca/Info/pas/gard99m.htm.

Gardner, R. A. Parental Alienation Syndrome, www.familycouts.com/pas.htm.

Gardner, R. A. Response to Kelly/Johnston Article. Speak Out for the Children: a publication of the Children's Rights Council: 17 (2):6-10. www.rgardner.com/refs/ar15.html

Gardner, R. A. The Empowerment of Children in the Development of Parental Alienation Syndrome. www.rgardner.com/refs/ar14.html

Gardner, R. A. The Role of the Judiciary in the Entrenchment of the Parental Alienation Syndrome (PAS). www.rgardner.com Pas References.

Gardner, R. A. (1998) Parental Alienation Syndrome. Cresskill, NJ: Creative Therapeutics, Inc. http://www.rgardner.com

Gardner, R. A. (2001) Should Courts Order PAS Children to Visit/Reside with the Alienated Parent? A Follow Up Study. www.fact.on.ca/Info/pas/gard01a.htm. The American Journal of Forensic Psychology, 19(3):61-106.

Gardner, R. A. (2002) The Empowerment of Children in the Development of Parental Alienation Syndrome. Cresskill, NJ: Creative Therapeutics, Inc.

Georgetown Family Center Website. http://www.georgetownfamilycenter.org/pages/murraybowen.html

Ginger. Email:gingersgood4u@aol.com. Home Again. Retrieved May 01, 2002.

Givens, D. B. (1998) Amygdala. Center for Nonverbal Studies. http://member.aol.com/nonverbal2/amydala.htm

Glod, M. (2003, May 13) For Father and child, Time to Get Acquainted, Daughter Returns After Nearly 8 Years. [Electronic Version] Washington Post. B01. www.washingtonpost.com/wp-dyn/aritcles/A8077-2002May 12.html

Grantsmanship Center, The. http://www.tgci.com/

Guidubladi, J. (1996, July) Minority Report and Policy Recommendations of the United States Commission on Child & Family Welfare. Received from Glen Sacs of sacs1@mindspring.com.

Hall, C. S., Gardner L. , Campbell, J.B. (1998) Theories of Personality, (4th Ed.). Canada: John Wiley & Sons.

Hall, N. 92002, April 3). Dad gets custody after mother's 'spiteful' lies. Judge says woman was also guilty of contempt of court, which merited a jail term. [Electronic Version] Vancouver Sun. www.canada.com/bancouver/vancouversun/story.asp?id={84DF8BDC-5D8D-4c2F-B72B-89E2B466EE1A}.

Hanna, S. M. & Brown, J. H. (2002) The Practice of Family Therapy, Key Elements Across Models. NY: Thomson Brooks/Cole Publishing.

Hawaii Family Service Agency, http://www.cfs-hawaii.org/more_about_cfs.htm

Hubin, D. C. (1999) Parental Rights and Due Process, The Journal of Law and Family Studies, University of Utah School of Law, Volume 1, Number 2, 123-150.

Human Services Collaborative. State of Connecticut. KidCare Institute for Community Based Care Program and Resources.

Indiana Civil Rights Council. Indiana Civil Rights Council Stats and Info. www.indianacrc.org/stats-info.html

Jefferies, M. & Davies, Dr. J. 2008. A Family's Heartbreak: A Parent's Introduction to Parental Alienation. Wilton, CT: Inergy Group.

Johnson, L.N. & Ketring, S. A. (2006, July) The Therapy Alliance: A Moderator in Therapy Outcome for Families Dealing with Child Abuse and Neglect. Journal of Marital and Family Therapy, Vol. 32, Number 3, 345-354.

Kemp, A. (1998) Abuse in the Family. An Introduction. NY: Brooks/Cole Publishing Company, Albany.

Kentucky Department of Mental Health and Mental Retardation. http://mhmr.chs.ky.gov/MH

Kentucky Family Service Agency,

Where Did I Go Wrong? How Did I Miss The Signs?

http://www.famchild.org/

Kiefer, R. A. PAS Victim. Stop PAS.yahoogroups.com

Kirkendale, W. What you do and don't do when as a loving parent you are confronted with a severe case of PAS in your child". On-line Posting. President of The Parental Alienation Syndrome Foundation & The family court Reform council of America. http://www.mall4us.com/parentnPAS.htm.

Kirkendale, W. (2002, Nov. 2). Family Courts. Parental Alienation Syndrome. <http://www.familycourts.com/pas.htm>.

Kirn, W. (2002, Sept. 16). I'm O.K. You're O.K. We're Not O.K. Time, p92

Kloth, J. To everyone who cares about our Children and Parents Rights. Putzangel@aol.com www.custodyreform.com. PasParents@yahoo.com

Koplen, B. (2002, May 26). Letter to Editor in response: Hymowitz, Schmyowitz... Family@cstone.net. Poetscry@gamewood.net.

Kassinove, H. (1995) Anger Disorders: Definition, Diagnosis, and Treatment. Washington, DC: Taylor & Francis.

Kounexki, E. F. MA. Resources for Fathers and Their Children. Koun0003@tc.umn.edu. http://home.earthlink.net/~koun0003.

Kuhl, B. (2002) Violence Knows No Gender. http://www.safe4all.org/essays/violencegender.html

Lee, D. For Parents in Active Custody case. http://childsbestinterest.org.

Lee, D. (2002, Aug. 11) http://childsbestinterest.org, Tennessee Court Declares CS Guidelines Unconstitutional.

Licht, C. & Chabot, D. (April 2006) The Chabot Emotional Differentiation Scale: A Theoretically and Psychometrically Sound Instrument for Measuring Bowen's Intrapsychic Aspect of Differentiation. Journal of Marital and Family Therapy, Vol. 32, No. 2.

pp.167-180.

Linde, C. (2002, May 10) A case For Fathers And Co-Parenting. http://tsw.odyssey.on.ca/~balancebeam/dadless/case.htm

Linehan, M. M. (1993a) Cognitive–Behavioral Treatment of Borderline Personality Disorder. New York: Guilford Press

Lowenstein L F: January 16, 1999, The Psychological Effects and Treatment of Parental Alienation Syndrome. Justice of the Peace Vol. 163. No... 3, p 47-50.

Lowenstein, L.F. 2005, How Can One Overturn The Programing of the Child Against the Parent?, Abstract, Southern England Psychological Services, http://www.parental-alienation.info/publications/30-howcanoneovetheproofachiagaapar.htm

MacKay, N. New law to stop divorcing parents turning children against each other. www.sundayherald.com/21120.

Major, J. A. Living Media 2000, "Parents Who Have successfully Fought Parental Alienation Syndrome", http://livingmedia2000.com/pas.htm

Manumit Exchange. (2002, Aug. 12). Dads On The Air - The Amazing Success of Dads In Distress. Dads On the Air (Sydney, AU).

Margiehomes@hotmail.com. (2002, Nov. 23). A Recipe for How to Stay in Touch with Your Kids. Message posted tostopPAS@yahoogroups.com

Marshall, C. (2002 May 2) Father's Rights Could change In Child Custody Cases, Ohio's Divorce Laws Could Be Reformed. www.nbc4columbus.com http://www.nbc4columbus.com/news/144817/deatil.html

Martin, J. PAS Victim. Stop PAS.yahoogroups.com website

Mason, P.T, M.S., & Kreger, R. 1998. Stop Walking on Eggshells. Oakland, CA: New Harbinger

Where Did I Go Wrong? How Did I Miss The Signs?

Publications.

Maslow, A. H. (1968) The Farther Reaches of Human Nature. NY: Esalen Books, Viking Press.

Maslow, A. H. (1968) Toward a Psychology of Being. NY: D.Vant Nostrand Company.

McGoldrick, M., Giordano, J. & Pearce, J.K. (1996). Ethnicity & Family Therapy. NY: The Guilford Press.

Myers, L. Berliner, J. Bricre, C.T. Hendrix, T. Reid, & C. Jenny (Eds.) (2002). The APSAC handbook on child maltreatment, 2nd Edition. Newbury Park, CA: Sage Publications. http://www.johnbriere.com/STM.pdf

child maltreatment, 2nd Edition. Newbury Park, CA: Sage Publications

Miller, S. (2002, Jan. 30). Associated with Raising a Child. Messages Posted at Afc@erols.com and family@stone.net

Milton Erickson Foundation. http://www.erickson-foundation.org/

Minor, E. Georgia man lives the good life in a converted corn bin. Parrot, GA: The Associated Press. www.farmandauction.com.

Misner, L. (2001) In the Children's Best Interest. Leonard Misner Publishing.

Muchnick, R. (2002, March 19). NOW took Clinton Cash Before Falling Silent on Sexgate. Children's Justice Forum. www.newsmax.com/shoinsidecover.shtml?a=2002/3/29/220751. www.childrensjustice.org.

National Institute of Mental Health, http://www.nimh.nih.gov/about/nimhbib.cfm

National Legal Research Group, NC., Divorce Source, (1995) Torts Arising Out of Interference with Custody and Visitation. http://divorcesource.com/research/dl/visitation/95sep192.shtml

National Mental Health Association, http://www.nmha.org/about/history.cfm

345

Nichols & Schwartz, 1998. Family Therapy: Concepts and Methods. 4th ed. Allyn & Bacon

Niggemyer, K. (1998) Parental Alienation is Open Heart Surgery: It Needs More Than A Band-Aid to Fix It, California Western Law Review, volume 34, 567-589. [Electronic Version]. http://fact.on.ca/Info/pas/niggerm98.htm.

Nova Southeastern University. http://www.nova.edu/ssss/QR/web.html, http://www.nova.edu/ssss/QR/QR2-3/schooley.html

Ohio Department of Mental Health, http://www.mh.state.oh.us/index-dept.html

PAS 2nd Wives Club, et.al. www.PAS2ndWivesClub@yahoogroups.com

Piercy, F. P., & Benson, K. (2005) Aesthetic forms of data representation in qualitative family therapy research. Journal of Marital and Family Therapy, 31(1), 107-119.

Peshkin, Dr. M.M. 1940's, original author of Parentectomy based on Asthma http://www.medterms.com/script/main/art.asp?articlekey=40066

Pisha, Lisa. (January/February 2009) Fear and the Family. Family Therapy Magazine. P.17-20

Pitchers, R. W. His story. http://ibduk.org/richard_v_state_of_california.htm.

Prevent Child Abuse America. Emotional Child Abuse. http://www.preventchildabuse.org/learn_more/research.html

Psychquel. http://www.psyquel.com/

Reagan, R. (1986, April 11). Proclamation 5467-A Proclamation on Fatherhood. www.reagan.utexas.edu/resources/speeches/1.

Rogers, M. R. (2002, May 23) A Brief Economic Critique of Virginia's Child Support Guidelines and Recommendations. Mark Rogers, Economic Consulting. www.GuidlineEconomics.com

Where Did I Go Wrong? How Did I Miss The Signs?

Rohner, R. and N. Research Center for Parental Rejection and Acceptance. www.ucc.uconn.edu~rohner

Sacks, G. J. Child custody system needs reform to respect fathers. www.dadsdirove.com/mag/essay.php/062Breform.html

Sacks, G. J. High-Profile 'Deadbeat Dad' Raids Won't Fix Child Support System Badly in Need of Reform. http://64.227.10.201/high_profile_deadbeat.htm

Sacks, G. J. (2002, April 2). Confronting Woman-Bashing in the Men's Movement. www.glennjsacks.com/confronting_women-bashing.htm.

Sacks, G. J. (2002, April 2). New Study Finds Myths, Misrepresentations In Women's Studies Textbooks. www.glennjsacks.com/new_study_finds.htm.

Sacks, G. J. (2002, April 8) Hate My Father? No Ma'am! She Thinks Magazine. www.glennjsacks.com/.

Sacks, G. J. (2002, April 15). Boys: The New Underclass in American Schools. www.glennjsacks.com/boys_the_new_.htm.

Sacks, G. J. (2002, May 2). Let's not 'Learn' the Same Lessons From Blake That We Learned From OJ. www.glennjsacks.com/lets_not_learn_pf.htm.

Sacks, G. J. (2002, May 7). Is There a Batterer in the US Senate? www.glennjsacks.com/is_there_a_pf.htm.

Sacks, G. J. (2002, May 10). California Child Support Bill Will Help Newly Released Prisoners Rebuild Their Lives. www.glennjsacks.com/california_child_support.htm.

Sacks, G. J. (2002, May 22) Stay-at-Home Dads: A Practical Solution to the Career Woman's Dilemma. www.glennjsacks.com/stay_at_home.htm

Safe 4 All. http://www.safe4all.org/resources/

Saltau, C. (2002, April 3). Boys Harmed by fathers' absence. The Age.

www.theage.com.au/news/2002/04/03/FFXYKE6J1LC.html.

Saponsneck, D. T. How Are the Children of Divorce Doing? www.mediate.com/fam/wintereditorial.cfm.

Sedam, S. (2002, May 22) Rebuilding broken bonds. Gazaette.Net. www.gazetter.net/200221/gaithersbrug/news/105393-1.html

Seward, R. R. How Fathers Contribute to their Daughter's Success. Department of Sociology at University of North Texas. Email: Seward@cmm.unt.edu

Sharf, R. S. (2000) Theories of Psychotherapy & Counseling. (2nd Ed.). USA: Brooks/Cole.

Simon, G. K., Dealing with Manipulative People. Excerpt from book: In Sheep's Clothing. www.rickros.com

Slater, L. (2002, March 17) The Trouble with Self-esteem. www.theage.com.us/articles/2002/03/17/1015909915787.html

Smith, C & Smith, L. 4 Lies & 4 Truth Talk Show, US-CAPF. Decatur, GA. www.paternityfraud.com

Smith, C. 2011, A Child's View, What would I think, How Would I Act? Reprinted with permission from author.

Smith, S. (2000, Nov 6). Parental Alienation. Message sent by author to state department of Connecticut for Child Welfare.

Sommer, R. Surviving Divorce. www.reenasommerassociates.mb.ca.

SPARC. Getting Access To Your Child's Report Cards and School Records. www.detabravo.net/cgi-bin/custody/reportcards.html

stnpride1@aol.com (2002, Aug. 12). Venting. Message Posted to www. PASparents/yahoogroups.com

Stop PAS organization and group.

Where Did I Go Wrong? How Did I Miss The Signs?

www.stopPas@yahoogroups.com
Streit, W. The Lakutis v Greenwood Case. Wilbur@TheFaceOf.com.
Stuart-Mills, P.A122 (2000, Nov.). The Rachael Foundation. http://www.rachaelfoundation.org
Substance Abuse & Mental Services Health Association On Grant Writing. http://grantstraining.samhsa.gov/
Sue, D. W. & Sue, D. (2003) Counseling the Culturally Diverse. Theory and Practice. (4th Ed.). NY: John Wiley & Sons, Inc.
Surgeon General, http://www.surgeongeneral.gov/library/mentalhealth/chapter2/sec7.html
Thompson, D. (2002, March 21). Child Support: Guilty Until Proven Innocent. CNSNew.com Commentary. www.CNSNEWS.com/ViewCommentary.asp?Page=\Commentary\archive\200203\COM20020321a.html.
Thompson, D. (2002, March 22). Want To Help Children? Stay Married. CNSNews.com Commentary. www.cnsnews.com/ViewCommentaary.asp?Page=\archinve\200203\COM20020322a.html.
Thompson, K. Sharing the Blame for Child Abuse. Men's News Daily. www.mensnewsdaily.com
Thompson, T. G., (2002, Jan 17). Regarding the Promoting Safe and Stable Families Amendments of 2001. www.dhhs.gov/news/press/2002pres/20020117b.html.
Tong, Dean (2002).Elusive Innocence: Survival guide for the falsely accused. Lafayette, LA: Huntington House Publishers.
Trelfall, P. B.A., Grad.Dip.Psych., I.A.M.F.C. Messages posted on Pas 2nd Wives Club.yahoogroups.com
University of Idaho Medical Class 2003 http://www.sci.uidaho.edu/med532/amygdala.htm

University of Sydney, http://www2.fhs.usyd.edu.au/arow/

Vacc, Nicholas A., (2000). Professional Orientation to Counseling. (3rd Ed.). Philadelphia, PA: Brunner-Routeledge.

Vaknin, S. (2001, Sept. 3). Narcissistic Personality Disorder. The Weapon of Language. www.suite101.com/article.cfm/npd/77822

Wakefield, H. & Underwager, R. (1990, March 30). Personality Characteristics of Falsely Accusing Parents in Custody Disputes. Institute for Psychological Therapies, Minnesota. Sixth Annual Symposium in Forensic Psychology, Las Vegas, www.deltabravo.net/cgi-bin/printapage.cgi?doc=/cusotyd/wakefield.htm.

Wallace, B. (2001, July 1). On the Death of a Friend. www.LewRockwell.com. www.lewrockwell.com/wallace/wallace49.html

Walsh, M. R. and Bone, J. M. (1997, June) Parental Alienation Syndrome: An Age-Old Custody Problem. The Florida Bar Journal. [Electronic Version] www.fact.on.ca?Info/pas/walsh.htm.

Warshak, R., A. Child Custody Resources. http://home.att.net/~rawars/shopcart.htm

Warshak, R. A. Remarriage as a Trigger of Parental Alienation Syndrome http://www.fact.on.ca/Info/pas/warsha00.htm

Warshak, R.A. (2001) Divorce Poison. NY,NY: Regan Books, HarperCollins Publishers.

Warshak, R. A. (2002, Jan 14-16) Keeping Kids Out of Parental Fights. SmartKids.com Family Resource Center. Keep Kids Out of Parental Fights. www.DivorcePoison.com

Warshak, R. A., (2002, Feb. 2). Dealing with "Divorce Poison". CBSNEWS.com. New York Area. www.cbsnews.com/stories/2002/02/01/earlyshow/Saturday/printable327911.shtml.

Warshak, R. A., (2002, May 2). . Richard Warshak:

Children often manipulated in custody fights. The Dallas Morning News. [Electronic Version] http://fact.on.ca/news0005/da00502.htm

Willenz, P. Children likely to be better adjusted in joint vs. sole custody arrangements in most cases. Living situation not as influential as time spent with parent. Pwillenz@apa.org. American Psychology Association. [Electronic Version] www.eurekalert.org/pub_release/2002-03/apa-clt031902.php

Wittenberg, C. & Insel, T. R. Male Suicide: Willful or Benign Neglect? http://groups.yahoo.com/group/menshealth/messages/630

Wood, G. (2001, June) Getting Your Message Across. The Insider: Number 284. [Electronic Version] www.policyexperts.org/insider/2001/jun01

Worth, J.B. (2004, Sept/Oct) Treating Anger in Therapy. Family Therapy Magazine. VA: The American Association of Marriage and Family Therapy. 40-45.

Zanard, C. R. E. (1996, July to present) Victims Account of Abuse- I have not seen my children in close to 8 years.

Printed in Great Britain
by Amazon